Secondary science

Science educ
within the su
co-authors di
the balance o
the nature of
resource for
of science te

- planning
- differentia
- assessmer
- practical
- problem-s
- informatic
- handling
- building

Throughout,
activities for
at helping the
Students wil
references to

Jerry Welli
and the edito

Secondary science
Contemporary issues and practical approaches

Jerry Wellington
with contributions from
Jenny Henderson, Vic Lally, Jon Scaife,
Stephen Knutton and Mick Nott

London and New York

First published 1994
by Routledge
11 New Fetter Lane, London EC4P 4EE

Simultaneously published in the USA and Canada
by Routledge
29 West 35th Street, New York, NY 10001

Typeset in Times by Michael Mepham, Frome, Somerset

Printed and bound in Great Britain by
Mackays of Chatham PLC, Chatham, Kent

British Library Cataloguing in Publication Data
A catalogue record for this book is available from the British Library.

Library of Congress Cataloging in Publication Data

[copy to follow]

ISBN 0–415–09843–2 (hbk)
ISBN 0–415–09844–0 (pbk)

1000 301144

Contents

Theme C Enriching science teaching

Illustrations

TABLES

Contributors

Jenny Henderson is lecturer in science education at the University of Sheffield. She has primary responsibility for the initial training of graduate science teachers and her particular interests are in personal and social education and health education.

Stephen Knutton is lecturer in education at the University of Sheffield. He is currently a member of the Examinations Council of NEAB and chairs the Chemistry Committee. Personal interests include science education in the developing world and distance education.

Vic Lally is lecturer in education at the University of Sheffield. He has research interests in education and ethics, in-service education, problem-solving and multimedia computing. He is currently working on the development and evaluation of multimedia teaching materials and school-based collaborative INSET.

Mick Nott is senior lecturer in physics and science education at Sheffield Hallam University. His main interest lies in the nature of science and its place in the science curriculum, and he is currently doing research into teachers' knowledge of the nature of science.

Jon Scaife is lecturer in education at the University of Sheffield. He taught for thirteen years in the secondary and tertiary sectors. His doctorate was in the physics of continua. Current interests include learning and meaning.

Preface

This book has been written both for students on initial teacher education courses and for in-service teachers who wish to read about and reflect upon their own practice. It is recognised that there is no substitute for classroom observation and teaching experience. On the other hand, time is often needed to stand back and reflect upon this experience. The aim of this book is to encourage and help with that process of reflection in the hope that it will improve and enrich practice.

A lot has happened in science education in recent years. This book aims both to cover contemporary issues in science education that have a direct bearing on science teaching, and to present and discuss practical approaches in science education. Contemporary issues such as the balance between process and content, the interpretation of the National Curriculum, the role of practical work, the nature of science, assessment of learning, the place of information technology and problem-solving, children's prior learning, and the handling of sensitive topic areas are all considered. In parallel with those discussions, practical approaches for teaching and learning are offered which, it is hoped, will be of value in the classroom or laboratory.

Science exists as part of the whole curriculum and therefore reference is made, wherever possible, to the cross-curricular themes and skills of the National Curriculum. The dimensions that cross the whole curriculum are those of providing equal opportunities for all pupils and of educating pupils for life in a multicultural society. These should be seen as an essential starting point for all the chapters whether the subject matter is assessment, learning, class management or language in science.

Space is limited, so none of the discussions or suggestions goes into the depth that could be achieved if a single book were written on just one of the areas – e.g. practical work, problem-solving, children's learning. Consequently, ample references and suggestions for further reading are given throughout. The book, like science teaching for all, is designed for a mixed-ability and mixed-motivation readership so it provides for the possibility of differentiation, special needs and interests, and ample scope for extension work! Some may not have the time or inclination to follow up the references and further reading, but we hope that others will.

Finally, not every issue or practical approach in science education could possibly be covered in a book of this kind – the main aim here is to introduce readers to the basic questions of why, what and how that occur so frequently in the teaching and learning of science.

Jerry Wellington

Acknowledgements

The authors and publisher would like to thank the following:

the Northern Examinations and Assessment Board for permission to reproduce the questions in Figures 5.2a, 5.2b, 5.2c, 5.2d and the INSET materials in Figure 10.2.

Thomas Nelson for permission to reproduce extracts from *Exploring the Nature of Science* in Chapter 1.

Oxford University Press for permission to adapt Figure 20.2, Natural Recycling, from page 78 of Tony Partridge (1992) *Starting Science Book 3*, used here in Figure 11.1.

Theme A
Thinking about the science curriculum . . . and science

1 Interpreting the Statements of the National Science Curriculum: graded tasks, upward spirals or conceptual dolly mixtures?

> The National Curriculum (NC) is here – in black and white, and occasionally pink and orange. The job of the teacher is first of all to make sense of it, to give it personal meaning. Without this personal interpretation, how can one teach from it? To an extent the NC is obligatory and given, not open to question. However, it is also the case that teachers can help to make sense of it by looking critically at its words and phrases. The aim of this chapter is to assist teachers in this process of interpreting and analysing the National Curriculum in order to do more than simply 'deliver' it.

MASS READING ACTIVITIES

One of the outcomes of the advent of the NC has been a relatively new phenomenon in peacetime: the simultaneous reading of centrally produced documents by large numbers of people. Admittedly, most of those people are teachers, but other parties too have been grappling with the folders and now posters of the National Curriculum Council (NCC), trying to make personal sense of them. The NC has generated a 'mass reading strategy' across the land:

> Everyone with a professional interest in the matter finds themselves reading the same glossy curriculum documents at the same time, and waiting for the next ones to emerge. This means that huge sections of the teaching profession and the satellite occupations which encircle it – academics, teacher educators, textbook publishers, journalists, and Local Authority officials – are engaged in a common interpretive task at roughly the same time.
>
> (MaClure and Stronach, 1993)

The mass reading phenomenon could have been witnessed in any school staffroom in 1991 and 1992, and it continues. With it came a new mode of describing teaching – the 'delivery' of the National Curriculum. Thus teachers began to talk of delivering the National Science Curriculum and of the resources needed to deliver the various programmes of study and statements of attainment.

The line followed in this chapter and those that follow is that science teachers are more than deliverers of curriculum packages.

THE STRUCTURE OF THE NATIONAL SCIENCE CURRICULUM

We are not able to reproduce the NC here so it is assumed that readers will have a copy of the latest version readily available. The NC for science is divided into four attainment targets (ATs) with programmes of study (PoS) relating to each one. In turn, the programmes of study and ATs are divided into four key stages (KS), corresponding to different years of a student's compulsory school life, from year one (age 5) to year 11 (age 16). Each key stage relates to a range of levels in the statements of attainment (SoAs), which run from level one to ten (see figure 1.1). This chapter will focus primarily on KSs 3 and 4.

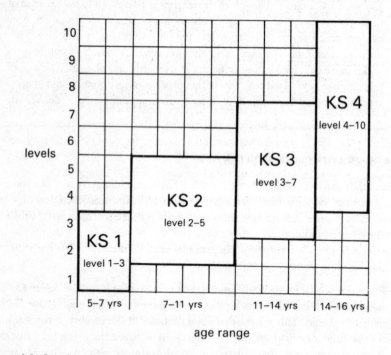

Figure 1.1   Levels, ages and key stages

INTRODUCING AND ANALYSING THE ATTAINMENT TARGETS

Attainment Target 1: scientific investigation

AT 1, scientific investigation, is designed to develop the pupils' investigative skills and their understanding of science through practical activities. These activities, according to the programme of study, should be set within their everyday experience and in 'wider contexts'. During KSs 3 and 4 pupils should gradually become more systematic in their approach, more precise and more quantitative. This should be reflected in their increasing ability to select and use more complex and more accurate measuring instruments and more systematic ways of recording data, including the use of computers. Herein lies the Progression (a key idea in the National Curriculum) in AT 1 at this stage. Pupils will also need to be able to plan and carry out investigations, and this has been a new aspect of practical work for many teachers. As Chapter 8 discusses, the use of science practical work in the past has rarely involved investigational work; more likely proving an existing law or at best a guided discovery lesson have been the norm. The problems that this new orthodoxy of investigation poses are explored fully there.

Alongside the PoS sit the statements of attainment and examples in italics intended to clarify them. It is a matter of some debate as to whether teachers actually pay more attention to the SoAs than they do to the programmes. A cynical view would suggest that if the primary concern of the teacher is for assessment then the SoAs are the focus of attention. These are stated for KS 3 largely in terms of items of behaviour which the pupil will be asked to exhibit – i.e. in behavioural terms such as: carry out a fair test (level 4); formulate hypotheses (level 5); use results to draw conclusions (level 6); and manipulate two or more independent variables (level 7). The problem of how these are actually exhibited in a school lab and how they are to be assessed is an issue for debate amongst teachers – the examples given in the NC document are rarely specific enough to be of practical value (again, see later chapter). I have been told at more than one meeting of teachers that they would like concrete 'exemplars' of the SoAs in AT 1 – i.e. examples of realistic school science lab investigations during which students can, for example:

1 Use a scientific theory to make quantitative predictions (level 9).
2 Collect data that enables them to make a critical evaluation of a law, theory or model (level 10).
3 Analyse data in a way that demonstrates an appreciation of the uncertainty of evidence (level 9).

Three identified strands run through AT 1 at both KSs 3 and 4 – together they make up the new model of practical work in school science. Practical work should be based on investigations which the pupils (not the teachers) plan and carry out and which involve these three elements:

1 asking questions, predicting and hypothesising
2 observing and measuring, and manipulating variables
3 interpreting results (the pupils' own results) and evaluating scientific evidence (It is not clear whether this is their own evidence or that of scientists.)

These strands make up practical work at KSs 3 and 4, and incidentally at stages 1 and 2 according to the NC document. From my own experience of talking to teachers, teaching, and observing other teachers, I feel that this model of practical work in AT 1 will pose more problems of interpretation than the other ATs – hence the need for a special chapter in this book (see Chapter 9).

Attainment Target 2: life and living processes

This is the AT of which people immediately say 'Ah . . . the biology one.' Its four main elements are shown in table 1.1.

Notice that these elements or 'strands' are phrased in terms of pupils' knowledge and understanding, as are those in ATs 3 and 4, as opposed to the more behavioural phrasing of AT 1. The aim here is not to go through the statements in detail, which readers can do at their leisure. It is worth saying, however, that most of the content in this AT is largely derived from traditional biology education. There is perhaps more of an emphasis on ecology, for example, feeding relationships in an ecosystem (level 4); and on the study of pollution, for example, the effects of pollution on the survival of organisms (level 5), than in traditional syllabuses. This is reinforced by the programmes of study in this AT that give further detail on the study required of, for example, the effects of human activity on our air and water, investigations into the local environment, on the nature of waste and the value of recycling, and on the 'major environmental issues facing society'. This AT has obvious links with two of the 'cross-curricular themes', i.e. health education and environmental education, that make up the National Curriculum (the other three themes are economic and industrial understanding, careers education and guidance, and citizenship). To an extent it also links with citizenship, in, for example, the PoS requirement to appreciate that beneficial products and services need to be balanced against harmful effects on the environment.

There are also many biotechnological processes and ideas in AT 2, for example genetic engineering, cloning, and artificial selection. These provide opportunities for links with the technology curriculum, for example, fermentation technology. Food production is another area which may be addressed in AT 2, in technology, and in the cross-curricular themes.

The second strand, on variation, also provides much substance for discussion of controversial issues. With properly structured teaching materials these issues may be tackled with mixed-ability pupils at KSs 3 and 4. Clearly, AT 2 also provides many opportunities for investigations and fieldwork.

Thus AT 2 is one of the more outward looking ATs, with clear links to other parts of the curriculum. To some extent all the ATs involve an element of economic and industrial understanding (theme one), especially in the general requirement in the PoS to consider the application and economic, social and technological implications of science.

Attainment Target 3: materials and their properties

As with AT 2, much of this area will be seen as familiar to those who have studied science, this time as chemistry. Thus three of the strands cover the properties, classification and structure of materials and chemical changes. A fourth strand,

Table 1.1 The science attainment targets and their main 'strands'

Attainment target 1: Scientific investigation	Attainment target 2: Life and living processes	Attainment target 3: Materials and their properties	Attainment target 4: Physical processes
Strand (i) Ask questions, predict and hypothesise	*Strand (i)* Life processes and the organisation of living things	*Strand (i)* The properties, classification and structure of materials	*Strand (i)* Electricity and magnetism
Strand (ii) Observe, measure and manipulate variables	*Strand (ii)* Variation and the mechanisms of inheritance and evolution	*Strand (ii)* Explanations of the properties of materials	*Strand (ii)* Energy resources and energy transfer
Strand (iii) Interpret their results and evaluate scientific evidence	*Strand (iii)* Populations and human influences within ecosystems	*Strand (iii)* Chemical changes	*Strand (iii)* Forces and their effects
	Strand (iv) Energy flows and cycles of matter within ecosystems	*Strand (iv)* The earth and its atmosphere	*Strand (iv)* Light and sound
			Strand (v) The earth's place in the universe

however, covers 'the earth and its atmosphere', and this may expose areas for which traditionally educated and trained science teachers may be less well prepared. Thus as early as level 4 one of the SoAs includes a knowledge of weathering, erosion and different types of soil. A later statement (level 6) includes an understanding of how different airstreams give rise to different weather as a result of their passage over land and/or sea (geography teachers please note). The same level asks for an understanding of the processes that form igneous, sedimentary and metamorphic rocks. At level 7, students are expected to understand how some weather phenomena – such as thunder, fog and frost – are driven in by energy transfer processes. Further work on the formation and deformation of rocks is part of level 8, and the weather reappears in level 9 where pupils are asked to explain changes in the atmosphere that cause various weather phenomena. The internal structure of the earth occurs at level 9 and resurfaces in level 10 where pupils, in the last SoA, are required to understand the theory of plate tectonics.

Thus an AT that appeared at first glance in the mass reading of the NC to be chemistry in fact contains elements of meteorology, geology and earth science, and another of the NC subjects, geography. AT 3 is thus the hybrid of the three knowledge-and understanding-based ATs. It links well with the cross-curricular themes, especially economic and industrial understanding (EIU), for example studies of radiation use in medicine and industry and project work on pollution or water conservation.

Attainment Target 4: physical processes

This is conventionally labelled as the physics component, although it does contain small sections on astronomy and even cosmology. The four main elements of this AT are shown in Table 1.1 – notice the inclusion of the earth's place in the universe. Most of the traditional areas of physics education are covered here, such as forces, energy transfer, electric circuits, light and sound, waves generally, motion, magnetism and electromagnetism. There is nothing particularly unexpected here or, as critics would point out, anything post-1900 except perhaps logic gates. It is largely Newtonian and classical. One welcome inclusion is the SoA requiring pupils to know that the earth goes round the sun (level 4). The solar system reappears in level 5, where pupils are expected to know the times and nature of the planetary orbits. In level 6 they need to know that the solar system is part of a galaxy which in turn is part of the universe. Later, in level 8, they are expected to speculate on conditions elsewhere in the universe, using available data. Satellite motion is covered in level 9, while in level 10 the ultimate statement of attainment requires pupils to relate current theories on the origin of the universe to astronomical evidence – no mean task for a 16-year-old.

Thus AT 4 does contain some 'untraditional' elements, though perhaps less so than does AT 3. Most teachers with a physics background will find it to be largely familiar ground. Once again, there is great potential for work related to the cross-curricular themes such as EIU, for example, the role of telecommunications in commerce and industry, the impact of robotics and information technology (IT) on employment patterns, and the future of the nuclear industry.

THE PROGRAMMES OF STUDY

We have glanced above at the ATs, largely by considering the statements of attainment. The programmes of study for each area and key stage provide an interesting comparison and sometimes contrast. The general introduction to the programmes for KSs 3 and 4 includes three areas in which pupils are expected to develop:

1   Communication: This includes the ability both to express ideas and to read 'purposefully' and to respond to secondary sources (practical ideas for this are presented in later chapters). It also includes the ability to use data from a computer system and an understanding of IT in communication. At KS 4 communication should develop further to include research skills, gathering and organising information from a number of sources, and the use of databases and spreadsheets. Indeed much of the IT skill and knowledge that formed an entire attainment target in the first NC document for science (old AT 12) are now contained – perhaps less visibly and less obviously – in this part of the PoS.

2   The appliance of science: Pupils should develop awareness of the use of science in everyday life and also look at the benefits versus the drawbacks of the application of science and technology. By following a programme of study in this area they should understand 'how science shapes and influences the quality of their lives'. At KS 4 they should go on to consider the use and effects of IT on individuals and society. Eventually, they should appreciate the 'power and limitations of science in solving industrial, social and environmental problems'.

3   The nature of scientific ideas: One complete attainment target in the original NC (old AT 17) which disappeared in the new version was concerned with the history and nature of science. For some people this had been a worrying AT because few had education or training in that area; for many, however, it was a challenging AT and a vital component of science education. Whatever the views and arguments, the outcome is that the nature and history of scientific ideas appears partly in the new AT 1, but more obviously in the programmes of study for KS 3 and KS 4 (though not KS 1 and KS 2). In their programme of study pupils should learn about the change of scientific ideas through time by studying the development of some important ideas in science. At KS 4 they should study the *context* in which the pursuit of science takes place – the 'social, moral, spiritual and cultural contexts'. They should learn that science is but one way of understanding the world, albeit an important way.

The nature of science is a vital part of science education, for both teachers and pupils, and Chapter 15 is devoted to it. Indeed, all the areas of the science curriculum outlined in these introductions to the programme of study are felt to be essential elements of a balanced science education. There is a danger, however, that some teachers will avoid or ignore them in their concern to cover the statements of attainment. This would be a great loss to science teaching.

More detailed programmes of study are given alongside each attainment target. Aspects of the three themes in the general introduction are spelt out in greater detail, for example, the use of IT, applications of the science in that AT, and considerations of the nature of science. Thus in AT 1, the PoS states that pupils should use sensors such as temperature, light and pressure in collecting data. They should use IT in displaying and communicating their own data and in seeking data from other sources. Later, they should look at the limitations of science and critically appraise their own investigation, and explore the nature of 'scientific evidence and proof'.

Unfortunately, the three key themes of the general programme of study, i.e. the communication, application and nature of science, are rather lost in the detailed PoS in ATs 2, 3, and 4. Here, the PoS refers largely to the content rather than the general themes on processes of science. The PoS in ATs 2–4 simply spell out in more detail the content to be covered, largely in terms of the knowledge and understanding required.

THE NON-STATUTORY GUIDANCE

In addition to the statutory documents of the NC, i. e. those setting out the PoS and SoAs which teachers are obliged to cover, the NCC has provided a large number of pages of non-statutory guidance to help teachers in planning and implementing the curriculum. These notes of guidance have proved helpful to teachers and are well worth studying. In particular they provide advice on two areas deemed to be 'new to some groups of teachers': earth science and the nature of science.

EVALUATING THE NATIONAL CURRICULUM

This chapter has attempted to provide a brief round-up, and to highlight certain features, of the programmes of study and the statements of attainment (some might say atonement) of the science curriculum. There can be no substitute for reading the relevant documents of the NCC, however, and these are listed later – they constitute several days reading! The aim of this book is to consider the issues that teachers will face in implementing (i.e. actively interpreting) rather than simply delivering (i.e. mindlessly transmitting) the NC, and to provide practical approaches to enrich this process. Before beginning those chapters, however, we should stop to consider briefly the positive benefits of the science NC, alongside the problems and difficulties posed by the existing framework. My suggestions on both aspects are given below; readers can surely add to them.

The value of a National Science Curriculum

The first benefit of the NC is that it can offer a framework and guidelines for the learning and teaching of science where previously none existed on a national scale. To some extent the science curriculum had been determined perhaps on a local scale (e.g. an Authority), at school level, or in extreme cases by an individual teacher. Thus the NC put an end to what some saw as a *laissez-faire* or do-your-own-thing policy on what science should be taught and to some extent how. Now at least there is some consensus on the curriculum, even if it has been reached with political interference (Graham and Tytler, 1992). Curriculum relativism has come to an end.

In particular, it has been argued, the NC has provided a mandate, a framework and a guideline for teachers in the primary sector (KSs 1 and 2) where previously the situation was far more unpredictable and patchy than in the secondary sector. In the secondary sector at least the content covered was laid down in practice by the exam syllabuses.

Secondly, it follows from above that two important features of any curriculum have now been made public and explicit. These are 'entitlement' and 'progression'. Both terms have become used widely since the Education Reform Act of 1988, and the ideas behind them will be considered more fully later. In brief, the first of these terms implies that pupils now have an entitlement, by law, to the 'broad and balanced curriculum' set out in the statutory documents. For many teachers this legal framework or 'right' for all pupils is one of the attractive features of the National Curriculum. Entitlement is often linked with the notion of 'access' for all, i.e. that every opportunity should be given to pupils with special educational needs (SEN) to have *appropriate access* to the programmes of study. This access is their entitlement. The term 'progression' implies that through a structured, published national curriculum pupils will experience continuity and progression as they move from one year to the next, from one teacher to another and even from one school to another. (In practice this is a difficult goal to realise.)

Thus, the introduction of a national, statutory curriculum has provided the possibility of a broad, balanced and carefully planned science education for all pupils (as an entitlement). The introduction of 'new' elements of science such as earth science, astronomy, ecology, and a dash of cosmology has enriched the traditional curriculum dominated by the big three sciences. Many were disappointed that this extra breadth was reduced in the new version of the ATs, but at least the possibility of greater breadth and therefore balance has increased to some extent. An important addition in broadening science education was the introduction of the nature and history of scientific ideas into the PoS, an innovation which is discussed in a later chapter.

Finally, the introduction of the NC did at least give an opportunity for people to consider why science is taught and what contribution it can make to a person's education. Just over a page is devoted to this in the non-statutory guidance, where six reasons are given for studying science. They will not be repeated here, but surely all teachers should examine why they are engaged in science education: Does it make for better, more well-informed citizens? Does it increase the public understanding of science? Is it of direct utility value to them in everyday living? Will it help them to get a job, or for a very small minority to become a scientist? Does science education, more broadly, contribute to a rounded educated person, capable of an improved understanding of the world? On the one hand, these questions are simply the topic of continuous academic debate. On the other, however, practising teachers could actually improve their lessons by considering why they are teaching what they teach and conveying that message to the pupils.

Difficulties in the National Curriculum

Interpretation

The first difficulty is the task of interpreting the NC and giving it personal meaning. This must be done in order to teach it creatively, lucidly and enthusiastically rather than 'delivering' it. In a sense, the problem is for the mass readership of the NC documents to read the minds and intentions of the small number of people involved in writing them. The problem sometimes degenerates into speculation of the kind: 'I wonder what they were thinking of there?' At other times some of the terms are, by their very nature, problematic. There is no consensus on the meaning of terms such as generalisation, predictive theory, causal link, variable, hypothesis, validity and model, yet they are freely used in NC documents, particularly in AT 1.

Variation in the SoAs

A second problem lies in the wide variation in the size and complexity of the statements of attainment. Some could be mastered in a double lesson. Others require study at post-doctoral level to begin to get to grips with them. For example, the SoA at level 9 which requires that pupils should understand the relationships between variation, natural selection and reproductive success in organisms and the significance of these relationships for evolution covers a large chunk of one of the most important hypotheses (or is it a theory?) in science. Contrast this with the ultimate statement of AT 4 which requires an understanding of momentum and its conservation or, at an earlier level, the law of moments.

Logical mish-mash

The third problem lies in the logical mish-mash of the various statements. Some are simply statements of required behaviour, for example, 'be able to . . .'. Some are statements of skills, for example, 'set up . . .', 'select . . .', 'manipulate . . .'. Some are statements of other processes such as theorising, communicating, speaking and listening. Other statements involve pure factual recall of the 'know that' variety. More confusingly, other statements of the knowledge kind involve far higher intellectual abilities such as understanding, application of knowledge, evaluation and in some cases quite abstract conceptual achievements. This difficulty is partly hidden by the occasional use of the word 'knowledge' when what is required is 'understanding' – and vice versa. When knowledge of terminology is needed it is sometimes at the level of a straightforward naming word, at other times to refer to a process, and occasionally to involve a complex concept such as work or energy (words which also have everyday usages). We must therefore be wary of the mixtures of 'know that . . .', 'know how . . .', 'understand that . . .' and 'be able to' statements in the NC (see Dobson, 1989).

Covering the statements: orienteering or mountain climbing?

A fourth problem lies in the apparent order or sequence of the SoAs. This problem has several parts.

First, according to the non-statutory guidance (section C8), the 'conceptual demand of an activity is indicated by the level of attainment' in a given AT. Yet when experienced teachers examine the document some of the later statements at (say) levels 8, 9 and 10 are actually less demanding than some at earlier levels. In AT 2, for example, the implication is that topics such as photosynthesis and respiration (level 7) are conceptually easier than genetics and evolution (levels 8 and 9). Is this the case? Does it not depend on how the topic is tackled? In addition, some SoAs seem to be inappropriately placed for a particular age group. Thus in AT 3, for example, rates of chemical reaction, which traditionally have been covered well into KS 4, are included at level 7. Moreover, from the children's point of view, they may reach level 4 in one strand of a particular AT, for example, electricity and magnetism, and level 8 in another strand, for example, light and sound.

Secondly, and more fundamentally, the statements are laid out in a linear, one-dimensional sequence in the National Curriculum document. It may not have been the intention of the working group to suggest that a science course or curriculum should proceed in this linear, sequential fashion. But this is certainly the message conveyed to teachers by the layout of the statements and the numbered levels. Whatever happened to the spiral curriculum? Most school science courses proceed in a cyclical, spiral fashion. Ideas are introduced at one level, discussed in a more refined way later, elaborated further at the next stage, and perhaps quantified at a higher level. This is true of many of the key concepts of science; unfortunately, however, it is not recognised by the structure and layout of the attainment targets and their division into ten seemingly sequential levels.

A collection of statements that may have been seen by the original authors of the National Curriculum as a map of the terrain which should be covered has thus gradually become reified into a sequence of hurdles in a supposedly objective order of increasing conceptual demand. From a pupil's perspective the greatest drawback in seeing coverage of the ATs as mountain climbing rather than orienteering is that for those pupils who do not 'aspire' to the higher levels, large important areas of science education will remain untouched. This practice will prevent the broad and balanced coverage of science, which seemed to be the main benefit of a planned curriculum for all. Thus in AT 2, for example, pupils who do not reach levels 8, 9 and 10 will not cover any of the ideas and theories (or hypotheses?) of genetics and evolution. In AT 4, ideas about the nature and origin of the universe, which fascinate children of all ages, are left to level 10. Yet many would argue that these key ideas could be introduced in some form or other to much younger pupils – this is the essence of the spiral curriculum (Bruner, 1962).

Entitlement breaks down if the curriculum is seen as linear and sequential, rather than cyclical or spiral.

Science in the whole curriculum: weft and warp

In their enthusiasm for the subject, science teachers may forget that science is just one element of a whole curriculum framework, with a weft and a warp. Additional subjects that make up the subject pillars or warp of the NC are the two other *core* subjects (maths and English) and other foundation subjects (technology, modern foreign languages, history, geography, art, music and PE). Religious education is also a compulsory element. The threads that cross the curriculum framework, the weft, are made up of themes (see page 9) dimensions and skills. Six skills have been identified in NC documents: communication, numeracy, study, problem-solving, personal and social, information technology. These are skills which teachers of all subjects can develop through their own subject, not least in science education.

The dimensions are, in a sense, more fundamental since they cover all aspects of equal opportunities and 'education for life in a multicultural society' (NCC, 1992). Thus, for science teachers and pupils, this might involve:

- challenging myths, stereotypes and misconceptions about other people or other societies
- making use of, and building upon, pupils' own backgrounds and experiences
- presenting positive images and role models
- extending knowledge and understanding of various cultures, technologies and faiths
- showing that science itself is not (and has never been) neutral or value-free, but is influenced by the society and the culture in which it is practised
- ensuring equal access for all pupils to science resources and the science curriculum

These dimensions or responsibilities fall upon all teachers. Many ideas for encouraging teachers to reflect upon them, and indeed for putting them into practice in science lessons, are contained in a manual called *Race, Equality and Science Teaching* (Thorp, 1991). The activities and suggestions in that manual can be used to support many of the subsequent chapters in this book.

REFERENCES AND FURTHER READING

Bruner, J. (1960) *The Process of Education*, Cambridge, Mass. : Harvard University Press.
DES [Department of Education and Science] and the Welsh Office (1991) *Science in the National Curriculum*, London: HMSO.
Dobson, K. (1989) 'Do You Understand? The Meanings of Terms Used in the Statutory Orders', *Education in Science*, September 1989, (134): 7–9.
Graham, D. and Tytler (1992) *A Lesson for All – The Making of the National Curriculum*, London: Routledge.
Hayle, P. (1993) 'Race, Equality and Science Teaching', in Smail, B. (ed.), *ASE Science Teachers' Handbook*, Hemel Hempstead: Simon & Schuster.

—— (1993) 'Science for Girls and Boys', in Smail, B. (ed.), *ASE Science Teachers' Handbook*, Hemel Hempstead: Simon & Schuster.

MaClure, M. and Stronach, I. (1993) 'Great Accidents in History', in Wellington, J. J. (ed.), *The Work-Related Curriculum*, London: Kogan Page.

National Curriculum Council (NCC) (1989) *Science in the National Curriculum: Non-Statutory Guidance*, York: NCC.

—— (1990a) *Curriculum Guidance Three: The Whole Curriculum*, York: NCC.

—— (1990b) *Curriculum Guidance Four: Economic and Industrial Understanding*, York: NCC.

—— (1990c) *Curriculum Guidance Five: Health Education*, York: NCC.

—— (1990d) *Curriculum Guidance Seven: Environmental Education*, York: NCC.

—— (1992) *Starting Out with the National Curriculum*, York: NCC.

Thorp, S. (ed.) (1991) *Race, Equality and Science Teaching*, Hatfield: Association for Science Education.

Watts, M. (ed.) (1991) *Science in the National Curriculum*, London: Cassell.

☆   ☆   ☆

Learning the lingo: a summary

Core subjects: Mathematics, science and English (and Welsh in Welsh-speaking schools).

Foundation subjects: The core subjects plus technology, history, geography, art, music, PE and a modern foreign language (for secondary-age pupils).

Key stages (KS):   The periods in each pupil's education to which the elements of the National Curriculum apply. There are four key stages, normally related to the age of the majority of the pupils in a teaching group. They are: the beginning of compulsory education to age 7; ages 7 to 11; ages 11 to 14; and age 14 to the end of compulsory education.

Programmes of study (PoS):   The content, skills and processes that must be taught to pupils during each key stage in order for them to meet the objectives set out in the attainment targets.

Attainment targets (AT):   Objectives for each subject, setting out the knowledge, skills, and understanding that pupils of different abilities and maturities are expected to develop. They are defined in detail at ten levels by means of appropriate statements of attainment (SoAs).

Statements of attainment (SoA):   More precise objectives than the broader attainment targets, which will be defined within statutory orders. They are related to one of ten levels of attainment on a single continuous scale, covering all four key stages.

Levels of attainment: The ten different levels of achievement defined within each attainment target, reflecting differences in ability and in progress, normally according to age.

Standard assessment tasks (SATs):   Tasks and tests used at or near the end of a key stage.

Strand: A sequence of related SoAs running through an AT or parts of a POS.

☆   ☆   ☆

Now take a seat (Science Education Assimilation Test)

Can you understand curriculum documents? Before moving on to the next chapter you should score at least 100 per cent in the following test.

1   What do the following initials stand for?
   (a) PoS
   (b) AT
   (c) KS
   (d) SoA
   (e) NCC
   (f) SAT

2   Define the following terms.
   (a) Attainment target
   (b) Statement of attainment
   (c) Level of attainment
   (d) Programme of study
   (e) Key stage

3   Which subjects or themes are included in:
   (a) the core subjects of the National Curriculum?
   (b) the foundation subjects?
   (c) the cross-curricular themes?
   (d) the cross-curricular skills?
   (e) the cross-curricular dimensions?

2 Breadth and balance in the Science Curriculum

'Thoughts without content are empty. Perceptions without concepts are blind.'
(Immanuel Kant, *Critique of Pure Reason*, 1780)

> We often hear and read about the notion that the science curriculum should be broad and balanced. But just what do the terms breadth and balance mean? How can a curriculum be designed to possess these features? Are they compatible with the sometimes deeply held views and educational background of the teachers who are responsible for breadth and balance? These are the questions addressed in this chapter.

WHY REFLECT ON THE SCIENCE CURRICULUM?

The purpose of this chapter is to encourage you to reflect upon science and the science curriculum and to examine your own attitude towards it. At first glance, this may seem a rather academic activity, given that there is now a statutory national curriculum (though only in England and Wales) and that the previous chapter has presented its outline and its structure. However, there are two good reasons for taking time for further reflection on the nature of the science curriculum. First, as argued earlier, teachers as professionals need to be far more than 'deliverers' of a science curriculum. They have an important role to play in shaping and interpreting science and in adapting the science curriculum for the future. It is not set in tablets of stone – that would make neither economic nor educational sense in a rapidly changing society based on science and technology. Secondly, the National Curriculum is laid down as a 'minimum entitlement' rather than a straitjacket or a set of immovable boundaries (although for many teachers it may feel like this). To use the metaphor adopted by the Association for Science Education (ASE), the national curriculum is a 'skeleton' which needs the flesh of the real world and the 'life force' of the teacher to bring it alive. Within its framework, teachers have flexibility in the way they present science, for example, as essentially about processes and methods or, in contrast, as a body of accumulated knowledge. They can also decide whether they present the various sciences as an integrated whole or as separate disciplines.

The aim of this chapter is therefore to consider what is taught in science, why it is taught and how the sciences should be presented.

DIMENSIONS OF BREADTH AND BALANCE

How many people reading this have experienced a broad and balanced education, let alone a balanced science education? Few, I would imagine. Many will have pursued an education biased towards the sciences perhaps from the age of 14 or earlier, and certainly from the age of 16 onwards. Within their science education, many will have followed a course geared either to the life sciences or to the physical sciences, with the choice of route depending on such fortuitous factors as the school, the teaching staff or their own gender. Some will have followed a science course that included little or no practical work (I recently spoke to a science graduate on a PGCE course who obtained the top grade in her O-level physics at school without ever doing a single physics practical – she was told that they never produce the right results anyway). Many will have gone through the system to graduate in a science without having studied earth science, cosmology, astronomy or ecology, let alone the nature and history of science.

So we need to recognise that many of those responsible for providing a broad and balanced science education to pupils have not had the benefit of such a curriculum themselves. Teachers need to be aware of their own background and the views and beliefs about science which they hold themselves – this is the basis of the activity which follows shortly in this chapter, and the one in the next. The activity here invites you to consider your own position on two issues: first, the question of whether the science curriculum should be seen as separated out into discrete sciences, or the study of science should be seen as an integrated whole; secondly, the question of whether the science curriculum should focus largely on the processes and methods of science rather than on the content or body of knowledge which science through the years has accumulated. The activity therefore focuses on the two poles of integration versus separation, and process versus content.

There are, however, other dimensions to breadth and balance that need to be remembered, principally that of the affective aspect of science education as opposed to the cognitive aspect. The affective element includes the pupils' attitudes and disposition towards science: interest, excitement, enthusiasm, motivation, eagerness to learn and openness to new learning. These are important dimensions of any science curriculum which are neglected at our peril (Claxton, 1989). Many critics of the National Curriculum accuse it of ignoring this dimension, though in fairness it is mentioned in the non-statutory guidance. The notion of different 'domains' of educational aims goes back to Bloom's (1956) taxonomy of educational objectives which is still valuable in considering a balanced science curriculum. A summary of these three elements is given in table 2.1.

Table 2.1 Groups of aims in science education

Cognitive	Psychomotor	Affective
Factual knowledge	Manipulative skill	Interest Enthusiasm
Understanding	Manual dexterity	Motivation Involvement
Application	Hand-to-eye coordination	Eagerness to learn
Synthesis		Awareness and openness
Evaluation		

In summary, then, there are three aspects at the very least which need to be considered in designing a broad and balanced science curriculum:

- process and content
- integration versus separation
- cognitive and affective

WHERE DO YOU STAND?

This section is designed to encourage you to reflect on your own views on the two poles introduced above: process/content and integration/separation. First of all, carry out the activity shown in table 2.2 – you might find it useful to photocopy that table first (you have permission!).

You should have considered each statement carefully and placed a number from – 5 to +5 in the unshaded boxes next to each statement (note that statement 4 has two unshaded boxes beside it). Now you need to add up your scores in order to establish your position. Follow these steps:

1   Add up the scores under each *column*, i.e. P, C, I and S, taking account of the sign of each score.
2   Calculate a value for (P-C) and (I-S), again taking careful account of the sign.
3   Plot your position on a graph as shown in figure 2.1. The value of (P-C) gives the *x*-coordinate; (I-S) gives the *y*-coordinate.

Look at your position on the graph in figure 2.1. You can give yourself a label according to which quadrant you fall into:

- process integrationist: northeast quadrant
- process separationist: southeast quadrant
- content integrationist: northwest quadrant
- content separationist: southwest quadrant

Table 2.2   Where do you stand?

- Consider each statement slowly and carefully.
- Numbers from +5 to –5 will indicate your agreement or disagreement with each statement.
- Place a number from +5 to –5 in the unshaded boxes according to the following scale:

+5	4	3	2	1	0	1	2	3	4	–5
agree strongly				agree		don't know don't care		disagree		disagree violently

You will be told what to do with those numbers when you have ranked each of the twenty statements.

	Statements	P	C	I	S
1	Each science has its own unique, separate identity.				
2	There is no such thing as 'the scientific method'.				
3	Science education is primarily concerned with transmitting a body of inherited knowledge.				
4	Science has its own unique processes and methods, common to all sciences.				
5	Science processes must be taught *explicitly* by teachers.				
6	Balanced science courses will only achieve status if the separate sciences are abolished.				
7	There is no such thing as a 'true scientific theory'.				
8	The abolition of separate sciences pre-16 would remove freedom of choice, a fundamental human right.				
9	Combined science courses should be taught only to less able pupils.				
10	By abolishing separate sciences before 16 the gender divisions in science education would be removed.				
11	'Processes need to be taught overtly . . . without the encumbrance of having to assimilate a body of facts at the same time' (Screen, 1986a).				
12	The separate sciences need to be preserved at 14–16 level to maintain standards.				
13	Science teachers should start from the pupils' ideas and build upon them encouraging them to develop their own theories.				
14	The scientific and technological elite needed for future economic growth can only be developed through a separate science curriculum (14–16).				
15	The processes of science can be identified, taught and assessed.				

Statements	P	C	I	S
16	The most valuable part of a scientific education is what remains after the facts have been forgotten.				
17	A good, solid grounding in basic scientific facts and inherited scientific knowledge is essential before young scientists can go on to make discoveries of their own.				
18	An integrated science programme is the only way to achieve an acceptable percentage of science within the overall curriculum.				
19	School leavers and future citizens will only be able to make decisions on scientific issues if they have basic facts at their fingertips.				
20	In the 'information age' all that matters is that pupils know *how* to access information and *where* to acquire the facts.				
		P	C	I	S

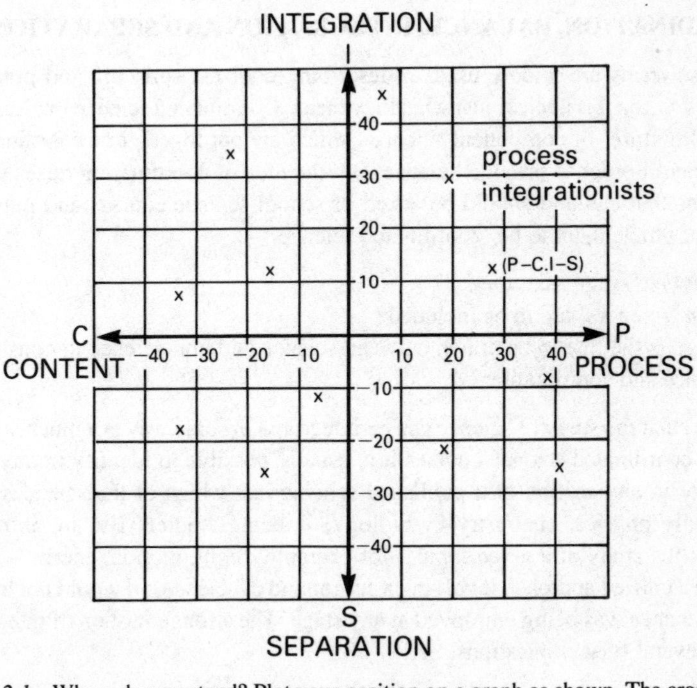

Figure 2.1   Where do you stand? Plot your position on a graph as shown. The crosses show some positions of teachers who have tried this activity.

Now is the time to reflect on the activity, and your position on the graph.

- Do you feel that this activity has wrongly placed you – i.e. are you in the right quadrant, according to your intuition? If not, then where do you feel intuitively that your position lies?

- If you are roughly in the right position, why do you feel that you hold such a view? Could you defend it, for example, to other science teachers? What argument should you use to support it?
- Does your view of science agree with that explicit and implicit in the National Science Curriculum?
- Indeed, what is the National Curriculum view of science – is it biased towards process or content? Is it integrationist or separationist? Which quadrant would NC science be in?

These are all points to ponder before reading the next two sections. There we consider the notions of balanced and integrated science by examining the nature of science, scientific method and the possibility of a unifying theme across all the sciences. Then we consider the arguments for and against a process-led view of the science curriculum, and conclude by suggesting a framework for a balanced science education.

COORDINATION, BALANCE, INTEGRATION AND SEPARATION

All these terms are widely used in describing courses, curricula and published schemes. Often it is unclear just what they mean. Coordinated science implies some sort of 'mixture' of component sciences which are put together or coordinated in some way in order to provide balance. But the idea of coordination raises several questions that can and should be asked of school science courses and published schemes which claim to be 'coordinated science':

- What is to count as a science?
- What 'sciences' are to be included?
- Where is the line to be drawn between science and non-science in considering balance and coordination?

The idea that the study of science can be integrated in some way is a much stronger one. In coordinated science courses it is usually possible to identify in any given lesson or in any section of a published scheme just which of the sciences (most commonly physics, chemistry or biology) is being studied. But in 'integrated science' the study of a given topic – for example, flight, motion, energy – would involve a unified approach involving a compound of sciences; it would not be clear which science was being employed at any stage. The stronger notion of integration raises several further questions:

- Is there some common feature shared by all sciences which could serve to unify them?
- Is it possible to combine or integrate these various studies into a new compound?
- . . . or will they merely form a 'mixture', separable at any stage?

The above questions are all important in that they have practical significance as well as philosophical interest. How can we construct and reflect upon a science curriculum unless we at least consider them? How can we talk about science education unless we have at least a rough idea of what science is? Indeed, why should there be a national science curriculum if there is nothing distinctive about science? And how can it be balanced if we have no criteria for considering balance? The remainder of this section offers a brief discussion of these issues which can be followed up from further reading.

What counts as a 'science'?

No one will ever state the necessary and sufficient conditions that must be fulfilled by a discipline or theory in order for it to qualify as a science. But the distinguishing features of a discipline or form of knowledge according to Hirst (1965) are as follows:

1   its own peculiar concepts
2   its own logical structure, i.e. the relationship between these concepts
3   its own testing procedures, i.e. procedures for testing the truth or falsity of factual statements emanating from this structure

These three criteria are still valuable and will be taken in turn.

1 The Concepts of Science

Two questions arise here: if a discipline is to count as a science, what must be the nature of its concepts? and, conversely, if science is to count as a *unified* discipline, is there a characteristic common to all its concepts? One philosopher of science has addressed himself to these questions at length. Korner (1966) argues that the concepts of science are necessarily *exact* in a sense in which everyday concepts of science are *inexact*. The concepts of science have no borderline instances – no greys, only blacks and whites. Scientific concepts are rigidly and clearly defined; without clear definition and sharp edges, quantification would be impossible.

Korner's analysis applied accurately to the exact sciences but would rule out the so-called 'inexact sciences'. These sciences may be inexact but many people would nevertheless wish to include them as sciences. In short, Korner's analysis seems to be *prescriptive* (based on a view of what science should be) rather than *descriptive*.

So is there anything else special about the concepts actually employed in science? It seems impossible to find a common feature. Many concepts employed in physics are abstract, idealised, and therefore without observable instances (point masses, rigid bodies, frictionless surfaces, particles and so on). At the other extreme some of the concepts of psychology are often inexact and 'intentional' in nature ('desiring', 'wanting', 'feeling', 'striving', etc.); they are unobservable for different reasons. Somewhere between these two disciplines lies biology – some of its concepts are exact, some inexact, some teleological in nature.

It seems that there is no characteristic common to all concepts in science. At best they bear some kind of 'family resemblance' to each other.

2 *Logical Structures and Paradigms in Science*

The structure of a science is often described as 'hypothetico-deductive'. Scientists are supposed to arrive at their laws and theories by a mixture of inspired guesswork, hunches, flashes of insight, 'hypothesising' and even a dash of (much maligned) induction, i.e. generalising from particular instances to a universal rule. From this body of laws and theories they are then able to deduce observationstatements which can be tested against experience. The hypothetico-deductive structure of a science is neatly summed up by Medawar (1979) as a 'mixture of guesswork and check-work'.

This structure of a science leads to the claim that scientific observations are theory dependent, i.e. existing theory directs scientists towards certain observations rather than making one observation rather than another. What a scientist observes is always only a small part of the whole domain of possible objects of observation.

This links with T. S. Kuhn's view (1978) that, in a true science, scientists work within a certain 'paradigm'. Kuhn uses the word paradigm to mean the central theory, the research tradition, the existing framework, 'the disciplinary matrix' or the current orthodoxy of a science. Kuhn suggests that without a paradigm a discipline cannot be considered a 'science', though it may be in a state of 'prescience'.

These considerations lead to three criteria for deciding whether or not a discipline is a science:

(a) The discipline should have a hypothetico-deductive structure relating theory to reality.
(b) Its observations should be theory dependent.
(c) It should have its own prevailing paradigm.

But perhaps these three criteria are too stringent. They would probably rule out psychology, sociology, psychiatry and even medicine as 'true sciences'.

3 *Scientific Procedures and 'Scientific Method'*

Are the testing procedures of a science sufficient to distinguish it from other disciplines? Is there something unique about scientific method which sets it apart from other rational activities (assuming that science is rational)?

Popper's notion of 'falsificationism' is often quoted as the hallmark of scientific method. No general statement can ever be *verified* – but it can be *falsified*, Popper (1968) points out. (This can be called the inherent *bias* of general statements.) A science deliberately exposes the observation statements (which follow deductively from its theories) to falsification. The more a theory exposes itself to falsification, the better the theory.

Popper's criterion clearly denies scientific status to the theories of both Freud and Marx. Both theories are so wide ranging and general as to be unfalsifiable. Any and every aspect of human behaviour can be explained by either Freudian or Marxist theory. If Popper's criterion is to be believed then these theories, and many others from psychology and the social sciences, will be classed as non-scientific (see Chalmers, 1986, where Adlerian psychology is used as an example, and, more recently, Chalmers, 1990).

Are there more features of 'scientific method' that serve to distinguish science from other kinds of activity? What are the characteristics of a *scientific* enquiry? Scientists observe, classify, measure, hypothesise, experiment and infer. These activities, it is claimed, constitute scientific method. Yet many philosophers of science and practising scientists would deny this. Feyerabend (1975) has argued that 'scientific method', as a unique process, does not exist. Anything goes, in his view (known as 'anarchic epistemology'). He even denies the rationality of science.

Medawar (1979) also denies that there is anything unique about the scientific process: 'Most of the everyday business of the empirical sciences consists in testing experimentally the logical implications of hypotheses – that is, the consequences of assuming for the time being that they are true.' Shortly afterwards he writes: 'These acts of mind are characteristic of *all* exploratory processes and are certainly not confined to experimental sciences. . . .'

Given that a satisfactory definition of scientific method may be impossible to attain, can science be defined by its purposes? A 'purposive definition' might provide a weaker criterion for what does, or does not, count as a science, i.e. the purpose of a science is both to explain and predict. It should explain one set of phenomena and predict certain others. This weaker criterion would admit more disciplines as sciences than any of the more stringent criteria discussed above. The theories of Freud and Marx, for example, are both (in intention at least) explanatory *and* predictive. Psychology strives both to explain and predict human behaviour. Economics might even be accepted as a science. Given the present accuracy of weather forecasting, however, meteorology would be pushed to qualify.

Where do we draw the line?

At least six criteria have been considered for deciding whether an activity or discipline is a science:

1   the unique nature of its concepts, for example, exactness, 'definability'
2   its hypothetico-deductive structure
3   the existence of a prevailing paradigm within it
4   the falsifiability of its observation statements
5   the uniqueness of its methodology (the 'scientific method')
6   its ability to explain *and* predict

Physics alone appears to satisfy all six conditions. Unless one is to admit that physics is the only true science (an unacceptable conclusion to most people), then these criteria cannot *all* be applied at once. Many disciplines that people would wish to call sciences satisfy one or two of the six conditions but not all, i. e. they are not all *necessary* conditions, therefore taken together they must be more than sufficient. However, a discipline unable to satisfy any of these conditions would surely be excluded as a science.

COORDINATION, COMBINATION, INTEGRATION . . . OR SIMPLY BALANCE?

The controversy over the distinguishing features of a science has continued for some considerable time, as the references cited above indicate. It is still alive and well, with many important recent discussions on the nature, philosophy and sociology of science (see further reading at the end of this chapter). The question that remains for science education is: how should the various parts come together to form some sort of coherent whole, i.e. a broad and balanced science curriculum? Balance and integration are not synonymous. It appears from the discussion above that there are insufficient grounds for a truly integrated science or science curriculum, i.e. there is no unifying principle involving the concepts, content or processes of science which can bring about integration. We are thus faced with a mixture rather than a compound in devising a balanced science course. What should this mixture contain?

My own suggestion, which is presented as an Aunt Sally, is that it should include the following:

- a study of the content and concepts of the sciences, giving a balanced coverage of the main sciences and some mention of the less commonly covered sciences
- consideration of the practices and processes of science, i.e. scientific methods and procedures (whilst remembering that there is no clear consensus on a single scientific method)
- study of the links between science, technology and society
- consideration of the history and nature of science

It does seem desirable that science education should be presented as a balanced, coherent and concurrent mixture of these parts, i.e. various sciences taught alongside their methods, their applications, their impact on society, with some consideration of their nature and limits. Is this expecting too much? It is certainly a goal that can be achieved within the framework of a national curriculum.

PROCESS AND CONTENT

Another key issue that concerns all those involved in planning science courses in schools and in designing science curricula is the balance between process and content. Should science courses place most emphasis on the skills and processes of science such as measuring, observing, hypothesising, predicting, and inferring (assuming that these are the processes of science)? Or should the emphasis be on the content of science – its laws and theories, the body of knowledge it has accumulated through the centuries? There was a huge swing towards 'process science' in the late 1980s with such schemes as Warwick Process Science (Screen, 1986a; 1986b), Science in Process (ILEA, 1987), the Suffolk Co-ordinated Science Development (Dobson, 1987) and others.

This swing had a lasting influence, and many of the arguments used to support it are still employed by those who favour process science. The aim of this section is to give the reader an opportunity to consider the arguments for and against both process and content as the dominant approaches in a science course. This has been done by presenting four arguments for process and offering counter-arguments to each one:

1 The content-led approach has failed.
2 'Science for all abilities' necessitates a process-based curriculum.
3 The 'information explosion' has made the teaching of facts highly questionable.
4 Scientific facts date too quickly to form the basis for science education.

1 The failure of the content-led approach

Science teaching has been dominated by the transmission of facts, the 'tyranny of abstractions' and the clutter of 'inert ideas' (Whitehead, 1932), according to its critics.

> If content-led science teaching had been successful, pupils would have acquired the intended understanding of public scientific knowledge and would have been able to apply this knowledge effectively in familiar contexts and creatively in open-ended problem-solving situations. The reality was otherwise. The majority failed to attain the level of mastery of school science which would allow them to proceed to certificate courses; of those who did, some failed to achieve levels which would allow any recognition of attainment, and many were awarded certificates on the basis of performances which, if described in criterion referenced terms, indicated that 50 per cent of their expected knowledge was either faulty or non-existent. Rote learning was widespread. Only a tiny minority of pupils gained the meaningful understanding which allowed them to use their knowledge effectively and creatively and there were justified complaints that even pupils who apparently *knew* a lot could do *very little*.
>
> (Simpson, 1987)

This is a strong argument for the necessity of change. It does not, however, imply that change should be process led. A second argument, which follows from this, does have that implication.

2 The 'science for all' argument necessitates a process-based curriculum

> School science can be made accessible to a much wider range of ability if it becomes less content laden and less abstract. . . . This widening of appeal can be achieved by emphasising and teaching skills and processes. If not everyone can understand scientific ideas, almost everyone, it seems, can be taught to observe, classify or hypothesise.
>
> (Jenkins, 1987)

This view is countered by Jenkins (1989) himself by arguing that scientific knowledge, if presented in an exciting and interesting context, can be equally appealing and accessible. In addition, the simplistic notion that all pupils can be taught to observe, classify, and hypothesise is strongly criticised by Millar (1989).

The belief that the processes of science are in some way simpler and more accessible to pupils of lower ability is based on a mistaken conception of science, which is followed up later. In brief, this misconception of science is based first on a belief that science proceeds inductively, i.e. from the concrete to the abstract, from the particular to the general; and the second that scientific observation, classification, and so on is independent of theory. Both beliefs are wide open to criticism.

3 The 'information explosion' has made the teaching of facts highly questionable

> With the developments of new information technology, facts can be retrieved from data bases with increasing ease – the role of science education is to develop the ability to access, use and ultimately add to the information store when required.
>
>   (see Screen, 1986b, as one exemplar of this argument)

It cannot be doubted that education should respond actively to developments in information technology that provide new devices for the storage and retrieval of information, and that the use of IT is and should be an integral part of the National Curriculum. However, to adopt 'the collection, retrieval and handling of information' as the dominant model in education is surely mistaken for at least three reasons.

First, it is an obvious fact, but worth stating, that thought involves far more than the processing of information. Second, thought is a creative, imaginative, and above all a personal process. This point was best expressed by Michael Polanyi in *Personal Knowledge* (Polanyi, 1958). Polanyi presented the notion of 'tacit knowledge' – knowledge that somehow exists and is constantly being shaped within a person but cannot be described or verbalised. Tacit knowledge joins together what we know with what we feel and experience – only this can lead to full 'understanding'. In other words knowledge is personal, involving a mixture of feelings, emotions, and responses to previous experiences. Two simple examples of personal knowledge might be the ability to ride a bike or the ability to play cricket strokes. Both types of knowledge are personal and often harmed by attempts to verbalise and analyse them (for example, the test-match cricketer who tries to analyse his own batting technique). The tacit or personal knowledge described by Polanyi is one of the most valuable aspects of human life and therefore of the school curriculum and education. Yet it will remain untouched by an education based solely on information skills. Third, learning and education do not involve the *passive* handling and acquisition of information. Human beings are not information-absorbers any more than they are information-processors. Active and meaningful learning involves selecting, interpreting, and transforming information according to the learner's previous experiences, present needs, preconceived ideas, knowledge, and hypotheses. Information handling is not done with a completely open mind any more than scientific observation is, a point first made by Sir Karl Popper (1959).

Information retrieval is theory laden. So in addition to so-called 'information skills', the learner will require these previous ideas, experiences and hypotheses. These are the true concern of science education.

The weakness of using the 'information explosion' as an argument for no longer teaching facts is followed up by several authors in Wellington (1989). Jenkins, for example, points out that the inability of any one person to *know* more than a small fraction of existing knowledge is not a new problem. Other contributors (for example, Millar 1988) discuss Polanyi's notion of tacit knowledge and its importance for science education in more detail.

4 Science facts date so quickly that they should not form the basis of science education

> 'The processes of science learnt by pupils remain after the facts have become out of date or forgotten. It could be said that the most valuable elements of a scientific education are those that remain after the facts have been forgotten.
>
> (Screen, 1986a: 13)

These twin arguments are based on three assumptions, all of which are open to question. First is the assumption that scientific *knowledge* is of a provisional nature and becomes out of date within a short period. This is hardly true of any of the science taught at school level, much of which has been with us for a century or more, including virtually all the laws and theories taught in the three separate sciences and in particular physics. Admittedly motion (for example) is no longer taught along Aristotelian lines (although many pupils and adults think in this way), but it is taught largely within the framework set by Isaac Newton 300 years ago. It could be argued that if the scientific knowledge of the twentieth century were taught in school science, the subject might have broader appeal. But if science education is to be relevant to the outside world it must be accepted that Newtonian mechanics (to continue with that example) should be taught – after all its application helped to put people on the moon. Similar examples can be found throughout the physical, biological, and human sciences.

Second, the argument relies on the belief that although scientific knowledge is provisional, scientific skills and processes are not. This belief has little philosophical or historical evidence to support it. The scientific method adopted by Descartes in his search for certainty bears little resemblance to the processes and skills of Galileo. In fact Descartes' approach is perhaps most similar to the 'thought-experiment' scientific method of Einstein in the twentieth century. Similarly the nature of current scientific activity within the traditions and paradigms first examined by Kuhn (1963) is vastly different from the 'learned gentlemen' scientific fraternity of the last century. In short, then, the processes of science are at least as provisional as its products.

Finally, there is no empirical and little intuitive evidence to support the belief that skills and processes are retained more readily than knowledge. Certainly if the skills and processes learnt in school science are never subsequently used or applied, pupils are unlikely to retain them any more than they will retain isolated facts, disconnected knowledge, or 'inert ideas'.

These are just four of the arguments and counter-arguments for process science. They will be considered again later in the book when we examine the role of practical work in science education – you will probably also hear and read about this ongoing debate in other contexts. It can be seen that there is an interesting and valuable dialogue between process and content in the science curriculum. The two poles provide an excellent way of seeking balance in science education.

STRIKING A BALANCE

It cannot be doubted that the traditional, content-led approach to the science curriculum with an overemphasis on factual recall, inert ideas, irrelevant laws and theories and difficult abstractions has been long overdue for change. But a swing or backlash towards an exclusive emphasis on processes and skills is equally undesirable, philosophically problematic and probably as likely to fail its students as a content-led approach. Particularly dangerous is the belief that processes could and should be taught in isolation from content.

As we have seen in this chapter, there are various ways of conceiving balance, none of which is definitive but all of which can be valuable aids to thinking about the goal of a balanced science curriculum as an entitlement for all pupils. A final framework for considering balance in both science lessons and schemes of work is offered in table 2.3. It presents three kinds of knowledge (Ryle, 1949) as being important in science education: knowledge *that*, i.e. traditional factual recall and the experience of events and phenomena in science; knowledge *how*, i.e. processes

Table 2.3 A balanced science education

Science education can be seen in terms of three categories of knowledge that people who have received a science education should possess:

Knowledge that

   . . . facts, 'happenings', phenomena, experiences

Knowledge how (to)

   . . . skills, processes, abilities

Knowledge why

   . . . explanations, models, analogies, frameworks, theories

A 'balanced' science education will not focus on *one* of these three categories at the expense of the others.

---

and skills; and knowledge *why*, i.e. a knowledge of explanations, laws, frameworks and theories.

Science teachers and curriculum planners could usefully employ these three categories in considering their teaching, science courses and curricula for the future. This framework, and the others presented earlier in the chapter, can certainly be valuable within the context of a national curriculum, however it evolves.

REFERENCES AND FURTHER READING

Bloom, B. S. (1956) *Taxonomy of Educational Objectives*, Cambridge, Mass. : Harvard University Press.

Chalmers, A. F. (1986) *What Is This Thing Called Science?* , Milton Keynes: Open University Press.

—— (1990) *Science and its Fabrication*, Milton Keynes: Open University Press.

Claxton, G. (1989) 'Cognition Doesn't Matter If You're Scared, Depressed or Bored', in Adey, P. (ed.), *Adolescent Development and School Science*, Lewes: Falmer Press.

—— (1991) *Educating the Inquiring Mind: The Challenge for School Science*, London: Harvester Wheatsheaf.

Dobson, K. (1987) *Co-ordinated Science: The Suffolk Development*, London: Collins.

Feyerabend, P. (1975) *Against Method*, London: New Left Books.

Hirst, P. H. (1965) 'Liberal Education and the Nature of Knowledge', in Archambault, R. D. (ed.), *Philosophical Analysis and Education*, London: Routledge.

Inner London Education Authority (ILEA) (1987) *Science in Process*, London: Heinemann.

Jenkins, E. (1987) 'Philosophical Flaws', *Times Education Supplement*, 3 April: 18.

—— (1989) 'Processes in Science Education: An Historical Perspective', in Wellington, J. J. (ed.), *Skills and Processes in Science Education: A Critical Analysis*, London: Routledge.

Korner, S. (1966) *Experience and Theory*, London: Routledge.

—— (1959) *Conceptual Thinking*, New York: Dover.

Kuhn, T. S. (1963) *The Structure of Scientific Revolutions*, Chicago: Chicago University Press.

—— (1978) *Essential Tension*, Chicago: Chicago University Press.

Medawar, P. B. (1969) *Induction and Intuition in Scientific Thought*, London: Methuen.

—— (1979) *Advice to a Young Scientist*, New York: Harper & Row.

Millar, R. (1989) 'What is Scientific Method and Can It Be Taught?', in Wellington, J. J. (ed.), *Skills and Processes in Science Education: A Critical Analysis*, London: Routledge.

Polanyi, M. (1958) *Personal Knowledge*, London: Routledge.

Popper, K. (1959) *The Logic of Scientific Discovery*, London: Hutchinson.

—— (1968) *The Logic of Scientific Discovery*, 3rd ed., London: Hutchinson.

Ryle, G. (1949) *The Concept of Mind*, London: Hutchinson.

Screen, P. (1986a) *Warwick Process Science*, Southampton: Ashford Press.

—— (1986b) 'The Warwick Process Science Project', *School Science Review*, 68 (242): 12–16.

Simpson, M. (1987) 'Suspect Psychology', *Times Educational Supplement*, 3 April.

Smail, B. (1993) 'Science for Girls and for Boys', in Hull, R. (ed.), *ASE Secondary Science Teachers' Handbook*, Hemel Hempstead: Simon & Schuster.

Whitehead, A. N. (1932) *The Aims of Education*, London: Williams and Norgate.

Wellington, J. J. (ed.) (1989) *Skills and Processes in Science Education: A Critical Analysis*, London: Routledge.

3 Science teachers, the nature of science, and the National Science Curriculum

Mick Nott and Jerry Wellington

> As teachers we do not just act as the gateway to knowledge. We ourselves represent, embody, our curriculum. And, in our teaching, we convey not just our explicit knowledge, but also our position towards it, the personal ramifications and implications which it has for us.
>
> (Salmon, 1988: 42)

A teacher's view of what science is may well affect the way they teach science. Also, the nature of science is now an essential element of the science curriculum – can teachers handle this part of the curriculum without at least some reflection on their own view of the nature of science? This chapter encourages you to reflect upon your own view of science and then to consider it in the context of other views of what science is.

WHY CONSIDER THE NATURE OF SCIENCE?

The nature of science in the National Science Curriculum

One very obvious and practical reason for considering the nature of science is the fact that it is present in the National Science Curriculum. At key stages 3 and 4, the understanding of the nature and history of scientific ideas is deemed to be an essential element in the study of science. This element seems to have three essential components, each of which will be explained in more detail shortly. They are:

1 the idea of the limits of science, i.e. it is not the only way of understanding experience
2 the study of changes in scientific ideas over time and across cultures
3 the importance of the context of science, moral, spiritual and cultural; the idea that science is a cultural activity

These components – limits, changes and context or LCC as a mnemonic – are present in both the general PoS and the programme for Science Curriculum 1 (Sc

1) (though sadly not in the other ATs). Thus the PoS for KS 3 requires that pupils should consider the 'benefits and drawbacks of applying scientific and technological ideas' and that they should begin to understand 'how science shapes and influences the quality of their lives' (limits and context). They should also develop their knowledge of how 'scientific ideas change through time' (changes). In the PoS for Sc 1, pupils should be given 'opportunities to understand the limitations of scientific evidence and the provisional nature of proof (limits again). At KS 4 the requirement to study the change of scientific ideas through time is repeated (change). The way in which the use made of science is affected by its social, moral, spiritual and cultural contexts is also added at this level (context). Pupils should also examine 'the power and limitations of science in solving industrial, social and environmental problems' (limits). The PoS relating to AT 1 requires that pupils should explore the nature of science and be able to 'distinguish between claims and arguments based on scientific considerations and those which are not' (limits of science) and that they should study examples of scientific controversies and the way in which scientific ideas change.

These, in brief, are the main elements on the nature of science in the National Science Curriculum with the three clear components (LCC). Teachers are required to include these in their courses and schemes of work – hence the need for teachers to consider their own view of the nature of science.

The importance of the teacher's view

There are many factors which affect the way that science teachers teach. Some are pressures, some constraints, while some will assist and enhance their teaching. Figure 3.1 gives a crude summary of some of the main factors involved:

It is generally accepted that the teacher's own view of the nature of science is one of the important factors although there is some debate as to the level of its importance (Lederman, 1992). In this book we will be considering various notions of science: scientists' science, children's science, National Curriculum science, and of course teachers' science. These are just four of the different locations where different bodies of scientific knowledge reside (Gilbert *et al.*, 1985). Imagine them as different repositories of science, all of which have importance for science education. Everybody forms their own personal construct of what science is. The activity of science teaching involves the interaction of these personal constructs. As Salmon (1988) puts it: 'Education is the systematic interface between personal construct systems.' This is an interesting definition and an important one for this book. It shows that successful teaching must achieve some shared meaning between the various parties involved, some sort of common ground between teachers' science, children's science and accepted scientific knowledge and process (see figure 3.2 and Novak, 1981).

A later chapter looks at children's science and the well-known dictum of David Ausubel (1968): 'The most important single factor influencing learning is what the learner already knows. Ascertain this and teach him accordingly.' This chapter,

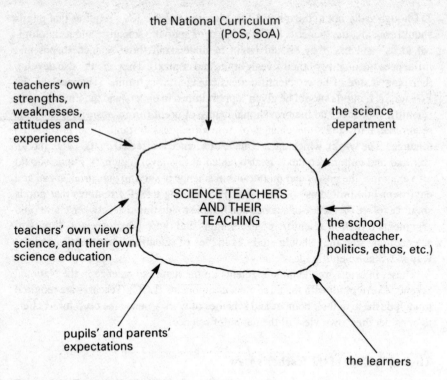

Figure 3.1 Factors affecting science teaching

however, is premised on the belief that what the teacher already knows is a factor affecting teaching. As Shuell puts it, perhaps too strongly:

> 'The conceptions and assumptions we hold about the nature of knowledge, the way knowledge is represented and the manner in which new knowledge is acquired determines what we study in science education, what we teach in science classrooms and the way in which the teaching of science is carried out.'
>
> (Shuell, 1987)

The starting point here is that the teacher's own image or view of what science is does have implications for the way that they present and teach science in the classroom – both on content and process. With this in mind we present the activity below.

YOUR OWN 'NATURE OF SCIENCE' PROFILE

The aim of the activity that follows is to encourage readers to reflect upon their own view of the nature of science. It is intended to be a way of getting you to think, learn and reflect rather than a valid measurement of your position on some sort of objective scale. So don't worry if, at the end of the activity, your profile is not as

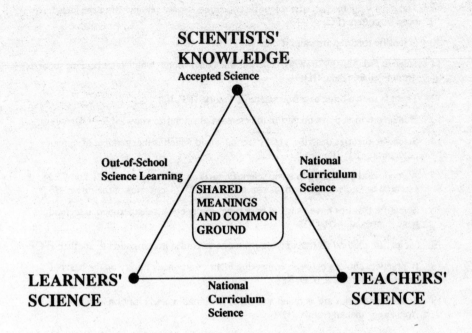

Figure 3.2   Common ground and shared meanings in science education

you expected. The thing to do then is to consider why – this is an important part of the process.

The 24 statements

Please read each of the statements shown in table 3.1 slowly and carefully.

Table 3.1 The 24 statements

---

1   The results that pupils get from their experiments are as valid as anybody else's. (RP)

2   Science is essentially a masculine construct. (CD)

3   Science facts are what scientists agree that they are. (CD, RP)

4   The object of scientific activity is to reveal reality. (IR)

5   Scientists have no idea of the outcome of an experiment before they do it. (ID)

6   Scientific research is economically and politically determined. (CD)

7   Science education should be more about the learning of scientific processes than the learning of scientific facts. (PC)

8   The processes of science are divorced from moral and ethical considerations. (CD)

9   The most valuable part of a scientific education is what remains after the facts have been forgotten. (PC)

10   Scientific theories are valid if they work. (IR)

11   Science proceeds by drawing generalisable conclusions (which later became theories) from available data. (ID)

12   There is such a thing as a true scientific theory. (RP, IR)

13   Human emotion plays no part in the creation of scientific knowledge. (CD)

14   Scientific theories describe a real external world which is independent of human perception. (RP, IR)

15   A good solid grounding in basic scientific facts and inherited scientific knowledge is essential before young scientists can go on to make discoveries of their own. (PC)

16   Scientific theories have changed over time simply because experimental techniques have improved. (RP, CD)

17   'Scientific method' is transferable from one scientific investigation to another. (PC)

18   In practice, choices between competing theories are made purely on the basis of experimental results. (CD, RP)

19   Scientific theories are as much a result of imagination and intuition as inference from experimental results. (ID)

20   Scientific knowledge is different from other kinds of knowledge in that it has higher status. (RP)

21   There are certain physical events in the universe which science can never explain. (RP, IR)

22   Scientific knowledge is morally neutral – only the application of the knowledge is ethically determined. (CD)

23   All scientific experiments and observations are determined by existing theories. (ID)

24   Science is essentially characterised by the methods and processes it uses. (PC)

Give each statement a number from 'strongly agree' (+5) to 'strongly disagree' (−5) and place it next to the statement. A score of 0 will indicate a balanced view. (For the time being, ignore the initials in brackets.)

Working out your profile

Having 'scored' each statement you now need to work out your own profile. Look closely at figure 3.3:

Each statement has at least two letters in brackets after it – for example, PC; some have four – for example, RP, CD. Put your score for each question into the appropriate box or boxes in figure 3.3, i.e. some score once, some twice. Note carefully that some scores have to have their sign reversed (i.e. − becomes + and + becomes − before they can be entered into the box).

After you have entered all your numbers into the boxes add up the totals, then transfer the totals from the columns to the correct position on each of the five relevant axes. Join up the five options with straight lines to show your profile of science. Are you a raving relativist? A proud positivist? Or a coy contextualist? What do all these terms mean anyway?

Your nature of science

Many of the terms used may be unfamiliar. In fact, many of them are problematic and a matter of debate. Their meanings change and shift and can be seen as insults or praise depending on to whom you are talking.

Definitions for the meanings attached to the five axes in the figure are offered below. In doing this we have consulted Bynum *et al.* (1983), Wellington (1989) and Ziman (1980).

1 Relativism/Positivism Axis

Relativist: You deny that things are true or false solely based on an independent reality. The 'truth' of a theory will depend on the norms and rationality of the social group considering it as well as the experimental techniques used to test it. Judgements as to the truth of scientific theories will vary from one individual to another and from one culture to another, i.e. truth is relative, not absolute.

Positivist: You believe strongly that scientific knowledge is more 'valid' than other forms of knowledge. The laws and theories generated by experiments are our descriptions of patterns we see in a real, external, objective world.

To the positivist, science is the primary source of truth. Positivism recognises empirical facts and observable phenomena as the raw material of science. The scientist's job is to establish the objective relationships between the laws governing the facts and observables. Positivism rejects inquiry into underlying causes and ultimate origins.

2 Inductivism/Deductivism

Inductivist: You believe that the scientist's job is the interrogation of nature. By observing many particular instances, one is able to infer from the particular to the general and then determine the underlying laws and theories.

According to inductivism, scientists generalise from a set of observations to a universal law 'inductively'. Scientific knowledge is built by induction from a secure set of observations.

Deductivist: In our definition this means that you believe that scientists proceed by testing ideas produced by the logical consequences of current theories or of their bold, imaginative ideas.

IR

Statement	Score
10	−
21	−
4	+
12	+
14	+
Total	

PC

Statement	Score
7	−
9	−
17	−
24	−
15	+
Total	

CD

Statement	Score
2	−
3	−
6	−
8	−
13	+
16	+
18	+
22	+
Total	

ID

Statement	Score
5	−
11	−
19	+
23	+
Total	

RP

Statement	Score
1	−
3	−
21	−
12	+
14	+
16	+
18	+
20	+
Total	

Add up the scores in the right-hand columns to give you a grand total for each grid.

N.B. Some statements score positive, some negative.

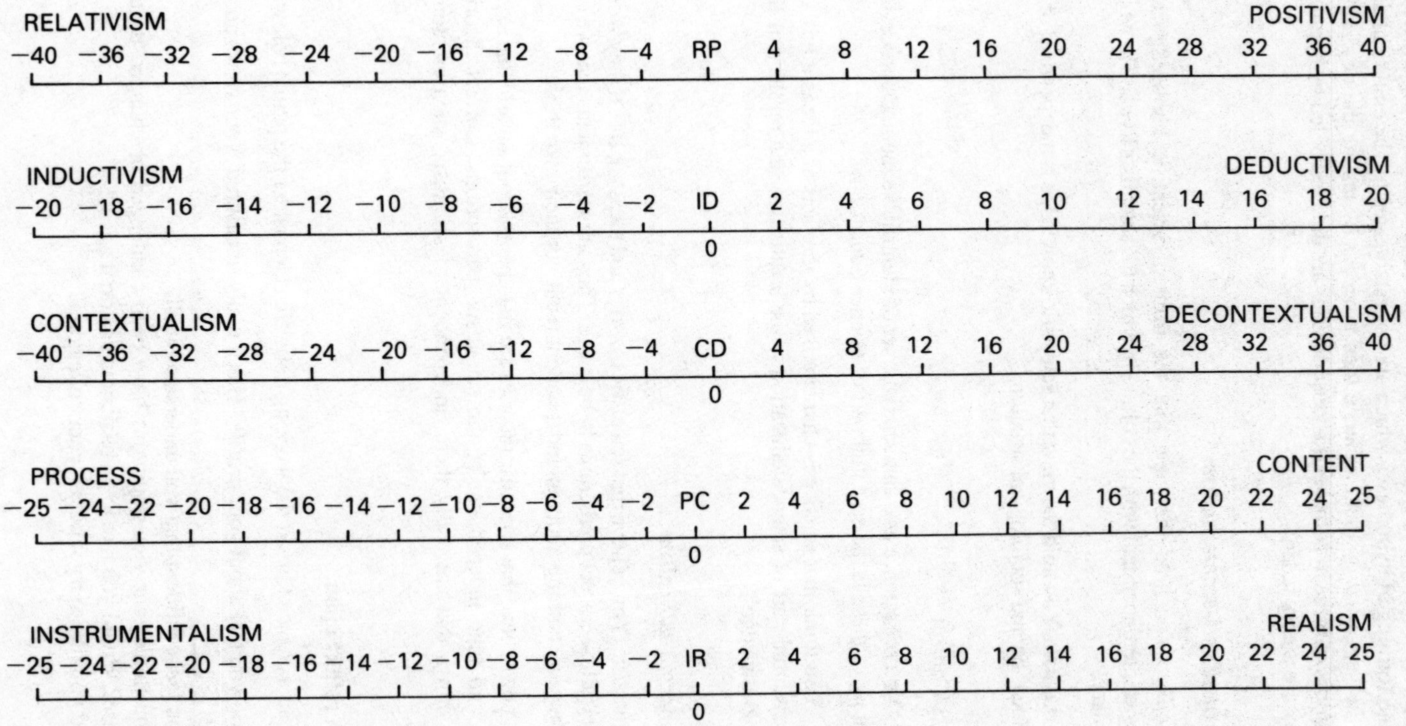

RELATIVISM −40 −36 −32 −28 −24 −20 −16 −12 −8 −4 RP 4 8 12 16 20 24 28 32 36 40 POSITIVISM

INDUCTIVISM −20 −18 −16 −14 −12 −10 −8 −6 −4 −2 ID 2 4 6 8 10 12 14 16 18 20 DEDUCTIVISM

0

CONTEXTUALISM −40 −36 −32 −28 −24 −20 −16 −12 −8 −4 CD 4 8 12 16 20 24 28 32 36 40 DECONTEXTUALISM

0

PROCESS −25 −24 −22 −20 −18 −16 −14 −12 −10 −8 −6 −4 −2 PC 2 4 6 8 10 12 14 16 18 20 22 24 25 CONTENT

0

INSTRUMENTALISM −25 −24 −22 −20 −18 −16 −14 −12 −10 −8 −6 −4 −2 IR 2 4 6 8 10 12 14 16 18 20 22 24 25 REALISM

0

Figure 3.3 Plotting your profile

According to deductivism (or hypothetico-deductivism), scientific reasoning consists of the forming of hypotheses which are not established by the empirical data but may be suggested by them. Science then proceeds by testing the observable consequences of these hypotheses, i.e. observations are directed or led by hypotheses – they are theory laden.

3 Contextualism/Decontextualism

Contextualist: You hold the view that the truth of scientific knowledge and processes is interdependent with the culture in which the scientists live and in which it takes place.

Decontextualist: You hold the view that scientific knowledge is independent of its cultural location and sociological structure.

4 Process/Content

Process: You see science as a characteristic set of identifiable methods/processes. The learning of these is the essential part of science education.

Content: You think that science is characterised by the facts and ideas it has and that the essential part of science education is the acquisition and mastery of this 'body of knowledge'.

5 Instrumentalism/Realism

Instrumentalist: You believe that scientific theories and ideas are fine if they work, that is they allow correct predictions to be made. They are instruments that we can use but they say nothing about an independent reality or their own truth.

Realist: You believe that scientific theories are statements about a world that exists in space and time independent of the scientists' perceptions. Correct theories describe things that are really there, independent of scientists, such as atoms, electrons.

Points to reflect upon

Having had a chance to read the working definitions, consider the points below:

- How do you feel about your profile? Has it really 'measured' your views about science?
- Do you feel confident that you understand it all?
- Do you think your views/opinions have been challenged or changed by the exercise? Would you like to go back now and do it again?
- Would you like to try it out on your colleagues?

Whatever the shape of your profile, please do not worry and do not panic! There are many 'natures of science'.

CONCLUDING REMARKS

One of the messages that runs through the PoS of the National Curriculum is that scientific knowledge is provisional, i. e. its ideas, laws and theories are subject to change. This is even more true of views on the nature of science. There is no general consensus on what science is – neither is there a commonly agreed view of what constitutes 'scientific method'. Many people argue that the way science is viewed and conceptualised varies from one discipline to another, for example, from life science to physical science (Lederman, 1992). There is certainly a wide variation in view amongst well-known philosophers on the nature of science, ranging from Popper (1959) and Kuhn (1963) to Feyerabend (1975), with the latter arguing against the idea of there being any such thing as scientific method (see further reading). Other commentators on the nature of science such as Collins (1985) and Woolgar (1988) have focused on the way that scientists actually work. A single common message is that scientists do not have a rigid or fixed view of what science is, or of what constitutes scientific method.

In short, the message for teachers and curriculum planners is that there is no definitive view of what science and scientific method are, any more than science itself is fixed and absolute. It therefore makes no sense to accuse teachers of having an inadequate conception of science, nor to berate them for it (as has happened in the past: Lederman, 1992). What can be expected of teachers, however, is that they do recognise in their teaching that science as a body of knowledge is provisional and that there is no single accepted view of scientific method. They should also emphasise that science and technology are not neutral or value-free activities. They are pursued within the context of a culture or society with its own economic and political pressures and constraints (Thorp, 1991: 135).

This chapter has attempted to encourage readers to reflect on their own view of science within those terms. Chapter 15 offers practical suggestions and guidelines for dealing with the nature of science in the classroom.

REFERENCES AND FURTHER READING

Ausubel, D. (1968) *Educational Psychology: a Cognitive View*, New York: Holt, Rhinehart & Winston.
Bynum, W. F., Browne, E. J. and Porter, R. (1983) *Macmillan Dictionary of the History of Science*, London: Macmillan.
Collins, H. (1985) *Changing Order: Replication and Induction in Scientific Practice*, London: Sage.
Gilbert, J., Watts, D. and Osborne, R. (1985) 'Eliciting Students' Views Using an Interview-about-instances Technique', in West, L. and Pines, A. (eds), *Cognitive Structure and Conceptual Change*, pp.11–27, New York: Academic Press.
Kuhn, T. S. (1963) *The Structure of Scientific Revolutions*, Chicago: Chicago University Press.

Lederman, N. (1992) 'Students' and Teachers' Conceptions of the Nature of Science: A Review of the Research', *Journal of Research in Science Teaching*, 29 (4): 351–9.

Novak, J. D. (1981) 'Effective Science Instruction: The Achievement of Shared Meaning', *The Australian Science Teachers Journal*, 27 (1): 5–13.

Popper, K. R. (1959) *The Logic of Scientific Discovery*, London: Hutchinson.

Salmon, P. (1988) *Psychology for Teachers: an Alternative Approach*, London: Hutchinson.

Shuell, T. (1987) 'Cognitive Psychology and Conceptual Change: Implications for Teaching Science', *Science Education*, 7 (2): 239–50.

Thorp, S. (ed.) (1991) *Race, Equality and Science Teaching*, Hatfield: Association for Science Education (ASE).

Wellington, J. J. (ed.) (1989) *Skills and Processes in Science Education: A Critical Analysis*, London: Routledge.

Woolgar, S. (1988) *Science: The Very Idea*, London: Tavistock Ltd.

Ziman, J. (1980) *Teaching and Learning about Science and Society*, Cambridge: Cambridge University Press.

More reflection

Three other activities which readers could consider on their own, or better still do with other consenting adults, are:

1 What is science?
2 What is science education about?
3 Culture in the classroom.

The above activities are in Thorp, S. (ed.) (1991) *Race, Equality and Science Teaching*, Hatfield: ASE, pp. 24–32.

FURTHER READING ON THE NATURE OF SCIENCE AND TEACHERS' VIEWS

Brickhouse, N. W. (1991) 'Teachers' Content Knowledge About the Nature of Science and its Relationship to Classroom Practice', *Journal of Teacher Education*, 41 (3): 53–62 (an intensive study of three science teachers with varying backgrounds and experience showed that their understandings about science not only influence explicit lessons about the nature of science but also shape an implicit curriculum concerning scientific knowledge).

Duschl, R. A. and Wright, E. (1989) 'A Case Study of High School Teachers' Decision-making Models for Planning and Teaching Science', *Journal of Research in Science Teaching*, 26: 467–502 (found that the science teachers in their study were committed to a hypothetico-deductive view of scientific method and to teaching the factual knowledge of the discipline. They put little emphasis on the nature and role of theories).

Koulaidis, V. and Ogborn, J. (1989) 'Philosophy of Science: an Empirical Study of Teachers' Views', *International Journal of Science Education*, 11 (2): 173–84 (showed that teachers vary in their views of science but that few are naive inductivists).

Lakin, S. and Wellington, J. J. (1994) 'Who Will Teach the Nature of Science?', *International Journal of Science Education*. Forthcoming (a study of teachers' views of science and the difficulties they face in teaching the nature of science).

Lantz, O. and Kass, H. (1987) 'Chemistry Teachers Functional Paradigms', *Science Education*, 71: 117–34 (studied three chemistry teachers using the same basic chemistry curriculum and found that they taught very different lessons on the nature of science following their own differing views).

Millar, R. (ed.) (1989) *Doing Science: Images of Science in Science Education*, Lewes:

Falmer Press (a collection of articles on, broadly speaking, the relationship of science education to images and studies of the nature of science).

Theme B
Teaching, learning and assessing science

Theme B

Teaching, learning and
assessing science

4 Learning and teaching science

Jon Scaife

Traveller:	'Excuse me – could you tell me how to get to the London Palladium please?'
First person:	'No, but I'll tell you how *I* got there.'
Second person:	'Yes, but not from where *you* are.'
Third person:	'Practise, practise, practise!'

> Pity the poor traveller! This chapter is about trying to improve the journey. Some basic questions are asked, such as: What's the problem? How are you travelling? Have you been this way before? Do you know these parts? And then: What can be done to help the traveller on the journey?

INTRODUCTION

Picture one or two science classes that you have been in most recently. If you could put 'yes' or 'no' in any of the boxes in figure 4.1, what would you put in order to represent what you saw going on in these classes? Would you put 'yes' in the top left box, for example, to indicate that you saw teaching done by teachers?

	TEACHERS	PUPILS
TEACHING?	*yes*	*yes*
LEARNING?	*yes*	

Figure 4.1   Teaching/learning in class

It is highly likely that many of us *would* put a 'yes' in the top left box. Some people who have been asked about this also put 'yes' in the upper right box, because they have seen pupils teaching. Some people with teaching experience put 'yes' in the lower left box, feeling that while they are teachers they are also learning. Each of these choices has resulted in a measure of consensus among teachers. The last box, 'pupils learning', seems to be more problematic. There have been less agreement and less confidence among teachers about what to put in this box. There is uncertainty about *whether* pupils *are* learning, *what* they are learning, whether they are learning what they *should be* learning, *how to tell* what they are learning and *how to affect* what they are learning. Perhaps the reason for this is obvious: as teachers we have continual first-hand experience of both the 'teaching' row and the 'teachers' column in figure 4.1. Our experiences of the 'pupils learning' box, however, are second-hand or are confined to our own past.

The mysterious contents of this box have been the subject of increasing interest in recent years.

> Some educators and researchers in education have come to the conclusion that, as a foundation for their activities, they must develop some theoretical ideas as to how children build up their picture of the world they experience. They believe that unless they have a model of the student's concepts and conceptual operations, there is no effective way of teaching.
>
> (von Glasersfeld, 1991: 21)

The remainder of this chapter is based on the idea that if more could be learnt about how people learn, then pupils and teachers would both benefit. The chapter sets out to give a brief introduction to some theories of learning, to some ideas that children have in science and to some possible approaches for teachers. Suggestions for further reading are given at the end.

WHAT'S THE PROBLEM?

Most science teachers are well qualified in science and have completed school science courses with considerable success. Does this show that science teaching and learning are on sound footings? Consider this report, from the *Times Educational Supplement*:

- 24 per cent of the GCSE age group managed grade F or above in GCSE chemistry in 1988 compared with 74 per cent in English.
- only about 15 per cent of 14-year-olds will reach the National Curriculum target for average pupils in science at KS 3 (levels 5/6).

These startling statistics, reported by Michael Shayer, need to be seen in a context in which science at upper secondary level (age 14 and above) has shifted from being an option for those with sufficient interest and aptitude to an 'entitlement' for all pupils (an entitlement that they are not entitled to refuse!): 'The implementation of the National Curriculum will ensure that all pupils have access to science education from the age of 5 to the age of 16. . . . Every pupil is entitled to a broad and relevant science curriculum' (National Curriculum Council, 1989). In the past, many pupils who selected science also succeeded at it. They evidently found effective ways of learning in science. Shayer's evidence suggests that this cannot be expected of *all* pupils, or even the majority, despite the introduction of a national curriculum designed for all.

Another perspective (see, for example, Millar, 1993) on the impact of science education on the population as a whole might be gained by judging the level of public understanding of science in, for example, the quality of debate of scientific issues in the daily press (see Wellington, 1991) or the coverage of science in news broadcasts.

There is evidence, then, of a serious mismatch between actual learning and learning targets. What can be done?

- Should the National Curriculum be revised again?
- Should pupils' learning be rewarded more generously?
- Should we try to find out more about how pupils learn?

The third option lies within the scope of this chapter.

HOW DO CHILDREN LEARN?

This is an open question, to which we are unlikely to find a single 'right' answer. There are, though, several useful and interesting *theories* about learning. Theories are constructed by people and they are shaped by forces that shape people, forces associated with culture, ideology, training, needs and so on. It is probable that everyone reading this book both has their own personal theories of learning and applies them, even if only in informal ways. One theory might be: 'A good way to get children to learn is to tell them things.'

This chapter can only contain a selection of brief theoretical ideas from the research literature. I will offer a selection that is explicitly personal: three theories that have helped me to construct for myself a model of children's learning.

Development

As people grow they develop intellectually as well as physically. Their powers of reasoning and their capacity to experience ranges of emotions increase. As they grow they are able to learn new ideas. What kinds of tasks and problems can children solve at different ages? This question was studied in detail by Jean Piaget (see note 1). He drew inferences about the cognitive processes employed by individual children as they attempted to solve various kinds of problems. The result of this experimental work, together with Piaget's view of intelligence as an adaptively favourable characteristic in natural selection, led him to propose a theory of children's cognitive development. The impact of Piaget's ideas on teaching in Britain has been very considerable; according to Edwards and Mercer (1987: 36) Piagetian theory 'legitimised the pedagogy' of the Plowden Report. Edwards and Mercer found that teachers generally identified themselves with this pedagogy through their everyday actions.

According to Piaget, children make meaning for themselves; they learn through actively constructing knowledge. A new experience might be *assimilated* by a child into her or his current cognitive structure. The experience might, however, be in conflict with the child's current cognitive structure, resulting in the structure changing or *accommodating* to the new information. Piaget saw these processes of assimilation and accommodation as helping to bring about 'equilibrium' between the child's cognitive structure and the environment. Teachers might use the associated idea of 'cognitive conflict' to stimulate learning in children. Here is an illustration: some children connect an electric bell to a battery. They can hear it ringing loudly and see that the arm of the bell is moving. The teacher then produces a second, similar bell inside a glass jar. Everyone can see that the bell is connected to a battery and that its arm is moving like the first bell, but it can only just be heard. Why is this? (first cognitive conflict). Pupils might assimilate the experience by suggesting that the glass is stopping the sound or that the arm is not hitting the sounder. The teacher, who has earlier pumped air from the jar, opens a valve to let air back in and the bell can now be heard clearly (second cognitive conflict). This is harder to assimilate! The intention is that pupils will accommodate a new idea, in this case that air can carry sound.

Piaget believed that although cognitive development in children is a continuous process, it does not take place smoothly, at a steady rate. He identified three principal *stages* of development, which occur in a definite order, as illustrated in

Cognitive development

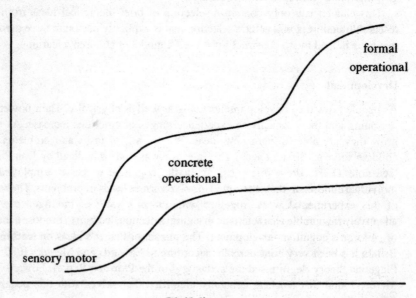

Figure 4.2   Piagetian stages of development

simplified form in figure 4.2. Children of school age have normally reached either the concrete operational stage or the formal operational stage.

Concrete operational thinking involves processes such as classifying, sorting and ordering objects. The child has developed ideas of conservation and revers-ibility; when a ball of Plasticene is moulded into a new shape and then rolled back into a ball, the child may know that the amount and weight of Plasticene remain unchanged through the cycle. Driver (1983: 55) illustrates the type of inferential logical problem that might be solved at this cognitive stage: If water in beaker A is hotter than water in beaker B, and water in beaker B is hotter than water in beaker C, which beaker has the coldest water in it?

Formal operational thinking is associated with the use of hypothetical models for the purpose of explaining things. It is characteristic of situations involving several variables and also of the use of the mathematical notions of ratio and proportion.

The significance of these cognitive stages of development for science teachers, then, is that some forms of learning cannot be achieved until children reach the formal operational stage. Piaget's experimental work led him to believe that formal operational thinking can take place in 12-year-olds, but subsequent research (Shayer *et al.*, 1976; Lawson and Renner, 1978) indicates that most children develop formal thinking much later than this and some do not develop it at all.

It has been argued that familiarity with the idea of stages of cognitive develop-ment will allow teachers to devise approaches to the science curriculum with greater insight (Shayer and Adey, 1981). A science scheme, 'Thinking Science', which has been designed with explicit reference to Piaget's model, will be described later in this chapter.

Active construction of knowledge

A major scientific debate took place during the late nineteenth and early twentieth centuries. The question was: Is space full of ether? Ether was an attractive idea because it gave a sense of absoluteness to space and it helped to overcome difficult puzzles such as how light travelled through space from the sun to the earth. A famous experiment by Michelson and Morley in 1887 was designed to show the effect of the earth moving through the ether. No effect was found. Within twenty years Einstein proposed that we cannot detect *absolute* physical properties of space; the only properties we can detect are *relative* ones – people's views of the physical universe depend on their relative circumstances (such as whether they are moving relative to each other). The ether is a property of absolute space; Einstein's ideas imply that we cannot know if ether, or absolute space, exists.

There are some similarities between the evolution of these ideas in physics and those in some fields of psychology and philosophy. For a long time, a dominant cultural view in the West has been that there is a universe 'out there' and that scientists are gradually uncovering fragments of truth about it. This perspective is sometimes called 'inductive realism' (see, for example, Selley 1989 and other chapters in this volume). At the same time, the dominant model of science teaching has been that teachers draw their pitchers from the wells of truth and pour knowledge from them into the empty vessels which are their pupils' minds. Another name for this model of teaching is the 'tabula rasa' or blank slate approach (which used to be commonplace in undergraduate lectures). The inductive realist view has been seriously challenged by numerous writers for many years. So far, in this field there is no equivalent of the Michelson-Morley ether experiment, but this has not stopped people from questioning the relevance of the idea of an *absolute* universe: 'I have never said (nor would I ever say) that there is *no* ontic world, but I keep saying that we cannot *know* it' (von Glasersfeld, 1991: 17).

In the view of von Glasersfeld and others who describe themselves as 'constructivists', people do not acquire knowledge about an independent reality; rather they *construct* knowledge to fit what they experience: 'the world we come to know (is) assembled out of elements of our very own experience'. (von Glasersfeld, 1991: 19).

How do people construct knowledge? Jeanne Bamberger and Donald A. Schon reported a study in which they observed people constructing meaning for themselves while working with simple materials and objects:

> This process we were able to see among our participants: Looking for something they did not yet know, they most often found it. And most often it emerged through a 'piton effect', like the process of pulling yourself up through your own power to a new position (and view) on a mountain.
>
> (Bamberger and Schon, 1991: 188)

Bamberger and Schon coined the term 'knowledge-in-action' to represent a person's current state of mental constructions. Knowledge-in-action is mobile and unstable. It includes what is gathered in passing and also what the individual knows *how* to do but cannot necessarily *say*:

> knowing *how* is most often hidden in the knower's actions; it remains silent – expressed in the builders' *work* but not in words. And since most of us are prone to equate 'knowledge' with what can be expressed in our conventional tongues and symbol systems, it seems quite natural to consider knowing how as if it were not knowledge at all.
>
> (Bamberger and Schon, 1991: 207)

By learning to see knowledge-in-action, Bamberger and Schon were able to understand how their 'builders' built new knowledge.

Driver and Bell (1985), working in the context of the school science curriculum, identified a set of key points which they referred to as a *constructivist view of learning*. These points are:

- Learning outcomes depend not only on the learning environment but also on the prior knowledge, attitudes and goals of the learner.
- Learning involves construction of knowledge through experience with the physical environment and through social interactions.

- Constructing links with prior knowledge is an active process involving the generation, checking and restructuring of ideas and hypotheses.
- Learning science is not simply a matter of adding to and extending existing concepts, but may involve their radical reorganisation.
- Meanings, once constructed, can be accepted or rejected. The construction of meaning does not always lead to belief.
- Learning is not passive. Individuals are purposive beings who set their own goals and control their own learning.
- Students frequently bring similar ideas, about natural phenomena, to the classroom. Some constructed meanings are shared by many students.

For a short, readable discussion of this constructivist view of learning see Scott (1987).

Active construction, active learning and activity

The previous section put forward the view that people actively construct new knowledge of their own, rather than being passive recipients of someone else's knowledge. This apparently simple idea could have very significant implications for teaching (and also for parenting and for some of the ways in which we try to persuade people to change their views). How is the notion of active construction related to 'active learning'?

If the job of a science teacher were simply to *transmit* knowledge to a class, then the teacher might rate the following lesson characteristics highly:

- quiet, attentive class
- a lot of work 'got through' in each lesson
- efficient coverage of the syllabus
- students able to demonstrate knowledge in written tests

Such a teacher would tend to operate in 'transmission mode' and would cast her or his students into the role of 'passive learners'. Clive Carre (1981) lists several reasons why a teacher might choose this mode of teaching:

- Time: If the teacher talks and students listen the curriculum appears to be covered much more quickly.
- Tradition: Transmission mode was often 'good enough' for the teacher so it is good enough for the students.
- Student pressure: Many students indicate that they prefer the teacher to do the work – and in particular, the thinking.
- Security: Transmission mode allows the teacher to keep tight hold of the reins and feel secure in what is going on in the lessons.
- Status: Transmission mode allows the teacher to maintain the role of 'expert'.

Contrast the 'passive learning' environment with what Bentley and Watts (1989) described as a necessary set of requirements for 'active learning':

- a non-threatening learning environment

- pupil involvement in the organisation of the learning process
- opportunities for learners to take decisions about the content of their own learning
- direct skill teaching
- continuous assessment and evaluation
- relevance and vocationalism

Contrasted above are two types of learning *environments*. I do not believe that these environments create two types of learning *processes*, one active and one passive, because I think that learning is essentially an active process. But different environments can and, I believe, inevitably do result in the construction of different kinds of new knowledge. An appropriately designed learning environment can *focus* learning; it can help to concentrate the energy of active knowledge construction towards a particular domain of thought and experience. In an inadequately designed learning environment, children still have intellectual energy and they still construct new ideas, but the focus is uncertain – it *could* be the carbon cycle but it could equally be determined by any of a whole spectrum of personal needs of each individual child.

Neither of the environments described above can be guaranteed to bring about focused learning, because this depends on more than the environment. As to which is the better designed, each will have its supporters.

In much the same way, *activity* is not, in itself, any guarantee of focused learning. Students may be on their feet in a laboratory, handling scientific apparatus, talking and listening to each other, writing observations and so on, but this guarantees very little about the nature of the learning that is taking place. Activity may be necessary for some forms of knowledge construction but it is by no means sufficient. In particular, as is pointed out by Driver and elsewhere in this volume, science practical activity is rarely an end in itself:

Many . . . practical lessons end abruptly when the prescribed task is complete and little, if any, time is given to the interpretation of the results obtained, although this is just as important as the activity itself. Pupils need time to think around and consolidate the new ideas presented to them. After all, they may have developed their own ideas as a result of many years of experience. It is unlikely that they will easily adopt new ways of thinking as a result of one or two science lessons. . . . [P]erhaps the time has come to help children make more sense of those practical experiences. What is being suggested is not a return to a more didactic teaching, but an extension of the range of types of activities in science classes.

(Driver, 1983: 83).

Shared ideas and new knowledge

No man is an Island, entire of it self; every man is a piece of the Continent, a part of the main.

(If John Donne were writing today, hopefully he would have included women and children too!) Up to now, intellectual development and knowledge construction have been considered from the point of view of the individual. But we are a social species, the more so by virtue of our possession of language. Is this significant? Do *interpersonal* processes influence how and what we learn? Humberto Maturana (1991: 30) certainly thinks that they do: 'Science is a human activity. Therefore, whatever we scientists do as we do science has validity and meaning, as any other human activity does, only in the context of human coexistence in which it arises.' Central to this coexistence is language. For Maturana, we exist in language, experience takes place in language and we know what we know through its constitution in language.

Maturana may be regarded by some as holding a radical view but the underlying point, that knowledge is constructed by individuals through interpersonal processes, is now shared by many people. Jerome Bruner (1964) stressed the importance of language in cognitive development nearly thirty years earlier. Around this time, the work of L. S. Vygotsky began to appear in the West, having been suppressed for two decades in Russia. Vygotsky (1978) believed that 'children undergo quite profound changes in their understanding by engaging in joint activity and conversation with other people'. This view is shared by Edwards and Mercer (1987), who regard knowledge and thought as 'fundamentally cultural, deriving their distinctive properties from the nature of social activity, language, discourse and other cultural forms'. The implication is that *meaning* is constructed not only through processes operating on individuals – such as the stimulation of senses or the mediation of prior knowledge – but also through processes of social communication (see note 2). This being so, it is no surprise, according to Joan Solomon (1989), that the alternative meanings brought by children into the classroom contain many *common* threads and ideas.

In one respect, the currently established practical approach to school science in Britain stands out for having legitimised learning through social interaction, since pupils almost always carry out experimental work in small groups and it is generally accepted that they will talk to each other in the process. Whether this talk results in meaningful learning in science depends greatly on the design of the practical task and its context in the lesson. Practical tasks which are designed on a recipe basis, or with the principal aim of simply occupying the class, are likely to result at best in rote learning – and if that is what is wanted then there are surely better ways of promoting it.

The affective domain

> Don't know much about science books, don't know much about the French I took. . . .
> But I know that one and one makes two, and I know that if you love me too. . .
> .

The discussion in this chapter has, up to now, been dominated by consideration of the cognitive domain, to the exclusion of the emotions or the wilfulness of the child. This may simply reflect the relative amounts of work that have taken place in these fields in recent times, rather than their relative significance in contributing greater understanding of how children learn. John Head (1989) predicts, however, that the focus of research interest is set to change: '[T]he affective area . . . will prove to be crucial, in research and curriculum planning, in the next decade.' This surely should be the case. If we are serious about improving our understanding of how a person's future learning is influenced by her or his past and present then we should be looking at the *whole person*, not just at the person's history of cognitive construction. We can reflect on this here: do you sense any influences, acting on you right now, competing with each other to determine what your mind dwells on next? I am aware of several current influences: I want to finish this chapter, I am thinking rationally about what I'm writing, and I would like another mug of coffee! Are children's thoughts in the classroom all that different? In the appositely titled paper, 'Cognition doesn't matter if you're scared, depressed or bored', Guy Claxton (1989) describes a set of pupil 'stances' that determine not only the 'amount' of learning that takes place but also the direction or domain in which it takes place. Claxton's labels are deliberately evocative: swot, thinker, boffin, socialite, dreamer, rebel and sinker. This classification is not based on any empirical data; nonetheless the stances have some 'chalk-face' appeal and they lend support to the argument that 'attitude' and 'motivation' are key elements in determining learning.

The 'zone of proximal development'

One of Vygotsky's ideas helps me to link the three main themes of this section: (1) cognitive development, (2) active construction of knowledge, (3) social interaction. Vygotsky coined the phrase (in Russian): 'zone of proximal development', which some authors have shortened to 'zoped' or ZPD. One description (Vygotsky 1978: 86) is that a child has a personal zoped that represents 'the distance between the actual developmental level as determined by independent problem-solving, and the level of potential development as determined through problem-solving under adult guidance or in collaboration with more capable peers'. Interpreted in this pragmatic way, the zoped is an *extra* amount of constructing that can be done by the child, and its 'size' depends on:

- the child's current level of development
- the child's current mental constructions
- the discourse between the child and her or his environment

Region 1 in figure 4.3 is a zone which represents the child's current development (cognitive and affective). Region 2 is the child's zoped, representing potential development in the near future. The arrows in figure 4.3 represent learning, leading towards new development. Since a central issue in teaching is the promotion and guidance of learning, the effectiveness of teaching could be judged according to how it assists (or otherwise) the construction and direction of these arrows.

The adult's action in guiding the child's learning has been likened by Bruner

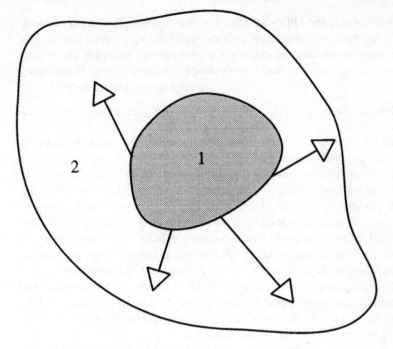

Figure 4.3 'Pragmatist' model of a zoped

(1985: 25) to the construction of scaffolding: '[T]he tutor in effect performs the critical function of "scaffolding" the learning task to make it possible for the child . . . to internalize external knowledge.' A word of caution is appropriate here, because the word 'scaffolding' can conjure up significantly different images. One image which is sometimes implied in discussion of Bruner's scaffolding idea is that of a temporary structural support; a 'buttress' would be a more accurate term for this. The purpose of scaffolding in the building trade is to support the *process* of construction, not to support the structure itself. Bruner's choice of word suggests process, but who does the building – the child or the adult?

Newman and Holzman are fiercely critical of 'pragmatic' interpretations of the zoped. They argue that 'the ZPD is not a zone at all' (1993: 88) but rather that it is 'a reorganising of environmental scenes to create new meaning and a learning that leads to development' (1993: 147). This is a much broader notion than the functional object described above: for example, 'Speaking (verbalizing, using a language) is, perhaps, the single human performance that best exemplifies . . . the form and substance of the life space of everyday human performance, the ZPD' (1993: 112). According to these authors the school by no means necessarily contributes constructively to development through learning:

> Traditional schools are not ZPDs; they teach children and adults alike to devalue and even destroy ZPDs. In the typical classroom children are taught to view the

major activities in the ZPD – working together, imitating that produces something other than mere repetition, collectively changing the total determining environment into something that is not predetermined, reshaping the existing tools of language and play into new meanings and discovery – as illegitimate.

(Newman and Holzman, 1993: 195)

I doubt that these authors would support a call to return to traditional schools with traditional values!

Vygotsky's view is that learning *leads* development in the zoped. When teaching, guidance or collaboration moves ahead of development it 'impels or wakens a whole series of functions that are in a stage of maturation lying in the zone of proximal development' (Vygotsky, quoted in Newman and Holzman, 1993: 60). This contrasts sharply with the idea that learning can take place until it reaches limits imposed by the current level of development, a view associated with Piaget.

The zoped represents current *potential* learning, leading to new development. It is not a characteristic of the child alone but rather it is an aspect of the large, complex *system* consisting of the child and her or his environment. 'Environment' is used here in the most general sense, including the child's peers, parents, teachers and school, the physical environment and also the social context, its history and the history of the child. Whether the child's potential learning is actually realised depends on the operation of the system as a whole.

So far, we have focused on children's mental processes of thinking and feeling. In the next section we describe some of the contents of children's thoughts in the field of science.

CHILDREN'S IDEAS IN SCIENCE

Alternative ideas

In an investigation of their understanding of the word 'plant', children were asked: Would you say any of these pictures are of plants? (Osborne and Freyberg 1985: 6). This response from a 9-year-old is not atypical: 'Grass is a plant; a seed is a plant – well it'll grow into a plant. Definitely not a carrot – it's a vegetable. And not an oak tree; it's a small tree then it's a big tree, not a plant.'

A response like this indicates that the child has definite ideas about the scientific topic (classification, in this case) and further, that these ideas are not the same as the scientific community's views.

Another study reported by Osborne and Freyberg used cards like those shown in figure 4.5 to investigate children's views about light. Concerning card (a) students were asked: Does the candle make light? What happens to the light? Where it was relevant, the children were then asked: How far does the light from the candle go?

Following the last question, four students said: 'one metre at the most'; 'about one foot'; 'just stays there and lights up'; 'stays there'. Two of these responses came from 10-year-olds and two from 15-year-olds. The 15-year-olds had studied light

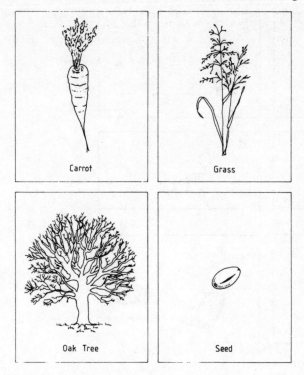

Figure 4.4 'Would you say that this is a plant?'
Source: Osborne and Freyberg, 1985

as a science topic and they could define terms like refraction and reflection reasonably well.

Commonality of alternative ideas

In the course of a major survey in England, Northern Ireland and Wales, (see note 3) the Assessment of Performance Unit asked 15-year-olds of all attainment backgrounds the following question (see figure 4.6):

> When the plunger of this syringe is pulled up, water goes into the barrel of the syringe. What makes the water go into the syringe? Explain your answer as fully as you can.

Here is a sample of students' written responses (including original spellings, emphases, etc.), reported in Holding *et al.* (1990: 42):

- The water goes up into the syringe because of two reasons: (1) atmospheric pressure pushing down on the water; (2) *the suction* and less atmospheric pressure inside the syringe.

Figure 4.5 'Does the candle make light?'
Source: Osborne and Freyburg, 1985

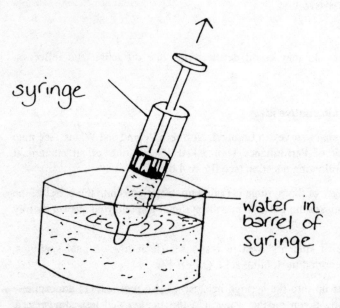

Figure 4.6 Diagnostic question: syringe
Source: Holding et al. (1990)

- The sucktion of the handle and the vaccum caused makes the water travel up the syringe.
- Air pressure on the surface of the water forces the liquid in to the barrel of the syringe.
- As the syringe is drawn up it creates a vacume thus somthing has to fill the vaccume. The watter is therefore sucked in.

Again, these responses show different views from those held in the scientific community, but this time there is evidence of a clear, coherent alternative idea, namely that *suction* is an active causative agency.

Commonality between some of the alternative views held by students about science has been revealed regularly in research carried out by the Children's Learning in Science (CLIS) team at Leeds University (see, for example, Brook *et al.*, 1984). The team found, for example:

- Many children use 'heat' and 'temperature' synonymously.
- The sensation of coldness is due to transfer of 'cold' towards the body.
- Particles swell: this explains pressure change and expansion.
- The word 'mixture' is often used for 'compound'.
- 'Food' for plants is anything taken in from the outside, e.g. water, minerals, air.

Some of these more commonly occurring ideas will be familiar to teachers. But sometimes the ideas seem so disconnected from the teacher's that their origins appear to be a complete mystery: 'They focus on things I would never dream of looking at!' said an experienced teacher about children's practical work.

The previous section in this chapter was an attempt to begin to see through the mystery of children's alternative ideas by suggesting how such ideas might arise. The early work of the CLIS team and others has contributed by describing some of the common alternative ideas. It has now become possible for teachers to use this knowledge to improve the quality of students' learning in science.

CHOICES FOR TEACHERS: THREE TEACHING APPROACHES BASED ON IDEAS ABOUT LEARNING

Three teaching approaches are described in this section. Two of them follow straight on from factors identified as central to children's learning: active knowledge construction and development. The third is a behaviourist approach, concerned with children's observable behaviour rather than with intellectual and physiological processes internal to the child. The three are not mutually exclusive. Although I may not have known it at the time, my own teaching has embodied, often haphazardly, elements of each approach. Had I been more aware of what I was doing in the classroom, perhaps my teaching would have had more coherence; it certainly would have been more controllable, in a scientific sense, and outcomes would have been easier to evaluate. The idea is not to replace intuition and 'feel' with some kind of pre-programmed teaching but to *supplement* them with a framework of choices for promoting learning.

A constructivist approach to teaching

Why not use the children's experiences as a resource?

(Ward, 1992)

The growth in awareness of students' ideas seems to be accompanied with a patience and a realisation by teachers that it is not what they teach that matters, it is what students learn.

(Driver, 1989)

Constructivist teaching involves finding out what students' views currently are and helping to focus construction of new knowledge towards ideas generally held in the scientific community. This is illustrated in the following example from the CLIS project (see Holding *et al.*, 1990: 83).

Conservation of Mass

Three year 8 classes had been working on the topic of dissolving. They had explored whether salt and sugar are still there when they dissolve. Most students had come to the view that salt and sugar *are* still there, even though they cannot be seen. The next topic, conservation of mass, was introduced with a worksheet (figure 4.7) which asks for students' views about whether dissolving affects mass.

Of 66 students, 27 held the scientific view (B), while 34 expected the side with dissolved sugar to be lighter. Now aware of these views, the teachers devised an activity to help move students' ideas from their current positions towards the scientific view. (Rosalind Driver likens this to someone phoning you for directions; you would probably say first: 'Where are you now?') The activity used the 'Balance' worksheet (figure 4.8) to take pupils through a 'predict – observe – explain' sequence.

Groups of students discussed and recorded their predictions and then watched the four demonstrations. After this they wrote down and attempted to explain what they had seen. These events were recorded by CLIS researchers. Here are short extracts from pupils' discussion during one of the pre-publication trials. The demonstration involved the addition of red blood to the water, and the discussion took place before pupils saw the outcome of the mixing:

Student 1: No, it won't balance.
Student 2: I think it will.
Student 3: It will balance because, er. . . .
Student 1: It won't.
Student 4: Maybe because it's a liquid.
Student 3: So? It'll still be the same amount of liquid, won't it?
Student 4: No, because the level will go *up* on that one there.
Student 3: Yeah, I know, but you don't add owt!

These pupils are evidently engaged with the scientific issue. The comments show perception and thought, and they are challenging to each others' views. The

Figure 4.7 Pre-task used to elicit understanding of mass of dissolved substance
Source: Holding et al. (1990)

key question, though, is this: can the 'predict – observe – explain' sequence result in learning in science? In order to test this, the students were asked to reconsider the 'Liz and Bob' worksheet (figure 4.7). If they wanted to change their view they were asked to explain why. One student who did change wrote: 'The four experiments we did it came to same because it is the same amount of sugar and it got

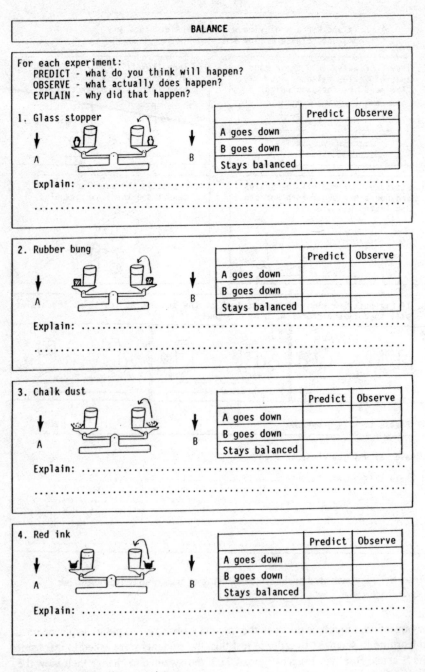

BALANCE

For each experiment:
     PREDICT - what do you think will happen?
     OBSERVE - what actually does happen?
     EXPLAIN - why did that happen?

1. Glass stopper

	Predict	Observe
A goes down		
B goes down		
Stays balanced		

Explain: ....

....

2. Rubber bung

	Predict	Observe
A goes down		
B goes down		
Stays balanced		

Explain: ....

....

3. Chalk dust

	Predict	Observe
A goes down		
B goes down		
Stays balanced		

Explain: ....

....

4. Red ink

	Predict	Observe
A goes down		
B goes down		
Stays balanced		

Explain: ....

....

Figure 4.8   Intervention experiments
Source: Holding et al. (1990)

dissloved it is the same. And that means norfing has been substracted or added so it is the same.' After this stage, almost unanimous agreement was reached that when salt or sugar dissolved, there was no change in mass.

An anxiety sometimes expressed by teachers about the approach described above is that it is time consuming. Would it not be better for the teacher just to do a simple demonstration, showing that mass is conserved? If such a demonstration were a reliable and effective way of promoting desired learning then it would indeed be hard to justify the constructivist approach. On the other hand, observations that seem unequivocal to teachers may be interpreted quite differently by pupils. As Asoko *et al.* (1993) point out, 'pupils do not always "see" what they are intended to see, and even minute movements of the balance pointer may be taken as evidence that supports their view and refutes the science idea'. When people are deciding whether or not the meaning of an observation is significant, they base their judgement on prior knowledge. This prior knowledge is generally different for each of us and so it is no wonder if we reach different conclusions about the meanings of the observation.

The teaching programme above contained an example of the effective use of cognitive conflict, a technique that was referred to earlier. A word of caution seems appropriate here. There is no guarantee that what appears to a teacher to be an elegant scheme embodying cognitive conflict and leading naturally to conceptual change will appear so to pupils! Carefully used, cognitive conflict may bring about desired learning, but conceptual change is not the only possible pupil response in this situation. If they feel under threat in some way, pupils may take steps to avoid losing self-esteem by, for example, disengaging from the task or from their peers. They may compensate for the sense of being under attack by defending their views with added zeal, becoming more rather than less entrenched. Others may feel indifferent to the conflict perceived by the teacher, or may be willing to operate in several separate domains of thought in which various sets of ideas are held apart and kept out of conflict.

This cautionary interlude illustrates that constructivist teaching can be challenging and demanding for the teacher, at least at first. However, as Rosalind Driver points out, 'Despite this there is general agreement that it is also more rewarding.'

Discovery Learning?

Much teaching now takes place within the constraints of prescriptive curricula, for example, the National Science Curriculum. A constructivist approach can be adopted by teachers whether or not a prescriptive curriculum is operating – in other words the teaching can, if necessary, be strongly goal directed. It is therefore quite different from teaching for 'discovery learning', a confusion that sometimes arises when constructivist teaching is first met.

Teaching Models

What are the key phases in a constructivist teaching programme? The constructivist sequence used by the CLIS team (for example, Needham, 1987; Driver, 1989; see also note 4) contains five phases: Orientation, Elicitation of Ideas, Restructuring of Ideas, Application, and Review. This model has been adopted in at least one secondary science scheme (Pople 1990: 7) where it is integrated into teaching schemes under the headings: Elicitation, Investigation and Consolidation. The 'generative learning' approach to teaching (Osborne and Freyberg, 1985: 109; see also note 5) contains four phases: Preliminary, Focus, Challenge, and Application. Although he did not describe it as such, John Head (1982) sets out what amounts to a constructivist approach for teachers in what he calls four possible teacher strategies designed to make learning as meaningful as possible. The four possibilities are: reformulation, in which pupils are encouraged to explain concepts in their own terms; application; making use of prior knowledge; and involving the learner in the teaching strategy. Much could be made of the last point; it could take the form of a brief orientation stage at the start of a new theme or topic, or it could be much more substantial. One functional possibility was suggested by the psychologist David Ausubel. Ausubel (1963) distinguished explicitly between meaningful and rote learning; and he introduced the notion of an 'advance organiser'. This is a general overview at the start of a new piece of work, with the aim of providing a framework in which the learner can fit, or 'subsume', new ideas. By fitting them in in an organised way, Ausubel argued that they become meaningful to the learner.

I have evolved (and am continuing to evolve) a *hybrid* of these approaches in my own teaching. It has met with some approval from critical adult learners in the following form:

- **Orientation**; activity or discussion to set the scene and focus initial attention and thinking; advance organiser of topic might be provided
- **Elicitation** of learners' current ideas
- **Challenges and changes**; the teacher interprets learners' ideas for her/himself and responds, questions and steers emerging ideas towards closer awareness and understai...ng of the science community's ideas
- **Application** of new ideas to new situations, problems or tasks; involves reflection and action in response to new ideas
- **Review** of the topic and of the learning

> *Learners contribute their ideas and are involved in the teaching strategies throughout the program.*

Whatever labels are adopted, constructivist teaching is underpinned by the idea that people actively construct their own new knowledge. Von Glaserfeld puts it like this:

> The most widespread effect has been achieved by the very simple constructivist principle that consists in taking whatever the student produces as a manifestation of something that *makes sense* to the student. This not only improves the general climate of instruction but also opens the way for the teacher to arrive at an understanding of the student.
>
> (Von Glaserfeld, 1991: 24)

Intervention

Does children's cognitive development take place at an inexorable rate, uninfluenced by external factors, or can it be speeded up? Some people believe that not only learning but also rate of cognitive development is dependent on the child's social and physical environment. Included in the child's environment, of course, is the school and the influence of teaching.

The Cognitive Acceleration through Science Education (CASE) project has grown from research which compared the stages of cognitive development typically found in secondary-age children with the cognitive demands of various attainment standards in science courses, including the National Science Curriculum. The research examined, among other things, the extent to which science curricula matched their customers' current capabilities. Materials from the project have been published as a teaching package known as 'Thinking Science' (Adey *et al.*, 1989). This package has been designed explicitly to encourage 'the development of thinking from concrete to formal operational' – in other words, it is based on the view that children's cognitive development *can* be accelerated through appropriate teaching. One reason for wanting to do this, according to the authors, is that students will be unable to achieve standards equivalent to GCSE grade D or above unless they can use formal operational thinking. The themes of the individual activities in the package are: control of variables, proportionality, probability, compensation and equilibrium, combinations, correlation, classification, formal models and compound variables (see also Adey, 1987a). As can be gathered from this list, the emphasis is on 'content-free' processes. The authors describe this approach in teaching as 'intervention', as opposed to instruction.

The CASE materials were used on a trial basis in several schools by dedicating approximately one science session per fortnight to the project, for a period of two years. This amounted to approximately one-quarter of the science curriculum time. Pupils from project and control classes were followed up to GCSE to investigate the nature of any effects arising from the intervention. At the end of the two-year intervention programme, there were no significant differences between the two groups, which at least indicated that the programme had not disadvantaged the project group through disruption to their science courses! After this, however, the project students began to out-perform the control students, gradually drawing ahead up to and including their GCSE year. More intriguing still was a 'far-transfer' effect reported by the CASE team. There was evidence of the project students' attainment advancing more rapidly than that of the control students not only in science but also in mathematics and in English.

Some people are sceptical about any claims of long-term and far-transfer effects. On the other hand, the point has been made elsewhere that if the potential pay-off is big enough, even the highly improbable is worth exploring!

For a detailed description of the CASE project and associated research see Adey (1987b) and Adey and Shayer (in press).

A behaviourist approach

A behaviourist approach in teaching focuses on *training*. Behaviourist theories emphasise the significance of *observable actions* rather than private consciousness. Behaviour is modified through a process known as conditioning, and change can be accelerated or inhibited by reinforcement.

Learning is defined as an observed *response* to particular *stimuli*. The aim in behaviourist teaching is therefore to identify and manage appropriate stimuli so as to bring about desired behaviour. Wheldall and Merrett (1989: 5) list what they call 'the five principles of Positive Teaching':

1   Teaching is concerned with the observable.
2   Almost all classroom behaviour is learned.
3   Learning involves change in behaviour.
4   Behaviour changes as a result of its consequences.
5   Behaviours are also influenced by classroom contexts.

They argue that good teaching involves the maintenance of an appropriate environment for desired learning to take place, a sentiment strongly supported by Marland (1975), Rogers (1991) and others: 'We have been concerned with methods of encouraging pupils to behave in ways which will maximise their opportunities for learning appropriate academic skills and knowledge' (Wheldall and Merrett 1989: 18). Wheldall and Merrett describe how teachers can set about systematically categorising their pupils' behaviour as either desirable or undesirable. Potential stimuli and reinforcers for these behaviours can be identified, and ultimately teachers' own behaviour can be modified so as to bring about desired changes in their pupils. A brief illustration, frequently found during initial teaching experience, is that of pupils repeatedly interrupting the teacher while he or she is carrying out a demonstration to the class. This is readily identified as undesirable behaviour! On closer observation it becomes apparent that whenever the teacher is interrupted in this way, he or she responds there and then to the pupil concerned. The teacher's response is acting as a reward to the pupil to continue behaving in the same way; the teacher is inadvertently 'reinforcing' the pupil's behaviour. As a result of this analysis, the teacher's action can be modified to prevent the reinforcement from taking place. (I am not aware of any single 'right' response in the situation described. Which of a range of alternative actions would be the most appropriate is impossible to judge outside of the teaching context.)

John Holt (1964) warns strongly that if undue emphasis is placed on desired behaviour, students will find it worthwhile to learn responses simply to please, so as to get the teacher off their backs. On the other hand, a behaviourist approach in teaching could be seen as *complementary* to either of the two approaches described earlier. It may be attractive in circumstances in which the applicability of the 'cognitive' approaches seems limited. Safety procedures in laboratories, maintenance (as opposed to negotiation) of social rules for class discussion and training in the use of equipment are examples which might benefit from this approach.

Punishment, used as a tool for managing pupils' behaviour, can be wearing and stressful for teachers. It can become a routine response, which does little, ultimately, to bring about the change for which it is nominally employed – that of improving the quality of the learning environment. As an alternative to punishment, Wheldall and Merrett's approach is likely to be less stressful, both to teachers and pupils, because it emphasises *positive reinforcement* of desired behaviour as a baseline teaching approach, rather than punishment of unwanted behaviour. Teachers who find themselves constantly repeating commands to pupils might, by reflecting on their actions in behaviourist terms, be able to bring about significant improvements not only in their pupils' learning but also in the quality of their own professional lives.

Which approach is best?

We live in a culture which celebrates being 'best', especially when being best is said to accord with common wisdom or current values. Complex systems like human beings, however, do not readily lend themselves to such a simplified measure. It is one thing to try to answer: Which is the best size for the print in this book? and quite another thing to address the question: Who is the world's best author?

None of the three approaches described above is claimed to be the best. It has not been an aim of this chapter to come to a judgement of 'best buy', for that would have been an artificial and misleading simplification. The three approaches have been included because there is merit in each and each merits consideration. My guess is that there will be times when each is tremendously effective in promoting learning.

REFLECTION

Several thousand words ago, this chapter began with a set of boxes, one of which referred to pupils' learning (figure 4.1). This box was empty. We asked: Could it be valuable to know more about pupils' learning?

Three theories about learning were described. They concerned children's cognitive development, the active construction of knowledge by individuals and the shaping of meaning through social interaction.

Children are not blank slates – they are full of their own ideas. Several examples were included of children's ideas in the field of science.

Finally some implications for teaching and some choices for teachers were examined in the light of the theories and the evidence.

NOTES

1 For a short summary of Piaget's theory of intellectual development see Donaldson (1978). Donaldson argues that children's thinking may be less constrained by stages of development than was proposed by Piaget. She suggests that a crucial factor is the set of interpersonal contexts in which children's thinking develops.

2   *Common Knowledge* by Edwards and Mercer (1987) contains detailed instances in which classroom discussion is analysed in terms of the *common meaning* made of it by teacher and pupils.
3   Large samples of children have been surveyed by the Assessment of Performance Unit (APU) to investigate, among other things, the knowledge and understanding that children have in science. Summary reports, describing main findings and implications for teaching, are available from the Association for Science Education, College Lane, Hatfield, Herts AL10 9AA.
4   Rosalind Driver's paper (Driver, 1989) takes a broad-based and pragmatic look at the implementation of a constructivist teaching scheme. She adds flesh to the bones described above, in the section on teaching models.
5   The generative learning approach to teaching described in Osborne and Freyberg (1985: 109) is based on Wittrock's 'generative' model of learning. There is much in common between this and the constructivist model of learning described by Driver and Bell (1985) and summarised above. For a summary of the generative learning model see Osborne and Freyberg (1985: 83).

GLOSSARY

Affective domain: Mental activity associated with feelings and emotions.
Ontology: Branch of metaphysics concerned with *being* in the abstract.
Pedagogy: The science, art and craft of teaching.

REFERENCES AND FURTHER READING

Adey, P. (1987a) 'Science develops logical thinking – doesn't it? Part 1. Abstract thinking and school science', *School Science Review*, June 1987: 622–30.
—— (1987b) 'Science develops logical thinking – doesn't it? Part 2. The CASE for science', *School Science Review*, September 1987: 17–27.
Adey, P. and Shayer, M. (1994) *Really Raising Standards*, London: Routledge.
Adey, P., Shayer, M., and Yates, C. (1989) *Thinking Science*, 1992 ed., Walton-on-Thames: Nelson.
Asoko, H., Leach, J., and Scott, P. (1993) 'Learning Science', in R. Hull (ed.), *ASE Secondary Science Teachers' Handbook*, Hemel Hempstead: Simon & Schuster.
Ausubel, D. P. (1963) *The Psychology of Meaningful Verbal Learning*, New York: Grune & Stratton.
Bamberger, J. and Schon, D. A. (1991) 'Learning as reflective conversation with materials', in F. Steier (ed.), *Research and Reflexivity*, London: Sage.
Bentley, D. and Watts, M. (1989) (eds) *Learning and Teaching in School Science: Practical Alternatives*, Milton Keynes: Open University Press.
Brook, A., Briggs, H., Bell, B. and Driver, R. (1984) *Aspects of Secondary Students' Understanding of Heat: Summary Report*, Leeds: CLIS Project.
Bruner, J. (1964) 'The course of cognitive growth', *American Psychologist* 19: 1–16.
—— (1985) 'Vygotsky: a historical and conceptual perspective', in J. Wertsch (ed.), *Culture, Communication and Cognition: Vygotskian Perspectives*, Cambridge: Cambridge University Press.
Carre, C. (1981) *Language, Teaching and Learning: Science*, London: Ward Lock.
Claxton, G. (1989) 'Cognition doesn't matter if you're scared, depressed or bored', in P. Adey (ed.), *Adolescent Development and School Science*, London: Falmer.
Donaldson, M. (1978) *Children's Minds*, reprinted 1985, London: Fontana.
Driver, R. (1983) *The Pupil as Scientist?* , Milton Keynes: Open University Press.

—— (1989) 'Changing conceptions', in P. Adey (ed.), *Adolescent Development and School Science*, London: Falmer.

Driver, R. and Bell, B. (1985) 'Students' thinking and the learning of science: a constructivist view', *School Science Review*, March 1986: 443–56.

Edwards, D. and Mercer, N. (1987) *Common Knowledge*, reprinted 1993, London: Routledge.

Head, J. (1982) 'What can psychology contribute to science education?', *School Science Review*, June 1982: 631–42.

—— (1989) 'The Affective Constraints on Learning Science', in P. Adey (ed.), *Adolescent Development and School Science*, London: Falmer.

Holding, B., Johnston, K. and Scott, P. (1990) *Interactive Teaching in Science: Workshops for Training Courses*, Workshop 9: Diagnostic teaching in science classrooms, CLIS project, Hatfield: Association for Science Education.

Holt, J. (1964) *How Children Fail*, revised ed. 1990, London: Penguin.

Lawson, A. and Renner, J. (1978) 'Relationships of science subject matter and developmental levels of learners', *Journal of Research in Science Teaching*, 15: 465–78.

Marland, M. (1975) *The Craft of the Classroom*, London: Heinemann.

Maturana, H. (1991) 'Science and daily life: the ontology of scientific explanations', in F. Steier (ed.), *Research and Reflexivity*, London: Sage.

Millar, R. (1993) 'Science Education and Public Understanding of Science', in R. Hull (ed.), *ASE Secondary Science Teachers' Handbook*, Hemel Hempstead: Simon & Schuster.

National Curriculum Council (NCC) (1989) *Science Non-Statutory Guidance*, York: NCC.

Needham, R. (1987) *Teaching Strategies for Developing Understanding in Science*, Leeds: CLIS Project.

Newman, F. and Holzman, L. (1993) *Lev Vygotsky: Revolutionary Scientist*, London: Routledge.

Osborne, R. and Freyberg, P. (1985) *Learning in Science*, Auckland: Heinemann.

Pople, S. (ed.) (1990) *Oxford Science Programme 1 Teacher's Resource File*, Oxford: Oxford University Press.

Rogers, B. (1991) *'You know the fair rule'*, Harlow: Longman.

Scott, P. (1987) *A Constructivist View of Learning and Teaching in Science*, Leeds: CLIS Project.

Selley, N. J. (1989) 'Philosophies of science and their relation to scientific processes and the science curriculum', in J. J. Wellington (ed.), *Skills and Processes in Science Education: A Critical Analysis*, London: Routledge.

Shayer, M. and Adey, P. (1981) *Towards a Science of Science Teaching*, London: Heinemann.

Shayer, M., Kuchemann, D. E. and Wylam, H. (1976) 'The distribution of Piagetian stages of thinking in British middle and secondary school children', *British Journal of Educational Psychology*, 46: 164–73.

Solomon, J. (1989) 'Social Influence or Cognitive Growth?', in P. Adey (ed.), *Adolescent Development and School Science*, London: Falmer.

Times Educational Supplement, 26 April 1991.

von Glasersfeld, E. (1991) 'Knowing without metaphysics: aspects of the radical constructivist position', in F. Steier (ed.), *Research and Reflexivity*, London: Sage.

Vygotsky, L. S. (1978) *Mind in Society: The Development of Higher Psychological Processes*, London: Harvard University Press.

Ward, J. P. (1992) 'Science for all?', unpublished P. G. C. E. assignment, University of Sheffield.

Wellington, J. J. (1991) 'Newspaper science, school science: friends or enemies?', *International Journal of Science Education*, 13 (4): 363–72.

Wheldall, K. and Merrett, F. (1989) *Positive Teaching in the Secondary School*, London: Paul Chapman Publishing.

5 Assessing children's learning in science

Stephen Knutton

For so it is, O Lord my God, I measure it;
But what it is that I measure I do not know.

St Augustine's Lament

This chapter is concerned with the role of assessment in school science. What is it for? Who benefits? What are the key issues in assessment? Some of the essential vocabulary and terminology of assessment is introduced. The first section describes some of the different forms of assessment including tests, examinations, unit accreditation and graded assessment and their relative advantages and disadvantages. This then leads into a brief discussion of assessment of the National Curriculum. The place of recording the achievements of students is covered, and finally there is a brief note on the role of assessment in the maintenance of standards. [The assessment of practical skills is dealt with in Chapter 10.]

THE BACKGROUND TO ASSESSMENT

What is assessment?

We are all familiar with the use of tests and examinations to determine achievement. To progress from school into higher education and then into the teaching profession has required the clearing of numerous hurdles. Have we got O level or GCSE certificates in English and mathematics, did we get sufficiently good 'A' level grades to secure a place in higher education, and did we satisfy our tutors and mentors of our capability to teach children in a classroom? These, and countless others, are examples of where our career paths have been dependent upon the assessments of others.

Deale (1975) has described assessment as 'an all-embracing term, covering any of the situations in which some aspects of a pupil's education is, in some sense, measured by the teacher or another person'. The essential information can be obtained in a variety of ways – some might be formal, such as examinations or tests, whilst others might be more informal (and possibly more subjective) through conversations and discussions. All too often assessment is rigidly associated with tests and examinations. The tyranny of this situation is well expressed by Holt, who states:

> At best, testing does more harm than good; at worst, it hinders, distorts, and corrupts the learning process. . . . The threat of the test makes the students do the assignment. The outcome of the test enables us to reward those who seem to do it best. The economy of the school, like that of most societies, operates on greed and fear. Tests arouse the fear and satisfy the greed.
>
> (Holt, 1969: 52)

Rowntree (1977) gives a useful definition in which

> assessment . . . can be thought of as occurring whenever one person, in some kind of interaction, direct or indirect, with another, is conscious of obtaining and interpreting information about the knowledge and understanding, or abilities and attitudes of the other person. To some extent it is an attempt to *know* that person.

This definition recognises the applicability of assessment outside the educational system in a myriad of situations.

The National Curriculum (TGAT) Report (1988) recognised that assessment is a natural part of teaching since teachers are constantly assessing pupils to determine their progress and to plan the next stage of their learning. This involves a continuous comprehensive examination of all aspects of the pupil's learning, drawing on a wide variety of evidence from many sources to arrive at a general picture.

Where assessment is too closely coupled with testing it can so easily be perceived as constraining. This is particularly so with respect to its influence on the curriculum where educationalists sometimes talk of the 'assessment tail wagging the curriculum dog'. This should be avoided and assessment be regarded as 'the servant of the curriculum and not its master' (SSCR, 1984). In any case a much broader approach to assessment transforms it into an enabling and facilitating exercise.

Why assess?

Why should teachers engage in assessment activities? The following reasons for assessing can all be put forward and argued for:

- to allocate pupils to different sets or groups
- to provide information to parents on progress
- to motivate pupils and give incentives for learning
- to give feedback on your own teaching effectiveness
- to identify individual weaknesses and problems
- to assist pupils in subject/career choice
- to reveal errors and misconceptions
- to inform HE/employers about attainment

- to give feedback to pupils on progress
- to maintain standards
- to rank pupils
- to entertain, for example, with a quiz

There may well be others. These purposes of assessment can be categorised into three major groupings:

(1) Looking Forward

Some of these purposes are primarily *forward looking*, where the results of the assessment are gathered for their predictive potential. Pupils' and parents' choices of subject are frequently influenced by test and examination performance. It is reasonable to ask: Do the results tell me that I have an *aptitude* for this subject? The validity of the judgements made are open to question – for example, the correlation between A level grades and future degree class is not particularly good.

(2) Looking Back

Other purposes are largely *backward looking* and concerned with pupil achievements, performance and attainment to find out the skills and knowledge that have been acquired from the course. The validity of such an assessment is dependent upon specifying the skills and knowledge through 'learning objectives' against which the assessment can be matched. Examples of this might include tests of cycling proficiency, driving and swimming.

(3) Guiding Action

Third, and educationally most important, are purposes concerned with remediation. The diagnosis of where pupils' learning is deficient is a crucial first stage to improving their learning (and performance) in the future. This can then be followed by the teacher deciding upon appropriate action to tackle the difficulties. These purposes are therefore both forward and backward looking.

An alternative categorisation of the purposes of assessment could be in terms of their professional or managerial intentions. Some are clearly *managerial* in that their main objectives relate to the successful management of the education system, for example selection for higher education, certification. Others are primarily concerned with helping with the educational process (*professional*) and the learner, for example diagnosis, screening, motivation. Some purposes might operate in both of these categories.

This discussion has so far centred upon pupils and their future. However, the great value of assessment to the teacher should not be overlooked. In particular assessment provides teachers with essential feedback on their teaching. It is a flow of information about the effectiveness of teaching strategies and approaches. An indication that many pupils have failed to understand a particular concept or idea can help the teacher rethink the approach, time and emphasis given to particular topics. As such this should feed into future teaching strategies to the ultimate benefit of those being taught.

Finally, the 1988 TGAT Report, which was the blueprint for National Curriculum assessment arrangements, identified four distinct purposes of assessment. These were:

- Formative: To allow the recognition of positive achievements and make decisions about future steps
- Diagnostic: To identify learning difficulties to enable appropriate remedial help to be given
- Summative: To record overall achievements of the pupil systematically and allow their communication to others
- Evaluative: To enable aspects of the educational process to be assessed and/or reported upon

It is interesting to look at the current National Curriculum testing arrangements to see how these purposes have been weighted!

TEACHING, LEARNING AND ASSESSMENT

All too often assessment has been seen as an end in itself, as a 'terminal' process. It is, in fact, a dynamic process involving the continual interaction of learners, teachers, materials and the assessment instruments. This is shown diagrammatically in figure 5.1 below.

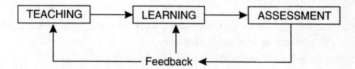

Figure 5.1 The teaching, learning and assessment cycle

Formative and summative assessment

In the above model the principal intention is the improvement of pupil learning. This occurs through reflection upon the teaching and learning process, informed by evidence from the assessment tools; these can be formal, such as tests or written exercises, or more informal, such as through question-and-answer sessions or discussions. This feedback can result in immediate remedial action for the present class and a consideration of alternative approaches in the future. This is essentially a *formative* approach to assessment which is capable of exerting a direct influence upon the learning process. It stands in stark contrast to *summative* assessment (for example, GCSE or A level), which comes at the end of the process where it is powerless to influence the learning process – it is an altogether blunter educational instrument. Summative assessment is used to make judgements at the end of the learning process through terminal examinations or end-of-module tests and leads to the assigning of a grade (or mark) to signify the level of performance achieved.

Norm- and criterion-referenced assessment

In the past most educational assessment in the UK has been norm referenced. As a result of the assessment the pupils are ranked and allocated to grades according to predetermined proportions. In public examinations such as GCSE, O and A levels, there is an element of norm-referencing based upon the reasonable assumption that in a large population there will be a spread of ability approximating the bell-shaped normal distribution curve.

Senior examiners then make professional judgements of the quality of answers in the light of the difficulty of papers, published grade descriptions (in the case of GCSE) and evidence of performance in previous years to give year-on-year consistency. The use of norm-referencing effectively means that the performance of a pupil is being compared to that of other pupils rather than upon some objective or absolute measure of performance.

The weaknesses inherent in a norm-referenced system have increased interest in criterion-referenced assessments. Within a criterion-referenced system the quality of the performance of the pupils determines their grade or score and is irrespective of the performance of other pupils. In order to be effective it is essential to provide teachers and pupils with clear descriptions of the levels of performance being required. Both GCSE and the National Curriculum aspire towards criterion-based assessment. The distinctive features of criterion-based assessment are as follows:

- It is concerned with individual children's work on a specified task and irrespective of the performance of other children.
- It represents what the individual child can do.
- It is directly related to the course and teacher objectives.
- It is designed to give explicit information on what children can or cannot do.
- It is ongoing and concerned with normal teaching situations rather than with special examination conditions.
- It can be repeated (i.e. it is not once and for all).
- It involves communication of criteria to pupils so that they can monitor their own progress.
- It can emphasise building on success and therefore enhance motivation.
- It can be related to pathways through the curriculum.

The criterion-based approach to assessment is closely linked with so-called mastery tests which are designed to focus upon specific skills to achieve success. In such a test it is perfectly acceptable for all the students to answer all questions correctly (compare this with objective questions where discrimination is sought). As teachers we usually want our pupils to succeed, and hence this approach represents a better match to our intentions. There are, however, a number of possible disadvantages. Consider the example quoted by Woolnough and Toh (1990) of a practical skill objective: 'Can read a voltmeter, not less than 100mm long, with unitary divisions, with no zero error, if the light is good, after a good night's sleep, to an accuracy of ±0.2V, more than 80 per cent of the time.'

Clearly the increasing specificity of the objective has been taken to ridiculous lengths in this case. As an objective becomes more and more complex it becomes increasingly difficult for the pupil to achieve the objective (negating any possible motivating effect) and more difficult for the teacher to determine whether the criterion has been achieved. It can also lead to the unnecessary and unhelpful disintegration of the holistic nature of the subject.

The use of criterion-referenced assessment is clearly most beneficial when viewed in the light of a formative assessment framework. There are obvious inbuilt means of enabling pupils to relate their learning to the course or teacher expectations and this can contribute to an increased awareness of their own progress and a realisation of what still needs to be done. There are, however, problems to be faced when attempting to interface a criterion-referenced system such as found within the National Curriculum and the summative grades required for GCSE. For example, must a pupil achieve all the criteria at a level to be judged to be operating at that level? Are gaps at a lower level acceptable?

Principles of good assessment

Thorp (1991) has summarised many of the above points in his five principles of good assessment. He suggests that assessment should:

- influence and inform future teaching and learning
- show what pupils know, understand and can do
- measure pupil progress
- provide feedback for pupils, teachers and parents
- give pupils a positive sense of achievement and therefore empower them

The INSET pack devised by Thorp goes on to list some of the actions that teachers need to take in devising and organising assessment activities.

FORMS OF ASSESSMENT

Assessment in school science teaching can take many forms, from oral questioning to the marking of exercises set for homework or short written tests of knowledge. Most often we think of assessment in the context of public examinations such as the GCSE and A level (the 'gold standard'). In these examinations a variety of different forms of question styles have been developed including objective questions (multiple choice, multiple completion and matching pairs), short-answer questions, structured questions, essays or extended-answer questions as well as comprehension materials. Each of these methods has different strengths and drawbacks with the result that most teachers utilise a range of different forms in combination.

Oral questions in class

Probably the most frequent assessment carried out by teachers is asking pupils questions during lessons – perhaps as many as 30,000 a year. This lesson-by-lesson interaction provides the teacher with valuable feedback about what pupils already know, can remember from a previous lesson and can understand or deduce. Good questioning can be a very powerful tool in helping teachers diagnose where to put most effort and energy in the teaching of a particular subject to a class. There are, however, dangers when the questioning is not so skilful in that it can become a game of 'guess what's in my head', or where assumptions about a correct answer from one pupil are assumed to be true of the whole class and then more difficult questions are asked based on the answer given (see Chapter 6).

The formal use of oral assessment has not been widely exploited in the sciences and yet could play a useful role in relation to certain objectives concerning the communication of scientific concepts and the demonstration of an awareness of the contribution of science to the economic and social life of the community (Wilson,1987).

Objective test questions

An objective test is one in which the pupil's score is independent of the marker. Typically the pupil marks a letter (often A–D) on an answer grid, which subsequently can be marked mechanically or by computer. Such a marking process can be very accurate and cost-effective for large-scale public examinations. However, this advantage is offset by the high cost and difficulty of setting good and discriminating questions. Another advantage of objective tests is wide syllabus coverage in a relatively short space of time. Whilst many pupils seem to enjoy answering these questions, this type of test can be open to the charge of encouraging guessing, and there is some evidence of gender bias in that girls perform slightly less well on these types of question.

Multiple choice questions

These are called 'Items'. Each item consists of a 'stem' and a number of 'options':

- The stem is the part of the item that states clearly the task required.
- The options are the alternative answers (usually four) to the item.
- The key is the correct option.
- The distracters are the incorrect options.

An example is:
    Which one of the following is a primary colour?   (stem)

 A Red   **B** White   **C** Black   **D** Indigo   (options or responses)

Of the responses to the item (question) the correct answer is A.   (key)

This is the most straightforward type of objective question. Its main weakness lies in the difficulty of writing questions where the distracters are effective in drawing pupil responses. Ideally each option should attract some responses; otherwise there are non-functioning distracters that do not contribute to the discriminating power and effectively make the question easier.

Matching Pairs or Classification Sets

These make use of the same set of responses (say A–D) for a number of questions. The responses (which might be numbers, words, definitions, equations, techniques, formulae, diagrams or statements) must then be matched to the particular item.

An example is:

Consider the following list of pH values:

$$\textbf{A} \quad 1 \qquad \textbf{B} \quad 4 \qquad \textbf{C} \quad 7 \qquad \textbf{D} \quad 14$$

Select from the above list, A–D, the number which best represents the pH of:

1 lemon juice
2 distilled water
3 oven cleaner
4 dilute hydrochloric acid

Multiple completion questions

These are slightly more complicated and often involve responses that cover several variables or statements that are connected in some way.

An example is:

Which of the following may be correctly classified as electromagnetic radiation?

    1 X-rays   **2** gamma rays   **3** beta rays   **4** radio waves

Select the letter A–E according to whether:

A 1, 2 & 3 only are correct
B 1, 2 & 4 only are correct
C 1 & 4 only are correct
D 2 only is correct
E 4 only is correct.

This form of question is useful because it can be used where fewer than four plausible answers are available and also allows for the interconnection of ideas. The answer code can be varied, and additional responses, such as 'none of these', 'all of these' or 'some other combination', can be introduced.

Even more complicated items, assertion-reason questions, can be set. These involve two statements, one an assertion and the other a reason, with the pupil being asked about the validity of them. These are much more difficult questions and not frequently used nowadays.

Item analysis of objective questions

It is usual for objective items to be pre-tested before large-scale use in public examinations and for the results to be statistically analysed. The two most important pieces of information obtained are the 'facility' of the item and its 'discrimination' – although the response pattern is usually also scrutinised for nonfunctioning distracters.

The *facility*, F, is a measure of the proportion answering correctly – usually as a fraction. A question with a facility of 1.0 has been answered correctly by everyone and has therefore failed to discriminate. It is probably too easy but may raise the morale of pupils especially if placed at the beginning. A facility of 0 indicates a very difficult question. Questions with facility values of between 0.5 and 0.55 are regarded as ideal for constructing objective tests which discriminate well and hence rank pupils effectively.

The *discrimination* or *biserial correlation*, D, is measure of the efficiency of an item in discriminating between high-ranking (good) and low-ranking (poor) students. For a valid item it is expected that 'better' candidates are more likely to answer it correctly than are 'weaker' ones. The discrimination index is obtained from the difference in facility values between good and poor students as determined by overall performance on the test. Thus D is obtained from

$$D = F \text{ (good)} - F \text{ (poor)}$$

where the good group represents the top third (or 27 per cent) and the poor group the bottom third (or 27 per cent). D can vary from 1.0 to −1.0, with a value of 1.0 indicating all the good and none of the poor answering the item correctly. A value of −1.0 indicates the opposite, and in fact any negative value is a cause for concern because it suggests that the question could be ambiguous and should be rewritten or abandoned. In general values of D greater than 0.2 are acceptable, with values of 0.35 and over providing good discrimination.

Short-answer questions

Short-answer question papers are usually distinguished by the fact that the questions are actually answered in the question book itself. The questions are often thematic in nature covering, say, the periodic table, Newton's laws of motion or the structure of the human skeleton. The activities may range from labelling diagrams, completing graphs and tables, giving definitions or short descriptions, supplying missing words from a short piece of text to completing simple calculations. Usually no choice of question is allowed (se figure 5.2a).

Structured questions

One of the weaknesses of both objective and short-answer questions is that whilst they are good for achieving syllabus coverage, they may sacrifice coherence. Structured questions are similar to short-answer questions in that they are answered

Questions A17–A19

The Warren Spring Laboratory monitors air pollution throughout the United Kingdom. The bar chart shows the sulphur dioxide content in the air in Manchester during 1987.

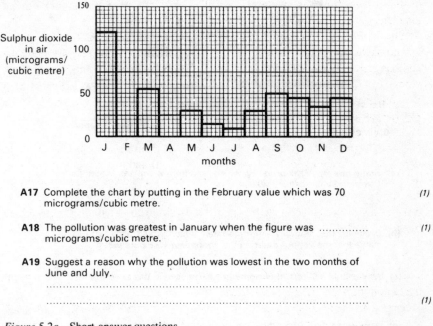

A17 Complete the chart by putting in the February value which was 70 micrograms/cubic metre. *(1)*

A18 The pollution was greatest in January when the figure was .... micrograms/cubic metre. *(1)*

A19 Suggest a reason why the pollution was lowest in the two months of June and July.

....

.... *(1)*

Figure 5.2a Short-answer questions

on the question paper. They usually tackle a single topic or theme from the syllabus but ask for a variety of different types of response – single words or sentences, identifying parts of a diagram by letters, simple calculations and slightly longer prose responses (see figure 5.2b). Some structured questions have been devised with an incline of difficulty so that a question starts easily and gradually becomes more demanding.

Essay or extended-answer questions

This type of question paper is not so common nowadays. This type of question, whilst easier to set, is necessarily longer and takes more examination time, the syllabus coverage is less good, and the marking is more difficult to standardise. In recent years there has been a tendency to reduce choice in science examination papers. Consider a section of a paper with four long-answer questions of which one must be answered. Each of these questions, in addition to differing in syllabus content, might also differ in the skills (writing versus calculation) required. Indeed it could be argued that because of the choice different candidates are doing different

C2 The diagram below shows how pure water can be obtained from sea water by distillation.

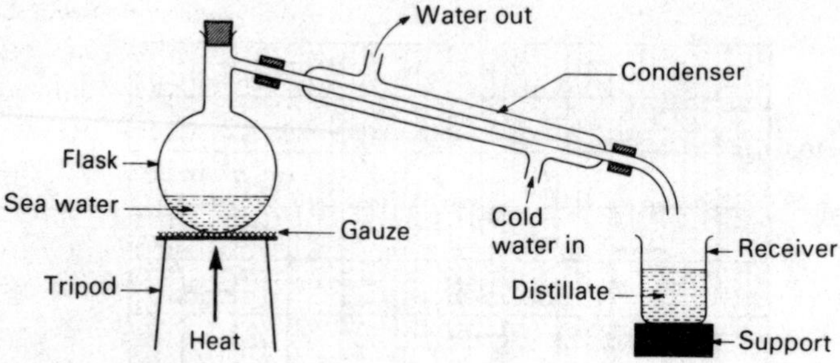

(a) State **one** physical property which is different for sea water as compared with distilled water.

....   *(1)*

(b) **Draw on the diagram** a thermometer which would allow you to check that the vapour entering the condenser was pure water.   *(1)*

(c) Why should a 0–50°C thermometer **not** be used in this experiment?

....   *(1)*

(d) What is the purpose of the cold water circulating in the condenser?

....   *(1)*

(e) State a safety precaution you would take when carrying out a distillation.

....   *(1)*

(f) Why is distillation more expensive than filtration?

....   *(1)*

(g) Why is the salt not removed from sea water by filtration?

....   *(1)*

(h) 1 cubic mile of sea water contains £1000 million worth of gold. Give a reason why gold is not extracted from sea water even though it is technically possible.

....   *(1)*

(Total 8)

Figure 5.2b   Structured questions

examinations! It is also difficult to ensure that questions are of equal difficulty and this could result in unfairness, especially where in the heat of the examination a student chooses unwisely. On the other hand, extended-answer questions can test the ability to marshal relevant information and write good English. Perhaps the ability to write fluently is one aspect that has not been adequately stressed in science examinations in recent years. Interestingly, essay questions are usually better answered by girls than boys (see figure 5.2c).

B3 Use your knowledge and understanding of chemistry to explain the following statements, **(a)** to **(c)**.

    (a) It is dangerous to use a butane camping stove in a caravan with the door and windows tightly sealed. (4)

    (b) Some indigestion tablets contain sodium hydrogencarbonate. (3)

    (c) Rust, iron (III) oxide, can be removed from an object by using dilute sulphuric acid. (2)

(Total 9)

Figure 5.2c Extended-answer questions

Comprehension passages

The use of text from newspapers or magazines can produce interesting material for setting examination questions; it is particularly helpful in setting a context for science which is economically, environmentally, industrially, politically and socially relevant (see Chapter 16). The text can act as a focus for asking a series of questions in which candidates can be asked to demonstrate their ability to cope with information (including numerical data), their comprehension of the science in the passage and their ability to relate new ideas to standard syllabus material as well as to make sensible inferences and deductions from the information supplied (see figure 5.2d).

Achieving differentiation through question setting

With the advent of the GCSE in 1988 came the necessity to provide opportunities for candidates to show 'what they know, understand and can do'. When dealing with pupils from a wide range of ability there are two particular dangers: (1) setting papers that are too hard for some and hence dispiriting, and (2) setting papers that are too easy, liable to be regarded as trivial by the able, and in which any discrimination is likely to be achieved through accumulation of small errors rather than positive evidence of ability. In practice differentiation can be achieved by *outcome* or by *task* (see Chapter 7). In differentiation by outcome common tasks that are accessible to all candidates are set and discrimination is based upon the range of answers given by candidates. Setting questions that can test and motivate both the most and least able is a challenging task. In differentiation by task different

A1   Read the following account taken from an article published in
the *Independent* on 21 January 1991, and answer the questions
which follow.

The molecule of the month, aluminium sulphate

ON 6 July 1988 a driver inadvertently polluted the water supplies of the Cornish town of Camelford by tipping 20 tons of acidic aluminium sulphate solution into the mains.

For more than a century water engineers have been using aluminium sulphate as a flocculating agent. When water is cloudy with silt and bacteria it can be made sparklingly clean by adding a small amount of calcium hydroxide and aluminium sulphate. This precipitates aluminium hydroxide which carries the impurities down with it.

Aluminium is a silvery metal found in combination with oxygen and silicon in rocks, and in clay. It requires a lot of energy to extract the metal from its ore, bauxite.

Forty per cent of Britain's aluminium is recycled, says Dr. David Harris, Secretary-General of the Aluminium Federation. "We use aluminium in more ways than any other metal. Aircraft, ships, containers, kegs, cars and cables are made from it".

(a)   Write the formula of aluminium sulphate. ....   (1)

(b)   Explain why it is **incorrect** to say that aluminium sulphate is
a **molecule.**

....   (1)

(c)   Give the formula of the two substances produced when
aluminium sulphate reacts with calcium hydroxide.

.... and ....   (2)

(d)   Explain why, even though aluminium is found combined in
most rocks and clays, it is not extracted from this source.

....   (1)

Figure 5.2d Comprehension passages

papers and different questions are set. This also poses problems for the teacher who has to make quite difficult decisions about paper choice, and also for examiners who have to place candidates from different overlapping papers on a common grading scale. Another approach is to set questions or papers with a built-in *incline of difficulty*. This is not easy to achieve and also makes the assumption that the incline of difficulty is the same for all candidates!

Criteria for Setting Effective Questions

Research conducted by the Inter-Group Research Committee for the GCSE (Joint Council for the GCSE, 1992) has identified a number of factors that contribute either positively or negatively to the effectiveness of questions, particularly with regard to differentiation. Among the features identified were:

- *Context/content of the question.* Unfamiliar contexts are advantageous and enable the syllabus to be assessed in an interesting manner. The context must be recognisable to candidates and obscure content areas avoided.
- *Structure and wording of the question.* Questions should be coherently structured and 'flow' well, i.e. have a logical sequence of sub-questions. Appearance is very important. Candidates need to be encouraged to want to do the questions. Any diagrams should be as simple as possible and avoid irrelevant detail. Language is vitally important if the questions are to be accessible – this means short, concise sentences and avoidance of ambiguous language.
- *Marking scheme.* It is crucially important that any marking scheme allows scope for the rewarding of different levels of response – especially where candidates are asked to 'explain'. Furthermore the exact requirements of any question should be clear to the candidates and the marking scheme should not have a 'hidden agenda'.
- *Mathematical skills.* Questions involving calculations should test science rather than mathematics and be placed in a scientific context. There is a danger that mathematical demands may not be accessible to lower-ability pupils even though the science might not be particularly difficult; such questions discriminate on the basis of mathematics rather than science.

Graded tests (criterion-referenced testing)

During the 1980s considerable energy was devoted to the development of graded schemes of assessment in science, the most notable being the ILEA Graded Assessments in Science Project (GASP) and the Oxford Certificate of Educational Achievement (OCEA). These schemes adopt a criterion-referenced approach and have the principal purpose of giving pupils credit for their positive achievements as they progress through the course rather than at the end of their school career. This is achieved by setting appropriate short-term objectives. These schemes therefore recognise success, and this can lead to student motivation. This can be further enhanced by a closer involvement of the students in understanding the goals to be achieved. Pupils can therefore participate in the assessment process by discussing with their teacher the extent to which they have attained the objectives. Pupils can also be involved in decisions concerning the next stage of objectives (target setting). The objectives are designed to match the rate of pupil development so that pupils are assessed at the right time.

The main characteristics of graded assessment schemes are as follows:

- The assessments are criterion referenced.

- The schemes are structured to provide objectives at different levels, with the lower levels being attainable by almost all at some stage.
- The emphasis is on process rather than content.
- Assessment is seen as integral to learning.
- Teacher-student interaction is encouraged.
- Student self-assessment is promoted.
- A wide variety of assessment techniques is used.
- Frequent assessment is required.
- Professional judgement by teachers is crucial, especially in the interpretation of criteria.
- A domain structure is used.

Graded tests are undoubtedly motivating for pupils but are also quite complex to administer, and there is a danger of pupils feeling that it is all assessment.

These graded assessment schemes have been well tested on a trial basis and form a good basis for review of the National Curriculum, requiring the assessment of rather similar statements of achievement in the areas of content knowledge and understanding, process skills and investigatory work.

Another approach has been to accredit units of work, and this shares some of the advantages of graded tests insofar as they are criterion related, pupil involvement is encouraged, short-term objectives are used and there are clear indications of increased pupil motivation. The most developed is the Unit Scheme operated by the Northern Partnership for Records of Achievement (NPRA). Each unit must specify the curricular area of the unit, the learning objectives and processes involved, the educational context and the outcomes to be accredited (skills, conceptual understanding, knowledge and experiences). This does not lead to a qualification, but pupils do receive a letter of credit from the Northern Examinations and Assessment Board (NEAB), which can then be included in their record of achievement.

ASSESSING THE NATIONAL CURRICULUM

During the setting up of the National Curriculum the Task Group on Assessment and Testing (TGAT) recommended that the sequence of pupil achievement through the ten levels between the ages of 7 and 16 should be expected to follow the bold line shown in figure 5.3.

The dotted lines at the ages of 7, 11, 14 and 16 give an indication of the range that might be expected for around 80 per cent of pupils. Typically an average 11-year-old will be at level 4, a 14-year-old between levels 5 and 6, and a 16-year-old between levels 6 and 7.

Key stage (KS) 3 assessment of the National Curriculum involves two components: (1) teacher assessment of their pupils' achievements, and (2) Standard Assessment Tasks (SATs).

1 Teacher assessment covers all four attainment targets and is a continuous process throughout the three years of the KS and is the only means of assessing

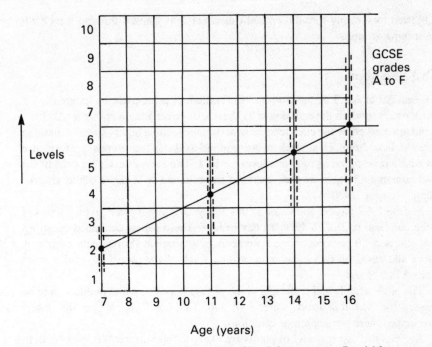

Figure 5.3 Sequence of pupils' achievement of levels between ages 7 and 16

attainment target 1 (Sc 1). The building up of evidence as the course progresses allows assessment to contribute to good teaching by enabling work to be better matched to pupils' capabilities and ensuring more orderly progression. To achieve this it is necessary to systematically gather, review and record evidence of attainment. This evidence might arise from diverse sources: classwork, homework, practical work and oral work as well as tests and examinations. A survey carried out by the Association for Science Education (ASE) in September 1992 (ASE, 1992) revealed that for Scs 2, 3 and 4 teachers used topic tests (56 per cent), classwork (26 per cent), homework/assignments (15 per cent), end-of-year exams (2 per cent) and pupil self-assessment (2 per cent). Once collected, evidence must be recorded and retained – especially important in the case of children moving schools. Teachers questioned in the survey revealed a variety of ways of keeping evidence: 43 per cent recording topic test marks and retaining associated mark schemes, 24 per cent doing the same for coursework, 23 per cent retaining examples of pupils' work and a further 7 per cent keeping teacher notes or comments made during the course.

2 The SATs are only used at the end of a KS and take the form of timed written tests for attainment targets (ATs) 2, 3 and 4 set on a national basis and marked by the class teacher to a centrally produced marking scheme. The assessments of pupil levels are then aggregated to give an overall level for science. These levels are then

subjected to scrutiny through an audit mechanism organised through the GCSE examining groups.

KS 3 Assessment

Assessment at KS 3 of the National Curriculum is principally by externally set written tests towards the end of year 9. These tests cover attainment targets 2, 3 and 4 and are marked by the class teacher in accordance with a highly specific marking scheme. In addition, class teachers are required to assess their pupils' performance on whole investigations to give a level for Sc 1. The overall levels for each of the four attainment targets are then averaged and rounded up if above 0.5 to give the pupil's science level.

For the 1992 pilot examination at this KS, year 9 pupils were given a series of three one-hour papers on the same day in June. These papers contained questions that assessed 50 per cent of the statements of attainment (SoAs) with each SoA being addressed on two separate occasions. Each of the papers covered content from ATs 2, 3 and 4.

The pilot schools had to decide which of four bands of paper pupils should be entered for. The four bands were: 1–4; 3–6; 5–8; and 7–10. Where the papers overlapped there were common questions.

At KS 3 the vast majority of pupils are likely to fall into the 3–6 level band. In science almost no pupils nationally could access the 7–10 band – principally because the content concerned falls outside the Programme of Study for KS 3 and is unlikely to have been taught! Special arrangements were made for pupils with special needs, for example, audio tapes were produced to help poor readers.

During the marking process teachers were required to fill in a grid to show where pupils had achieved individual SoAs. It was necessary for pupils to get only one of the two statement questions correct. The ticks on the sheet were then transferred down to the second bottom horizontal row to give an indication of the SoAs achieved. It was then deemed that a level had been achieved if a tick appeared in each column at that level in that AT. Furthermore, provided that at least half of the statements in a level had been achieved, compensation for a missing statement could be allowed by counting back a higher level statement.

A number of weaknesses were identified in this pilot exercise. These included:

1   The rigidity of the marking scheme: Because the marking scheme had to be applied by several thousand science teachers it was perfectly understandable that there was a desire to ensure uniformity of application. Unfortunately, the requirement for pupils to use a particular 'form of words' disadvantaged some pupils and ruled out some basically sound scientific answers.

2   The countback system to compensate for missing statements was thought to be reasonably fair but unfortunate in the band 3–6 papers, where the achievement of level 6 was particularly difficult because no countback mechanism could operate.

3   The alternative of giving such pupils the band 5–8 papers was not especially

happy because quite able pupils had not covered a lot of the science content and hence found the papers somewhat demotivating.

The 1992 KS 3 tests were a pilot. Since the completion of the exercise, the Secondary Assessment & Examination Council (SEAC) have produced exemplar material (SEAC, 1993), including pupils' answers to illustrate the types of question used and the nature of professional judgement decisions that teachers have to take in awarding credit.

The 1993 KS 3 science tests were massively disrupted by the refusal of teachers to cooperate with the vastly increased workload associated with the tests. Nevertheless, there were modifications in place to alleviate some of the difficulties identified in the pilot. These included addressing the rigidity of the mark scheme. It was emphasised that teachers could use their professional judgement to decide whether credit should be given where a pupil response:

- was equivalent to any of those listed
- conveyed the underlying ideas given in the highlighted section of the mark scheme
- matched the statement of attainment on which the question was based

Furthermore, the criterion used to determine whether or not a pupil had achieved a particular level of attainment was drastically altered. A numerical marking scheme was introduced with a threshold of approximately sixty per cent of the marks available being required for achievement of that level. Achievement of a higher level was not dependent upon success at lower levels.

KS 4 Assessment and Beyond

When the assessment arrangements for the National Curriculum were first formulated it was decided that the means of reporting pupil achievements at KS 4 would be through suitably modified GCSE examinations. This, in part, reflected some of the success that the GCSE. examination had achieved since its first examination in 1988. Furthermore the GCSE letter grade scale (A to G) had become well established and understood by parents and other users.

It was therefore proposed that the new ten-level National Curriculum and the GCSE letter grades be brought together by determining equivalences. Thus, for example, a GCSE grade B was equated to a NC level 8 and a GCSE grade F to NC level 5. The two scales are, however, reached by quite different methods and direct equivalences were not possible at all points (especially the historically important GCE Ordinary level pass of Grade C – crucial to the maintaining of standards) and there was considerable potential for confusion. In addition the Secretary of State for Education decided in 1993 that there was the need to introduce a new grade to represent the highest levels of achievement – the A* or super-A grade.

The major review of the operation of the National Curriculum commissioned during 1993 by the Secretary of State and carried out by Sir Ron Dearing (1994) made a large number of recommendations which have been accepted by the government. It has been agreed that the use of the National Curriculum ten-level scale will be restricted to the first three key stages with the consequence that GCSE gradings (including the A*) will be retained from 1995 onwards.

This decision opens up the opportunity to consider how the KS 4 curriculum might develop as part of a 14–19 continuum. The decoupling of achievement from the National Curriculum levels permits more flexibility in the post-14 curriculum. In particular the streamlining of required subjects at KS 4 has opened up the opportunity for pupils after the age of 14 to follow a variety of different routes. For large numbers of pupils the *academic pathway* will be most appropriate but for others a *vocational pathway* which maintains a broad educational component could be advantageous. Eventually an *occupational pathway* might also be designed for KS 4 pupils. The vocational route enables pupils to make use of General National Vocational Qualifications (GNVQs) which could lead to Vocational A levels post-16. The occupational pathway is designed to develop the competence to do a job or narrow range of jobs and these are accredited by National Vocational Qualifications (NVQs). The challenge posed by Sir Ron Dearing is to 'ensure that the alternative pathways are of equally high quality and that progression routes are assured'.

PROFILING AND RECORDING ACHIEVEMENT

The disadvantages of examinations as terminal judgements of achievement when it is too late to make amends has already been noted. The outcomes of perhaps two years of study are compressed into a single grade or mark with a consequential loss of information about a range of qualities which may have been exhibited during the course. In recent years there has been a growing interest in developing methods of recording achievement, and this has resulted in the statutory introduction of the National Record of Achievement (NRA) for school leavers from 1992 onwards. Profiles or records of achievement are not themselves methods of assessment but mechanisms for recording, reviewing and reporting achievements under a variety of headings. The use of a record of achievement can have many advantages for pupils and end users alike:

- They afford a much more comprehensive picture of the student's qualities and give a fairer picture of 'the whole student'.
- They provide information that can be readily interpreted and used by prospective employers or higher education admission tutors.
- They give credit for and recognition to the multi-dimensional achievements and abilities of students in a particular curriculum area. A single grade cannot do justice to such achievements.
- They provide students with increased motivation, better awareness of their own strengths, better teaching and learning strategies arising from diagnosis and review sessions, and there is potential to reward some qualities that would not otherwise gain recognition.
- They can be useful both formatively and summatively.

The use of profiling in a formative manner is of particular importance. This requires the involvement of the student in the learning and assessment process and results in feedback which can enhance future learning. As progress is made some data/comments become redundant and new challenges arise for the student until eventually, on the student's leaving school at age 16, a summative document can be prepared. It can therefore act as a tool of diagnosis and encouragement including strengths, achievements, evidence of progress as well as target setting for future work. The involvement of the pupils themselves in the assessment of their own progress is especially valuable. Pupils can be encouraged towards self-assessment through using their own copy of the sheets used for recording. Greatest benefits are achieved by the systematic reviewing of progress with the teacher on a one-to-one basis where comments can be discussed and targets set. Although time consuming, this is very worthwhile.

Pupil self-assessment

The involvement of pupils in the assessment of their own achievements is a vital part of enabling them to become self-sufficient learners. Pupils do have an idea of what they can do and what they understand. An important objective of teacher assessment must be to help pupils come to a realistic view of their own progress and capabilities. Sometimes pupils can be rather scathing of their abilities and need to be encouraged not to be unduly modest or superficial. This does not simply happen; it takes time, and pupils often need a lot of guidance and help. The use of checklists and prompt sheets at the end of lessons or units can assist pupils to structure their own assessment of the learning that has taken place. Examples of aids that have been developed to enable pupils to assess a variety of activities (for example, problem-solving, role play) can be found in the ATLAS Project (Centre for Science Education, 1992).

Another important learning experience is the one-to-one review session contributing to the recording-of-achievement process. Above all, involving pupils in the assessment process gives them a sense of *ownership* – assessment becomes something they are doing for their own benefit rather than something that others are doing to them. In the long term the ultimate value of assessment will only be gained if autonomous individuals are produced.

CURRENT ISSUES IN ASSESSMENT

The standards debate

At the present time there is massive government and media attention concerning the maintenance of standards in education. Much of the commentary places enormous and unwarranted faith in the ability of examinations systems to give absolute answers. The inevitable shortcomings of examinations are dismissed as either irrelevant or as a justification for incompetence on the part of teachers, examiners and those organising the system. Issues of validity and reliability are ignored and crude figures accepted at face value. Godley (1899) expressed doubts about reliability as follows:

Twixt Right and Wrong, the Difference is Dim:
Tis settled by the Moderator's Whim:
Perchance the Delta on your paper marked,
Means that his lunch has disagreed with him.

Within the educational domain there can be no *absolute* standard because we do not possess measuring instruments directly comparable to a ruler for length or a clock for time. An element of subjectivity is inevitable. In science examinations there are many fewer problems of standardisation than in some other subjects, say English or history. Most answers do not call for the subjective views of the marker. However, even in science, there are occasions when judgements must be made as to the interpretation of a pupil's response. Very often pupils fail to write in the manner predicted by examiners when drawing up the mark scheme – this was the case in KS 3 tests in summer 1992. Consequently there is a need for marking to be moderated so that, as far as possible, all mark to the same criteria. Nevertheless, there will always remain some variation.

Testing and the National Curriculum

Undoubtedly the National Curriculum has enormously increased the amount of testing of pupils and the bureaucratic record-keeping required of all teachers. Media attention, both nationally and locally, is intense because 'league tables' of schools are made possible by the publishing of results and make excellent copy. Has a situation of testing overload been reached? Are the demands of testing making quite unreasonable demands upon time that is required for teaching? The Secretary of State has belatedly accepted that a review of the testing regime is required. The merger of NCC and SEAC into the new School Curriculum and Assessment Authority (SCAA) has provided an opportunity to reconsider testing arrangements. This will include a reappraisal of the ten-level scale, a review of test administration and a look at possibilities for simplifying the tests themselves. Whether this will be enough remains to be seen.

REFERENCES AND FURTHER READING

Allay, M., Bennett, S., Dutch, S., Levinson, R., Taylor, P. and West, D. (1992) *Open Chemistry*, London: Hodder & Stoughton (a useful collection of articles covering a wide range of issues concerning the teaching of chemistry but likely to be of use to most science teachers. Includes two chapters on the assessment of chemistry).
Association for Science Education (ASE), (1992) 'Report on the Monitoring of Key Stage 3: September 1992', *Education in Science*, (150): 18–19.
Centre for Science Education, Sheffield Hallam University (1992) *Active Teaching and Learning Approaches in Science* (ATLAS project), London: Collins Educational (a useful collection of pupil activities designed to illustrate the potential of active teaching

approaches in science. The early chapters contain much valuable guidance on the adoption of the teaching strategies used).

Christofi, C. (1988) *Assessment and Profiling in Science*, London: Cassell.

Deale, R. N. (1975) 'Assessment and testing' in *Secondary School Council Examinations Bulletin*, (32): 19–27.

Fairbrother, R. W. (1986) 'How is science teaching evaluated, assessed and examined?' in Nellist, J. and Nicholl, B. (eds), *ASE Science Teachers' Handbook*, London: Hutchinson.

—— (1988) *Methods of Assessment*, York: Longman.

Godley, A. T. (1899) *The Rubaiyatt of Moderations*, quoted in Wiseman, S. (ed.), (1961) *Examinations and English Education*, Manchester: Manchester University Press.

Holt, J. (1969) *The Underachieving School*, London: Pitman.

Inter Group Research Committee of the GCSE Group (1992) 'Setting GCSE Science Papers Which Differentiate Effectively', London: Secondary Assessment and Examinations Council (unpublished).

Kempa, R. (1986) *Assessment in Science*, Cambridge Science Education Series, Cambridge: Cambridge University Press (tough going, but useful, for the enthusiast).

National Curriculum Task Group on Assessment and Testing (TGAT) (1988) *A Report*, London: HMSO, Department of Education and Science.

Rowntree, D. (1977) *Assessing Students: How Shall We Know Them?*, London: Harper and Row.

School Curriculum and Assessment Authority (1994) *The National Curriculum and its Assessment: Final Report by Sir Ron Dearing*, London: SCAA.

Secondary Assessment & Examinations Council (SEAC) (1993) *School Assessment Folder KS3 Science Sample Test Questions*, London: HMSO.

Skevington, J. (1993) 'Assessing and evaluating in science education' in Hull, R. (ed.) *ASE Secondary Science Teachers' Handbook*, Hemel Hempstead: Simon & Schuster.

Secondary Science Curriculum Review (SSCR) (1984) 'Assessment: An SSCR Central Team View', Working Paper No. 2, London: SCDC Publications.

Thorp, S. (ed.) (1991) *Race, Equality and Science Teaching*, Hatfield: ASE (useful activity on the 'principles of good assessment', pp. 101–2).

Wilson, C. (1987) *Better Science. Curriculum Guide 11 – Assessing Progress*, London: Heinemann/ASE for SCDC (one of a series of summary reports arising out of the Secondary Science Curriculum Review (SSCR) that gives an overview of assessment prior to the introduction of the National Curriculum).

Woolnough, B. and Toh, K. A. (1990) 'Alternative approaches to assessment of practical work in science', *School Science Review*, (71): 127–31.

6 Planning and managing learning in science

In a sense, the whole of this book is about planning and managing learning in science. This chapter, however, is aimed solely at offering practical ideas, frameworks and guidelines on preparing for and managing learning in science. They are presented for you to consider, with a minimum of discussion – suggestions for further reading therefore are important and lengthy.

PLANNING AND PREPARING

Schemes of work

The first task for many teachers is to prepare a scheme of work to cover perhaps from a half-term's to a year's work in science. This is usually a broad outline stating in brief *what* is to be taught lesson by lesson and often *how* it is to be taught, with perhaps additional notes on the resources needed. This is often a shared activity in a science department which achieves several aims:

- a shared, coordinated approach to the curriculum for a given year group
- a division and saving of labour amongst staff
- on a practical level, a guide which can help in the case of staff absence
- a record of the coverage of the PoS of the National Curriculum (which should form the basis of the scheme)
- a record which can be used in liaison between schools, for example junior to secondary

What might a scheme of work for secondary science look like? My own view is that it should be clear and concise with the detail coming in the lesson plan. The starting point is to examine the relevant PoS and then to divide it into convenient themes, topics or areas of study. A possible format is shown in table 6.1 below, but readers are encouraged to look around at other ideas and formats in order to develop their own, which they and the school they work in are happy with.

Table 6.1 Headings for a scheme of work

Area/Theme of study (for example, the environment, energy, force, health and diet)

LESSON ONE (for example, Your surroundings, What is energy? Feeling forces, Eating for health, etc.)

Lesson aims:
Content/activity
Learning and teaching ideas, for example, demonstration, circus, role-play
Resources needed (special notes on safety)
Assessment plans and opportunities
Links to other parts of the NC
SoAs covered

LESSON TWO . . . and so on.

These notes on creating a scheme of work have been necessarily brief – fuller guidelines are given in Section B of the Science Non-Statutory Guidance.

Planning individual lessons

Planning each lesson within a scheme of work is the next stage – a somewhat enigmatic activity in that beginning teachers find it extremely time consuming and demanding whereas experienced teachers are able to give the impression that there is absolutely nothing to it. Appearances are misleading: lesson planning is a vitally important part of good teaching, not only in producing a well-structured, varied, carefully paced, well-timed and scientifically correct lesson but also in ensuring good management and control. Good lesson planning is the first step to good control and discipline. Pupils can see for themselves if a lesson has been carefully thought through, clearly structured and pitched at the right level – indeed, it is a good teaching ploy to outline the what, the why and the how of a lesson at the outset. Surely teachers should tell pupils what they are about to do, how, why and for how long?

There are almost as many schools of thought on lesson planning as there are schools. This section offers a fairly traditional view and format for lesson planning for readers to consider. In another chapter an alternative view is offered from a 'constructivist' perspective, in which the lesson begins with the pupils' own conceptions of a concept or topic and the lesson is based upon that foundation. This obviously demands much greater flexibility and spontaneity on the part of the teacher. The ideas offered below take a much more content-and teacher-led perspective.

From this perspective, a lesson plan should include at least the following ten elements:

1 Basic information, for example, the class, time, room, etc.

2 The aims of the lesson, i.e. what the pupils should know/be able to do/understand at the end of the lesson which they did not know/were not able to do/did not understand when they walked in. These might be phrased in terms of cognitive aims, for example, recall, explain, understand, calculate, interpret, classify, etc.; or affective aims, for example, appreciate, enjoy, be aware of, gain a liking for, etc.; or 'doing' aims, for example, measure, observe, carry out, choose, etc.

3 The resources needed: What equipment will be needed? Which visual aids? How will it be organised and distributed in the room?

4 Safety notes – more on this later.

5 The overall structure for the lesson itself, for example, introduction, development, concluding.

6 Detail (greater or lesser depending on preference) within that structure. Some people like to write virtually a script; others confine themselves to listing the questions they will ask; others use the briefest of notes.

7 Indication of timing, perhaps in a margin in the side.

8 Notes indicating what the teacher and the pupils are doing in any given part of the lesson, for example, 'teacher activity/pupil activity'. This can be valuable in ensuring the variety and pacing of a lesson.

9 Homework ideas (where needed).

10 Space for evaluation (to be done after the lesson!): A short section is needed to consider the progress of the lesson, did it achieve its aims, to list points to remember for next time, how you would do it differently if you taught it again!

A possible format or pro-forma for constructing lessons is presented in table 6.2. Readers may wish to use it and gradually adapt it for themselves – lesson planning is quite rightly an activity which will vary from one teacher and one school to another. What is unacceptable, in my view, is not to plan at all.

A very different approach to lesson planning will be adopted by those who take a constructivist view of teaching and learning in science. This is explored fully in Chapter 4, but in brief the lesson will begin with the elicitation of children's ideas, for example, by getting children to explore their own conceptions and ideas (on, say, energy, force, pressure, the environment, health, fuels, growth, evolution) with each other and the teacher. This would form the starting point of the lesson (see The Oxford Science Programme, Teachers' Resource file and Pupils' books, for example).

Keeping a lesson file

One of the things that students on teaching practice are widely expected to do, and yet experienced teachers are strangely reluctant to be seen with, is a lesson file. In my view, it is a necessary part of professional teaching, even if seasoned teachers pretend that they don't have one or don't need one (in reality, they are either subtle or they have a filing cabinet instead of an arch folder).

Lesson files can usefully contain at least the following:

Table 6.2 A possible lesson plan format

A **Basic information**

Class ....   Date and time ....

Number of pupils ....   Place ....

Memo, e.g. homework reminder ....

Topic ....

B **Resources needed**

[NB Safety points:]

C **Aims and objectives**

Skills?   Knowledge?   Attitudes?

D **Lesson summary [main section]**

TIME	ACTIVITY	NOTES AND COMMENTS	AIMS
0–5 mins	Introduction/ appetiser	Space for notes	
5–10 mins etc.	Development	(further expansion on separate pages if if necessary)	
	Summary or conclusion		
e.g. 50 mins	Trailer for next lesson		

E **Evaluation and reflection**

How did it go? Did you achieve your aims? Feedback from pupils/other teachers?

- schemes of work for each year/class
- class lists and records, with essential information, for example on very special needs
- seating plans (if used)
- plans for individual lessons, and evaluations
- photographic records, for example, of posters produced, wall displays, practical work, problem-solving activities, etc.
- samples of pupils' work
- OHP transparencies
- worksheets, DARTS, etc.

ASKING QUESTIONS

One of the activities that teachers engage in whatever their view of learning or lesson planning is that of asking questions. Indeed there is probably no other context in life (except perhaps the Houses of Parliament) where so many questions are asked by so few of so many. One estimate is that teachers ask questions for one-third of their classroom time with a total on average of 30,000 questions per year. Some teachers ask sensible, useful probing questions of pupils spontaneously and naturally – I would suggest that these Socratic people are few and far between. Most of us need to plan and prepare our questioning even to the extent of writing them into the lesson plan. Time spent on this can avoid embarrassment and disruption in the classroom. A question such as 'Where can I find sea water?' is likely to lead to either dumb disbelief that any adult could ask such a thing, or worse still loud shouts of 'Skegness', 'Blackpool', or 'Hastings', depending on the region.

Teachers need to examine carefully four aspects of questioning:

1   *Why* they should ask questions at all?
2   *When* are the best times to ask them?
3   *How* should questions be posed and presented – i.e. what makes for a good questioning technique?
4   *What* types of question can teachers ask?

The four aspects are closely interrelated, for example, the time and reason for asking a question will determine the technique and tone used – this should be remembered as we take each aspect in turn. A large amount has been said and written about questioning (see further reading); what follows below is a brief, potted summary.

Why ask questions?

There are many good reasons for asking questions in a classroom, including the following:

- to gain and keep attention, i.e. as a means of control
- to get pupils to think
- to keep them active and attentive, i.e. to avoid spoon-feeding
- to stimulate curiosity and interest
- to test/confirm their knowledge or understanding
- to identify/diagnose any problems in learning, recall or understanding
- to lead a class step-by-step through a topic or an experiment, i.e. Socratic questioning, 'bringing things out'
- to elicit pupils' prior knowledge or conceptions, i. e. finding out where they are already
- to go over/revise a topic, for example at the end of a lesson or at the start of a new one
- to gain feedback on whether and what they have learnt, to evaluate the lesson, for example 'Have aims been achieved'?

When to ask questions?

The reasons for asking questions are connected with the best times to ask them, for example:

1   at the start, during the introduction, for example, to give a link with the previous lesson, to revise and reinforce earlier learning, to elicit pupils' ideas
2   during the development of the lesson, for example, using key questions to guide pupils' thinking or to formulate a problem, working out the right steps, procedures and sequence for a practical instead of simply giving instructions
3   during class activity, for example to sort out problems in small groups or with individuals
4   at the end of a class activity, for example, to pool results, to consider results, to work towards a conclusion
5   at the end of a lesson, for example, to go over, revise, reinforce, evaluate, lead up to the next lesson

What kind of questions can be asked?

There are two important ways of classifying questions:
1 Questions can be grouped according to whether they are open or closed. Closed questions usually have one correct, often short answer – for example, What is the symbol used for sodium? or What is the capital of England? The teacher usually wants pupils to give an answer which she or he already knows. If there is a particular correct answer which the teacher is seeking, such as trachea rather than windpipe, then closed questions often become a 'guess what's in my head' exercise.

With open questions a variety of responses can be acceptable, such as Why did London become the capital of England? They often ask what the pupils are thinking, and there will be more than one correct answer – however, for many teachers, some answers are more correct than others! In other words, except perhaps in a genuine brainstorming session, few questions are genuinely totally open. Thus a question like 'What did you notice about the copper as we heated it?' may invite many responses whereas the teacher may be seeking only one.

2 Questions can also be grouped by the intellectual demand made by the question. It may require any of the following:

* factual recall, for example, Which gas makes up 0.03 per cent of the air? or Which ore does iron come from? This will obviously involve asking closed questions.
* understanding and application of a formula, a rule, a law, a theory, etc., for example, If a person lifts a weight of 50 newtons from the ground onto a shelf two metres above it, how much work has she done? (These are generally closed questions.)
* analysis and evaluation of, for example, a process, a material and its use, an energy source, or a set of data. Analysis may sometimes have one correct answer, for example, in analysing data from a table, but evaluation may invite several

'correct' responses, provided they are based on careful consideration and analysis, such as, What are the benefits and drawbacks of using nuclear fission to provide energy?

- predicting and hypothesising, for example, What do you think will happen if. . .?
- interpreting and explaining, for example, Why did the wire become hot?
- inferring, for example, If we add more weights to this spring what will happen? (c. f. predicting)

These are just some of the ways of classifying questions; such a classification is not definitive and there is also much overlap between the categories. Often we cannot tell if we are predicting, hypothesising or inferring – the three go together. But a classification of this kind is useful for two reasons. First of all, in lesson planning and evaluation, teachers can prepare and examine their questions to see if they are asking a fair balance. Are all their questions of the closed, factual recall kind? Do they ask pupils to speculate, predict and hypothesise? Do they give opportunities for weighing up pros and cons, analysing points of view and assessing benefits and drawbacks, i.e. evaluation? These are all essential features of the science national curriculum.

Thus a classification of questions asked (in both spoken and written form) is useful in lesson planning and in ensuring coverage of the NC. It is also vital in considering assessment of students' learning. This is a topic followed up in full in a later chapter.

HOW SHOULD QUESTIONS BE PREPARED AND DELIVERED IN A CLASSROOM?

The final aspect of questioning is the 'how?' Table 6.3 offers a set of guidelines on preparing and phrasing questions, and on presenting them to a class.

SAFETY ISSUES

Safety in the lab is not just an important issue – it is the issue which overrides all others. In other words, whatever good reasons (educational, motivational or any other) there are for doing an activity or a demonstration, IF IT IS UNSAFE OR UNHEALTHY IN ANY WAY THEN DO NOT DO IT! This is the simple and cardinal rule.

Having said that, there are many activities that can be carried out safely in science, given the right precautions, management and conditions.

Precautions for teachers

In my view the biggest single hazard in the lab is that which comes in with the pupils – in short, their bags and coats. Few comprehensives have a cloak-or locker room where pupils can leave their paraphernalia. This means that many carry it

Table 6.3 Guidelines for questioning

Preparing and phrasing questions

- Prepare key questions in advance, using the categories above.
- Relate the questions to the aims of the lesson.
- Phrase the questions clearly and at the right language level.
- Avoid ambiguous wording.
- Beware of 'nonsense' questions, for example 'Why does a pig have four legs?'; general questions, for example 'Where can we find sea-water?', and other questions that invite stupid answers, for example 'What do you all do at least once a day?'
- Make sure that questions are carefully sequenced.

Presenting and delivering questions

- Position yourself and the class carefully – ensure that you can see and be seen.
- Insist on the use of hands rather than shouting out.
- Spread questions around the class – look for a balance, such as back and front, male and female.
- Use pupils' names in directing and responding to questions.
- Draw ideas out from the pupils – don't give too much too soon.
- If the classroom situation allows it, keep probing and prompting in order to extend pupils' thinking, for example 'What do you mean by that . . . ?', 'And then what might happen . . . ?', 'What makes you say that . . . ?', and so on.

Accepting and dealing with responses

- Be ready to record responses on a board, OHP or flip chart. This is a form of reward as well as a useful record, for example, of predictions.
- Encourage pupils to respond by body language, such as nods, hand gestures, smiles.
- Praise responses even if the answer to a closed question is incorrect – don't condemn answers to open questions purely because they don't coincide with what's in your head.
- Give leads and hints if responses are not forthcoming, perhaps by rephrasing and redirecting the question.
- Don't embarrass or humiliate by waiting too long for a response.
- Don't allow others to ridicule a pupil for an incorrect answer to a closed question or a strange answer to an open one.
- Open questions, although educationally desirable, lead to responses which can be far harder to manage and control than closed ones, such as long monologues from pupils or totally unexpected or zany replies. Developing a good questioning technique that includes asking and responding to open questions takes time and reflection.

around with them all day. Thus teachers can expect pupils to carry into a lab any or even all of the following: overcoat, bag, sports kit, saxophone/guitar/clarinet etc., cooked produce or cooking containers, hockey stick, boots. . . . You name it. These are the first hazard in the lab and every teacher will need a strategy or set procedure for dealing with it before any active work can begin. Different schools and departments will have different tactics but the universal rule is that no practical work can begin safely until all unneeded belongings are safely away from aisles, stools, benches and tables. Pupils themselves will need to feel safe and secure with this arrangement.

There are a number of other hazards in the lab which teachers need to be aware of and prepared for. They may be chemical, biological, electrical or physical. Fortunately, the advent of the Health and Safety At Work Act in 1974 forced schools to examine safety in science labs in a much more systematic, open and responsible way. One of its subsequent outcomes has been the production of a large and valuable range of documents, leaflets and books on safety in science from a number of sources. These are essential reading for science teachers and are listed at the end of this chapter. No attempt is made to summarise them here as there is no substitute for reading them in full. A selection from a valuable checklist published by the Association for Science Education is given as an appendix to this chapter.

Training pupils for safety

In addition to teacher precautions, pupils need to be given safety training, sometimes as lessons in themselves and sometimes within certain practical lessons. Students must have a clear set of lab rules and guidelines, both in their books and on display – but this is not enough. They should also be trained at the very least to:

- spot all potential hazards (chemical, biological, etc.)
- consider and if necessary revise the lab rules
- heat substances safely
- wear safety goggles whenever at all desirable, i.e. when heating liquids, observing flames, etc.
- identify electrical dangers, for example that a person's electrical resistance drops from about 10,000 ohms with dry hands to around 300 ohms with wet hands
- use a bunsen burner correctly
- know all the hazard warning symbols (which they actually quite enjoy learning)

Fortunately there are a number of useful published materials on safety that can be used with pupils, not least the *Safety Matters* collection from Philip Harris.

MANAGEMENT AND CONTROL

The subject that perhaps most concerns all beginning teachers, and that relates to lesson planning, asking questions and safety, is the management and control of pupils during the lesson. This topic is another on which a vast amount has been said and written, some of which is useful and practical (see further reading), part of which is too vague to be of value, and an element of which is pure scare-mongering.

Let us therefore start by putting classroom management issues into perspective. An important report in 1989 (HMSO, 1989) showed that, in its sample of over 2,000 teachers, the five behaviours most commonly reported as a difficulty, in the order shown below, were:

1 pupils talking out of turn
2 work avoidance or idleness

3   pupils hindering other pupils
4   pupils not being punctual
5   pupils making unnecessary, non-verbal noise

Take a careful look at these, the top five. They do not include swearing at the teacher, acts of vandalism or physical attack – all of the incidents which a gullible reader of the popular press would infer are common in schools. The Elton Report and other published studies show clearly that those 'newsworthy' types of behaviour may sell newspapers but are relatively rare in the real, non-tabloid world. Thus we start here from the premise that the most common management goals for the teacher are quite simply to organise and control pupil talk in the classroom, and to keep pupils to task.

As mentioned earlier, a large number of books have been written about classroom management, and although they can never be a substitute for experience and observation they can give teachers at all stages useful frameworks for analysing their own practice. Many of the books (listed at the end of the chapter) offer practical advice on class management: Robertson (1989), for example, gives a useful checklist for 'successful teaching'; McManus (1989) provides a summary of 'teaching skills for classroom management'; Marland (1975), in one of the most widely read books in initial training, offers a guide to all aspects of the classroom component of a teacher's job. It would be impossible to distil all the practical wisdom from the wide range of books in this area. However, I have offered below a checklist which might be valuable to teachers to consider before and after a lesson. These points are a summary of much of the agreed wisdom on planning, preparing, presenting and managing lessons. They are offered to readers in a clear and direct style, but please do look carefully and critically at them.

Planning

- Plan a varied, interesting lesson.
- Make sure the pupils are busy throughout, according to your lesson plan, i.e. give them plenty to *do*.
- Plan some time fillers, such as a quiz, spelling test, word-search or cross words.
- Plan a lesson that makes sense and has some sort of logical pattern, sequence, or structure to it. Make it clear to the pupils *what* you are trying to teach them and *why*!

Preparation

- Try all experiments and demonstrations before the lesson.
- Prepare some blackboard work and/or OHP diagrams beforehand, if possible.
- Check all the apparatus *before and after* each lesson. Count it all out – count it all back in again.
- Ensure that ventilation and lighting are adequate.

Presentation

- Try to *look* confident and professional: – don't slouch, mumble, look at your feet or stare out of the window.
- Speak clearly, at a sensible speed.
- Project yourself.
- 'Scan' the group and make eye contact. Don't talk just to the front row.
- Put some life into it, for example, move your lips, don't stand in one place like a statue; appear enthusiastic.
- Be aware of what's going on ('with it'); – look for feedback, such as yawns, glazed looks.

Relationships

(These are both a cause and an effect of good classroom management. Also, they do take time.)

- Be pleasant but never friendly – it's totally false.
- Be firm but not 'stroppy'. Pupils hate teachers who shout and moan at them all the time.
- Occasionally show that you're human (this is probably safest outside the classroom, such as on the games field).
- Don't court popularity.
- Try to enjoy what you're doing, but don't smile too much (don't spend two minutes getting the class quiet, then tell them a joke).
- Start learning names immediately (by studying the class list in advance and using silly mnemonics; when handing out books; as pupils answer questions; using a seating plan, etc.).
- Use names as soon as you can (i.e., don't use 'You at the back', 'Yes, you').
- Use praise, both public and private.
- Respond positively to correct answers – don't just grunt or nod imperceptibly (for example, 'Very good' or 'Yes, well done').

Gaining attention

- Insist on silence when you are talking to the whole class – but don't overdo it (five minutes at a stretch?).
- Pick the right moment to address the class (for example, not while they're trooping out of or into the room).
- Give clear, positive starting signals to gain attention according to some sort of 'hierarchy' ranging from pleasant to curt. For example:

Pleasant: non-verbal signals, such as standing waiting for quiet
Pleasant: 'Can I have your attention please?'
Pleasant: 'Will you all listen now?'
Pleasant: 'Be quiet everybody.'

Curt: 'John – be quiet.' (i.e. pick on individuals)
Pleasant: 'Shut-up.'

- Don't start the lesson until you have complete silence, even if you have to work through this range and repeat these signals.
- If spoken words won't shut the class up, try written words or a definite task; such as:
'Copy these notes off the blackboard. . . .'
'Draw this diagram. . . .'
'Copy this OHP transparency.' (a good way of gaining attention because (1) you switch it on and light appears and (2) you're facing the class.)
- Never, ever use 'Ssshh . . . ssshh. . . .' It's ambiguous and usually ignored anyway.

Keeping control

- Don't expect a class to follow the same activity (for example, note-taking) for an hour, or to listen to you endlessly. Variety is the spice of a lesson.
- Try to decide in *your own mind* what standards and norms you want to enforce – this is half the battle. (Commands are obeyed in direct proportion to how much you mean them.)
- Stick closely to the school norms whenever you can – it's easier.
- Be *determined* in enforcing these norms.
- There is no need to insist on silence during class or practical work but you can, for example, insist that pupils only talk to the person next to them.
- Be consistent and predictable over what you want and what you expect.

Starting and ending a lesson

- Stand near the door and look at each pupil as he or she comes into the room. (Don't, for example, write on the board, fiddle with apparatus, engage in deep conversation with a pupil or the lab technician, or sort out books as the kids come in.)
- You may wish to make *brief* individual remarks as they enter, such as 'You're sitting on the front row today' or a similar witticism.
- Don't try to start a lesson *too quickly* (for example, explain Einstein's theory of relativity while they're still taking their coats off). Give them one to two minutes to settle down and get in the right frame of mind, with the occasional salutary remark from you (such as 'Put him down', 'Spit the chewing gum in the bin', etc.).
- On the other hand, don't start a lesson ten minutes late.
- Try to sum up, and round off every lesson, then tell them what they're doing next time.
- Don't dismiss the class until they are all sitting in silence. Dismiss one row at a time.

- Stand by the door and watch each pupil as he or she leaves. Save long conversations, and reprimands, until others have gone.

If things go wrong . . .

- Avoid one-to-one confrontation. It's very difficult to win.
- Use other staff, for example, to send one or two (at most) miscreants to (extracting one or two pupils can save a lesson for the other 26).
- If you send a pupil out, send him or her to somebody specific, such as Head of Department, with a specific task to do.
- Don't make empty, 'unkeepable' threats, such as 10,000 lines, 90 minutes' detention.
- You can make small, keepable threats, such as 50 lines, 10 minutes' staying in.
- Don't be afraid to make pupils move seats.
- Don't get physical *in any way*.
- Raise your voice to the roof if necessary, but above all don't overdo it – it soon loses its impact.
- Seek advice. Talk over your lessons with staff and other students.
- Above all, don't take it personally.

Your worst class

If all the above fail:

- Try a totally different tactic, such as individualised learning instead of class teaching, lots of colourful bandas and worksheets, video, slides, OHP . . . anything!
- Find out how other teachers cope with them, if at all.
- Have a cup of tea, drink, walk or run before you carry out a post mortem (evaluation) on your lesson.

Every professional benefits from colleagues' help. Teachers are no exception.

Even if teachers do follow all the rules, tips, dos and don'ts, and handy hints dished out to them by everyone from their mentor in school, to parents, press and politicians, there will be lessons that do not go according to plan. It is worth returning briefly to the Elton Report to see what teachers in their sample did when dealing with difficult classes or individuals. The most common strategies and sanctions used were, in this order:

- reasoning with a pupil or pupils inside the room
- reasoning outside the room
- setting extra work of some kind
- detaining a pupil or pupils
- sending a pupil or pupils out of the room
- referring a pupil or pupils to another teacher
- sending a pupil or pupils to a more senior teacher

These are likely to be the most common sanctions that teachers will continue to employ – it is unlikely that caning, hanging, drawing and quartering in return for deviant behaviour will make a comeback.

FEEDBACK AND MARKING

One of the clearest messages from studies of behaviour in classrooms is that although punishment has little effect in improving the behaviour of those punished (although it may have a deterrent effect on those who observe it), the use of praise can be extremely effective. Pupils like teachers who are well organised, interesting and humorous – there is also extensive evidence that they respond well to praise. Praise can be a tool for classroom control in encouraging pupils, keeping them to task, motivating them, and generally improving their self-esteem. Its value can not be over-stated.

In general, the feedback that pupils receive from the teacher is vitally important. Humiliation and condemnation are not productive – praise and encouragement are. This is also true of marking pupils' written work. More will be said on pupils' writing and marking in the chapter on language in science education, but it can be said briefly here that feedback on written work is as important as it is in the oral, classroom context. What guidelines can be offered on marking work? A short summary is given here which will be developed in the language chapter:

- Always mark pupils' work at frequent intervals, even if there is not time to mark it thoroughly, word by word, on every occasion. Some feedback, comment or praise is better than nothing. At least it shows pupils that the teacher cares and is keeping an eye on things.
- Use praise and encouragement as well as criticism. Find something positive to say about the work, however small. If appropriate, praise the work as you hand it back.
- The correction of spelling is a thorny and contentious issue. Spelling is important for at least three reasons: poor spelling inhibits the writer's fluency and distracts the reader from the content; the reader judges the content to be of lower quality, not least in a scientific context; spelling is seen in society as important, rightly or wrongly. For these reasons a teacher has a duty to consider a pupil's spelling when marking work in science and to use whatever strategy is best for that pupil in order to improve it. This is the nub of the issue. With pupils who make perhaps two spelling errors in a piece of work, correction of each is both practical and not too damning. With a pupil whose work is riddled with misspellings the situation requires tact. One strategy is to single out the more important errors and correct those tactfully but clearly. There may be persistent errors which a teacher can look for and attempt to remediate. Special help may be needed, for example through the use of IT. The process of correction and re-drafting is far easier to handle and far less painful if a simple word processor is used, perhaps with a spell-checker. Presentation and self-esteem can be greatly enhanced by using a computer system to reveal the true extent of a pupil's writing. Teachers

should not be misled into assuming that a poor speller, or a person with unsightly handwriting, is a poor writer.

There are many issues connected with marking and giving feedback to pupils that could be considered; the main message here, though, is that it should be based on reward, praise and encouragement rather than on negative criticism or condemnation.

HOMEWORK

The final job that falls to teachers at the end of the lesson is very often the setting of homework. Not only are teachers responsible for the learning and behaviour of pupils during school hours – they also extend their influence outside these hours by the tradition of homework! Like it or not, most secondary schools have a policy of setting and monitoring homework. It can be set for a variety of reasons:

- to finish work started in the lesson, such as finishing written work, writing up a practical
- as a new piece of work relating to the lesson
- as an assessment of the learning in a lesson, for example, a set of questions based on the lesson content
- as an extension to the work in the lesson, for example, a worksheet of information, reading and questions
- as an open, flexible piece of work that can be undertaken almost independently at home, such as a piece of mini-research, a project, an exploration. (This will obviously depend to a large extent on a pupil having access to resources at home or nearby.)

There may be other reasons and motives for setting homework. Ideally, a useful piece of homework should have the following features:

- It should be clear and manageable within a realistic time span.
- It should not make too many demands upon or assumptions about the home environment, for example, 'Look up the following words in *Encyclopaedia Britannica . . .*'
- It should be clearly connected to the lesson and the overall scheme of work.
- The purpose behind it should be clear to the pupil, i.e. why is this demand being placed upon them in their out-of-school time?

Homework can be valuable, and there might well be an outcry from certain quarters if the tradition of British homework disappeared. However, there are problems with it that have surfaced both in the everyday experience of teachers and in research studies of attitudes to it. The main, most common problems seem to be:

- pupils being unclear about what they had to do or how much, with no opportunity to seek clarification (this may arise from poor instructions in the lesson, not writing it down, not listening, not remembering, etc.)

- pupils not having the resources, such as secondary sources, or the equipment, such as a protractor or calculator, to carry out the work
- pupils unable to obtain secondary sources, for example, from the public library (which may, like my own, be closed down)
- poor working conditions at home
- badly written, unclear or poorly reproduced worksheets

These are all problems that the teacher needs to be aware of, even if they are not all within the teacher's sphere of influence. A later chapter considers the important and connected issue of children's out-of-school learning in science.

REFERENCES AND FURTHER READING

Management and control

There is a wide range of books on classroom management and control. Here is a brief list showing a selection of those books with short notes on each one. Although they cannot be a substitute for classroom practice and experience, they can help to provide a framework for analysing and reflecting upon them. There is nothing so practical as a good theory.

Cheesman, P. and Watts, P. (1985) *Positive Behaviour Management: A Manual for Teachers*, London: Croom Helm (discusses the background to behaviour problems and ways of assessing them. Puts forward practical advice on intervention and 'step-by-step' guide to positive behaviour management. The summary of suggestions for 'teacher behaviour' may be particularly useful [pages 80–84].).

HMSO (1989) *Discipline in Schools: The Elton Report*, London: HMSO.

McManus, M. (1989) *Troublesome Behaviour in the Classroom – A Teacher's Survival Guide*, London: Routledge Education (a detailed account of troublesome behaviour, its causes and remedies; draws extensively on research findings, but also has many practical activities to try. Useful for students and experienced teachers alike.).

Marland, M. (1975) *The Craft of the Classroom*, Oxford: Heinemann (reprinted many times, this book is a short, well-organised and very practical classic covering all aspects of the new teacher's job; valuable if a little dated.).

Neill, S. (1991) *Classroom Non-verbal Communication*, London: Routledge (Illustrates [with text and numerous drawings] the use of body language, facial expression and posture in the classroom. Very practical discussion and advice [based on recent research] offering suggestions for teachers on conveying enthusiasm, gaining attention, using space and interpreting pupils' body language.).

Robertson, J. (1989) (2nd ed.) *Effective Classroom Control – Understanding Teacher-Pupil Relationships*, London: Hodder & Stoughton (up-to-date, short but detailed, with much good advice on teacher-pupil relationships; over half of the book is devoted to analysing and dealing with unwanted behaviour in the classroom.).

Rogers, C. (1983) *Freedom to Learn*, Ohio: Merrill (a compendium of Rogers' research on person-centred learning, how to manage it and set it up so that pupils' curiosity and enthusiasm are not stifled. A stimulating and challenging book.).

Thorp, S. (ed.) (1991) *Race, Equality and Science Teaching*, Hatfield: ASE (has several useful activities involving looking at schemes of work [page 57], 'Looking at my classroom' [pages 15–17] and reflecting on 'Groupings in the classroom' [page 51].).

Questioning

Brown, G. A. (1975) *Microteaching*, London: Methuen (This book has been around for some time but has many useful points.).
—— (1984) 'Questioning', in Wragg, E. C. (ed.), *Classroom Teaching Skills* (1984), London: Croom Helm.
Kerry, T. (1982) *Effective Questioning*, London: Macmillan Education.
Sands, M. and Hull, R. (1985) *Teaching Science: A Teaching Skills Workbook*, London: Macmillan Education (A useful collection of practical ideas on not only questioning but management, control, marking and safety.).

Safety

ASE (1988) *Topics in Safety*, Hatfield: ASE.
—— (1988) *Safety in the School Laboratory*, ASE Laboratory Safeguard Committee (9th ed.), Hatfield: ASE. Brief, comprehensive and up to date.
HMSO (1985) *Microbiology: An HMI Guide for Schools and Non-advanced Further Education*, London: HMSO.
DES (1984) *Safety in Science Laboratories*, DES Safety Series 2 (3rd ed.), London: HMSO. The DFE (formerly DES) produce a range of free 'Memoranda' on a range of safety topics such as laser use, radiation, and AIDS from: The Publications Unit, DES, Honeypot Lane, Stanmore, Middlesex HA7 1AZ.
Everett, D. and Jenkins, E. (1990) *A Safety Handbook for Science Teachers*, London: John Murray (5th ed.). Covers the whole field of safety in science teaching and contains a comprehensive list (over 600 items) of all major hazards.

For classroom use:

Safety in the Lab, a leaflet for pupils, (2nd ed. 1982) Hatfield: ASE.
Safety Matters – A Resource Pack (1990), London: Philip Harris Ltd. Contains teacher's guide, worksheets, information sheets, cassette tape, board games, etc.
Croner's Manual for Heads of Science (1988), London: Croner Publications Ltd. (1988). Contains a large, useful section on safety in the school laboratory.

7 Meeting special needs in science

Although pupils with severe learning difficulties may not understand the more complex concepts underlying scientific activities, they must not be denied the opportunity of scientific experience.

(NCC, 1989: Section 5)

The statement above applies to all pupils with special educational needs (SEN), whether a difficulty they have in learning is severe or not. Indeed, we should remember that we all experience difficulty of some kind or another in learning, whether it is due to tiredness, saturation or simply that it 'won't go in'. One of the values of the Education Reform Act (ERA) of 1988 was that it established in law that all pupils should receive a broad and balanced curriculum, relevant to their individual needs. How this might be achieved is the subject of this chapter.

WHAT MAKES INDIVIDUALS DIFFERENT?

. . . special needs can best be met when a general concern for individual differences is uppermost in teachers' thinking.

(Postlethwaite, 1993: 21)

Everyone is different. This is a tautology, but it is worth emphasising before spelling out the differences that science teachers need to be aware of. The differences that matter can be divided and summed up as follows.

Educational differences

Children bring different preconceptions (alternative frameworks), different abilities, knowledge, understanding and skills into science education. There is extensive evidence that children have a wide range of preconceptions on notions such as force, pressure, heat, energy, plant nutrition, animal, burning and indeed most of the concepts that are the concern of the National Science Curriculum at key stage 3 (see Chapter 4). The important point for teachers is that these 'alternative conceptions' (so-called in that they differ from the accepted view of normal science) have served children in their life outside of the science classroom and are strongly held on to.

Children also have a huge variety of past experiences from home, parents, cubs or brownies, holidays, visits, etc. which leads to a wide and rich range of scientific experience, knowledge and understanding in any classroom of 20–plus people.

As for abilities, the Assessment of Performance Unit (APU, 1989) studies of secondary pupils showed that pupils varied enormously in their ability to:

- observe
- interpret observations
- interpret information
- plan investigations, including controlling variables

The APU studies revealed many other important differences, of course (see APU, 1988 and 1989).

Perhaps the most important difference, however, is the huge range of linguistic ability that pupils bring to the science room. Science teaching takes place almost exclusively through the medium of language, both written and spoken (see Chapter 11). Hence teachers need to recognise the pupils' differences:

- in writing ability (for example, in reporting practical work, taking notes, or written assessment)
- in speaking and listening ability (for example, when answering oral questions or reporting by speech; in group or class discussion)
- in reading ability (for example, in reading instructions for a practical or an account in a textbook or worksheet)
- in organisational ability (for example, in sequencing tasks or instructions, even in organising their own time)

Psychological differences

It is a statement of the obvious to any practising teacher that pupils exhibit psychological differences. However, it can be helpful to divide them up according to three general categories:

1   General intelligence: There are dangers, however, in taking too much account of IQ scores, as Postlethwaite warns: ' . . . an unfavourable score on an IQ test may alert us to the need to deal with a pupil in a different way, but it is not a trap which condemns that pupil to poor levels of performance' (Postlethwaite, 1993: 31).
2   Motivation, personality and attitude
3   Self-image and self-esteem: how many pupils shrug and say 'Well, I'm just no good at science'? This seems to be more common in the science area than in other subjects, and more true of girls than of boys. Past experience of failure in science will further lower self-esteem.

Learning difficulties and learning styles

Different people have different learning styles – some are 'holists' (looking for overviews and connections amongst different parts); some are 'serialists', preferring to take an element at a time (Pask, 1975). Pask argued that people learn most effectively if they are taught in a style that matches their preferred mode of learning – not an easy task for the teacher when actually teaching, but the difference should be borne in mind when arranging learning activities. From another perspective, it seems that some prefer to learn by moving from concrete specific examples to the abstract and the general; others prefer to start from the abstract and the general before meeting concrete examples. Both strategies are necessary for learning the powerful abstractions that make science important.

Similarly, some learners will experience difficulty of one or more kinds in learning science. Various types of difficulty will be encountered which cannot be discussed fully here, but they may include difficulties in: remembering, e.g. figures, abstractions, science knowledge; classifying; gathering information systematically; generalising from one situation to another; sustaining concentration. Postlethwaite (1993) gives a useful discussion of these difficulties and sensibly points out that they apply to most people at some time or another!

Physical differences

Examples include physically challenged pupils, for example pupils in wheelchairs and pupils with specific impairments such as visual, aural. There will be a wide range of physical difference between pupils in any secondary class. Perhaps the important point for science teachers is that practical work will need special attention, for example whilst giving instructions or in providing special resources/apparatus.

Social differences

Shyness, ability to listen to others, respect for fellow learners, willingness, enthusiasm, social skill, ability to work in a group, leadership quality – these are all important 'social differences' between pupils. They do relate to the four types of difference already listed, but there is not always a clear one-to-one connection (for example, 'not contributing to class discussion' may be attributable to a number of causes including shyness or introversion, lack of confidence, low self-esteem, or lack of knowledge).

Socio-economic differences

These include social class, family background, etc. This clearly relates to the final two points below.

Cultural differences

Different values, religious views, moral standpoints, attitudes to education, differing educational goals and aspirations – these are all factors that will affect science teaching and learning, not least in the treatment of controversial issues such as evolution, the origin of the universe, contraception and sex education.

Gender differences

Pupils' attitudes to the sciences appear to be gender-related (Postlethwaite, 1993), and hence gender affects choices they might make at crucial stages in schooling. There has been some evidence (APU, 1988) that boys are more competent than girls in some areas, such as using apparatus, and that girls better than boys in others, such as making and interpreting observations, but these generalisations are wide open to debate.

All the differences listed above are inter-related, for example prior experiences and socioeconomic background, but it can be useful to separate them out and summarise them in order to be aware of them and to attempt to address them.

RESPONDING TO DIFFERENCES

How can teachers respond to all these individual differences, characteristics and prior experiences which students of all ages and abilities bring to the class or lecture room? First, it needs to be recognised that every group is a mixed ability group. Teachers who are heard to make comments like: 'I don't hold with this mixed-ability teaching' ignore the truism that every group of every age presents different abilities, potential, experience and motivation. The only variable is the range of those differences in a given group.

The second factor for both teachers and learners is to decide how controllable and how pervasive these individual differences are (Postlethwaite, 1993: 44–5). In plain terms, the learner and the teacher can pose these questions:

- Which differences affect all aspects of a pupil's work, whatever the context? In contrast, which differences affect only some aspects of work, in some contexts?
- Which of the differences can be controlled, altered and influenced, i.e. which factors can teachers and learners themselves actually do something about?

Within these two questions there are two other questions:

1 Internal or external? If the difference can be controlled, altered or influenced is it something *internal* to the learner, for example the effort they put in? Or is it something *external*, such as economic status? Is the problem that of the child or a problem of the context and background?
2 Stable/permanent or unstable/temporary? Is the difference something which is constant, unchanging or permanent, or is it short term or temporary, such as a broken leg?

These are all questions that can be asked of individuals, often in connection with their success or failure at certain tasks or activities. The basic questions are summed up in figure 7.1 as a kind of continuum.

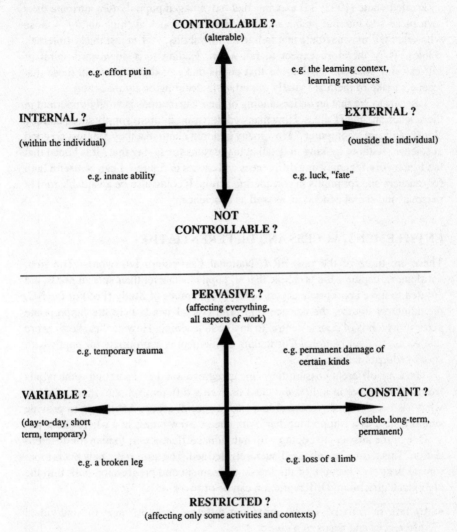

Figure 7.1   Why do people succeed or fail? Questions to ask of individuals' differences and attributes

We often do this with ourselves when we consider our own successes and failures and the reasons for them. Is your sheer brilliance due to pure innate ability (internal, stable, not controllable), or is it a result of your drive, motivation and dogged hard work at crucial times (internal, controllable and unstable)? If, like me, you are totally incapable of writing poetry, is it your English teacher's fault because she killed it stone dead for you as a teenager (external, stable and uncontrollable), or is it your own lack of creativity and insight (stable, internal and possibly pervasive)?

Postlethwaite (1993: 35) explains that 'advantaged pupils' often attribute their own success to internal, stable and pervasive factors such as 'high ability' – those who often fail may attribute that failure to 'low ability' – 'I'm just thick' (internal, stable). They therefore expect to fail again, leading to a downward spiral of self-esteem. Thus the attributions that pupils make of themselves and those that teachers make of them are vitally important in deciding on future action.

It seems to me that an understanding of these attributions is vitally important in the science and the IT areas. How many adults (few children) simply shrug and say 'I just can't use a computer'? How many children claim that they are 'just no good at science' without looking in detail at the reasons for saying that? It is hoped that the framework for analysing differences and causes in figure 7.1 can be useful both for teachers and for pupils in considering action. It could also be a valuable tool in personal and social education, as well as in science.

ENTITLEMENT, ACCESS AND DIFFERENTIATION

These are three of the post-ERA, National Curriculum buzzwords. The first, entitlement, captures the principle that all pupils, whatever their special needs, are entitled to have appropriate access to the Programmes of Study (PoS) of the NC, including, of course, the science PoS. The crucial words here are 'appropriate access', which is of course central to any good teaching. How can teachers ensure that access to their National Curriculum entitlement is appropriate for pupils with special educational needs?

There are different possibilities. One is segregation, i.e. separating some pupils from others, either in a different class or even a different school. This can allow what has been termed 'remedial help' for a special group. Another is to provide support, such as a 'support teacher' with one or a few pupils in a whole class.

One of the answers to coping with individual differences is to plan for differentiation. This term is widely used but rarely defined. The term is not new but is more topical than ever because of the levels, assessment and progression built into the National Curriculum. Differentiation can be of two kinds:

- by task or activity, i.e. by providing different tasks to meet the individual differences and needs of a group
- by outcome, i.e. by allowing different results or outcomes from activities or tasks

The former, by task, suggests that certain activities – such as on a worksheet or in a practical session – should be made special and different for some pupils in order to cater for all needs. The latter implies that different outcomes, such as submitted work, can be planned for and accepted for (say) assessment. Thus differentiation involves first identifying needs, then planning a variety of activities or tasks to meet those needs, then agreeing and setting a range of outcomes from the activities which can be evaluated or assessed (figure 7.2).

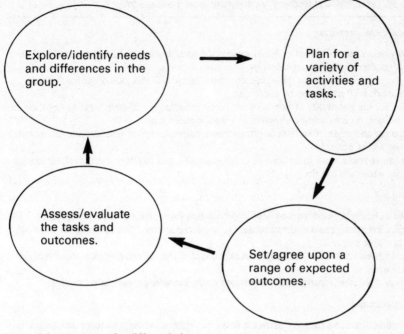

Figure 7.2 A strategy for differentiation

NCC Curriculum Guidance 10 (NCC, 1992b) gives a number of suggestions to teachers on planning for differentiation. The NCC guidance suggests two main principles that are indisputable and indeed apply to any lesson planning:

1 Teachers should define their objectives, taking into account knowledge, understanding and skills, i.e. in a given lesson what do they hope to achieve in terms of those three areas and what knowledge, experiences and skills will pupils leave the room with that they did not have when they entered?
2 Teachers should plan activities appropriate to the class, to groups within it, and to individuals. (This is easier said than done, of course.)

Practical suggestions are given for achieving this key feature of successful teaching: appropriateness. Table 7.1 gives a summary of guidelines on planning, pacing and communicating.

One of the problems, of course, is to put these guidelines into practice in the classroom. Differentiation by task is in many ways more of a challenge in the secondary school than in the primary. Primary teachers are experienced in organising and managing a classroom where a number of different tasks (practical, oral and written) are going on at the same time. In contrast, the norm for the secondary classroom is a group of children engaged in roughly the same activity, such as a practical task, following a worksheet or taking notes from an OHP or blackboard. The challenge for the secondary teacher is to introduce differentiated tasks that do

Table 7.1 Planning and teaching for differentiation: basic guidelines

Planning and preparing

- Provide a range of activities which ensure the participation and involvement of all pupils (differentiated by task); and/or
- Provide similar work for the whole group but allow different outcomes for different individuals (differentiation by outcome).
- Plan for the possibility of pupils' work being recorded in different ways to suit their capabilities, such as using computers or video or audio tape.
- Plan for and make effective use of classroom helpers, support teachers and lab technicians where possible.
- Organise some work to be done in small groups so that pupils can demonstrate to each other what they can do.

Pacing

- Use a clearly defined, step-by-step approach that promotes a gradual development of skills, knowledge and understanding, i.e. break the lesson down into a series of small, achievable steps.
- Ensure that the pace of the lesson takes account of the differing work rates of individual pupils.
- Allow sufficient repetition to consolidate skills, knowledge and understanding.

Communicating

- Communicate in a range of different ways, i.e. speech, writing, pictures and diagrams, to give all pupils the opportunity to learn in a way which best suits them.
- Adapt communications for particular special educational needs, such as enlarged print, clear uncluttered illustrations, worksheets on audio tape.
- Use a consistent presentation for written material and a format for practical work which will avoid anxiety and encourage confidence and participation.
- Break down class worksheets into clearly itemised small steps.
- Use jargon-free, simple, unambiguous language; start from the pupils' own language and introduce words as needed.
- Explain new words to pupils so that they understand them and can then use them; display words in regular use so that they can be copied accurately.

Source: Adapted from NCC Curriculum Guidance 10 (NCC, 1992b)

not create resentment, jealousy, distraction or obvious streaming within the classroom.

The next section gives further explanation and some more examples of approaches for coping with a wide range of differences.

SOME PRACTICAL POSSIBILITIES FOR THE CLASSROOM

Working with 'support teachers' in comprehensive schools

A number of schools can now benefit from the work of a teacher on the staff who may be commonly called the 'SEN teacher', the 'support teacher' or the 'special needs coordinator'. None of these terms does justice to the potential role of a fellow professional who can work collaboratively with a science teacher in achieving the differentiation and access discussed above (Dyson, 1991; King, 1989). Such teachers must first be regarded by the science teacher as more than just an extra resource in the room, or a non-teaching assistant. They should be seen as someone who can be a consultant and collaborator at all stages of providing access to the mainstream science curriculum:

- in planning and preparing lessons, i.e. in producing lesson plans and schemes of work for individual teachers and for the science department; in preparing materials, such as worksheets or DARTs, or resources, such as equipment or activities for class practicals
- in achieving differentiation both of task and outcome, for example, in building differentiation into curriculum planning at key stages 3 and 4
- in teaching the lesson itself and supervising classwork
- in post-lesson or post-scheme of work evaluation
- in joint assessment and recording of pupils' progress in both written and practical work

This collaboration is necessary whether the 'support' teacher gives in-class support or withdraws pupils, such as unusually able or timid pupils, for special work. Whatever the strategy, the cooperation/collaboration needs to be handled sensitively. The support teacher will often not be a science specialist and may often hold his or her science background in low esteem. Moreover, collaboration in the class will not work if the teaching style and environment is a purely didactic one, dominated by the 'scientist', the 'real teacher'. Collaborative teaching will work best in a resource-based, individualised learning approach in the classroom. But this in turn presents problems; problems of reading, for example of worksheets or instruction cards, and of writing, for example responses or write-ups, are often the most important source of learning difficulties in the lab. Collaborative teaching will need to find ways of making this approach work – suggestions are offered in the next section.

Reducing language barriers

Difficulties with language in some form or another are almost certainly the most common problem for learners and teachers in the mainstream, comprehensive school science curriculum. Most of the suggestions below are therefore connected with practical ways of trying to overcome language barriers in science learning.

1 Giving instructions

So many people are guilty of the 'I've told you so now you know' approach. This is not acceptable for learners with a variety of special needs (not least those with hearing impairment) and is poor practice anyway. Instructions should be given using a variety of visual or aural support materials, including:

- drawings, diagrams and pictures as support for the spoken word
- written instructions on a workcard/worksheet, the blackboard or an OHP
- for certain practicals, an example set up on the front bench that can be referred to
- In some cases, especially for those with specific needs, instructions in the form of audio tape can be an extra help.
- For some practicals, prepared pictures with words of different stages in an experiment can be given and pupils asked to sequence them correctly and perhaps label them (obviously the sequence will need to be checked before starting).

2 Worksheets

A separate chapter gives guidelines on producing written material for pupils. These apply to any group of mixed ability. With specific needs extra provision may have to be made, for example:

- Visually impaired children may need a Braille version of text and special aids for diagrams. An audio-tape version of the sheet will be a useful aid for both visually impaired and poor readers. Support may often be available to the science teacher in preparing these.
- Poor readers may need additional symbols and visual prompts to complete a task, such as filling in missing words. A symbol (for example, from the Rebus system) or simple diagram next to the blank may be a sufficient prod.

3 Variety in submitted work

As discussed earlier, differentiation by outcome implies that a range of submitted work will be accepted for, say, assessment. As well as hand-written work, teachers can consider more emphasis on diagrams and pictures; work printed from a computer that has been checked and corrected; audio-tape accounts or descriptions, such as of a process or an experiment; photographic records, such as of a practical or a product; video of, say, a group project on a topic or issue, or of an investigation.

4 Support with writing and spelling

Spelling is an issue that seems to generate more hot air than most. Spelling in science needs to be attended to and corrected but not in such a way that pupils are totally discouraged from attempting writing for fear of making spelling mistakes – a page of writing covered in red ink will not encourage. Certain guidelines can be followed by teachers and pupils in gradually improving spelling in science:

- If a large number of errors are made, teachers can select those which pupils are most likely to correct and learn successfully.
- Such errors can be identified with a 'Sp' in the margin and underlined. The pupil

should then look along the line, find the error, and then either use a dictionary, ask a reliable friend or ask the teacher so that it can be corrected.

• Other errors can be identified with a 'Sp', and the correct spelling written in the margin or at the end, such as specialist terms in science. These can be added to a student's 'Science Wordbank' (see Table 7.2). The whole of the correct word can then be written above the mistake; teachers should avoid altering the word.

The main idea is to get pupils to try to find their own errors, to learn from their mistakes, and to correct misspellings themselves – not have the teacher do it for them.

5 Wordlists and Wordbanks

A list of 'important', commonly used words in science could be produced and displayed in large lettering on the lab wall. These could be of great help to those who have difficulty in 'finding words' as well as those who need help with spelling. The word list could include common items of apparatus used in practical, such as bunsen burner, flasks of different kinds; important labelling words, such as parts of a device, parts of the human body; words for important concepts and processes, such as photosynthesis, electrolysis, evolution; difficult nomenclature, such as for chemicals; the common units, for example joule, newton, metre, etc. These key words could be referred to whenever pupils are doing a written task. For home use they could be written in a 'Science Wordbank' at the end of the pupil's book. For some lessons with especially new and difficult language, a sheet could be given out at the start with a clear list of all the words, terms, etc. which will be used during the course of the lesson.

Table 7.2 shows an example of a wordbank with a collection of about 300 words. This is a list that I have formed from examining the PoSs and SoAs of the National Science Curriculum and a sample of recent science textbooks and from talking and listening to pupils and teachers. In my estimation, this rather daunting list contains most of the words and terms pupils will encounter in their linguistic journey to key stage 4.

6 Using IT (for task and outcome)

Using computers for writing can be of enormous benefit not only to reluctant writers and poor spellers, but also to good writers whose handwriting is unreadable. The use of a word-processor can completely change attitudes to writing, correcting, redrafting and presenting written work (see Chapter 12). Laptops and portables, some costing less than £200, can be versatile and valuable tools for all pupils in the science lab.

The use of computers in data-logging (again see Chapter 12) can also be of great help to all pupils, including those with special needs. Learners who are slow and untidy at recording and presenting data can be helped by a simple-to-use system such as First Sense, which collects data, for example on light levels or temperature,

Table 7.2 Science wordbank: An A to Z of science words for KS3 and KS4

	Life and living processes (AT2)	Materials and their properties (AT3)	Physical processes (AT4)
A	accommodation absorption alimentary canal animal antibiotic aorta artery	acid alcohol alkali aluminium ammonia anode anthracite aqueous	acceleration alternating ammeter amplifier amplitude atmosphere atom
B	bacteria biceps biodegradable biomass biosphere	bauxite burette	barometer battery bi-metal strip Brownian motion
C	capillaries carbohydrates cardiac carnivore cartilage cell cellular chlorophyll cholesterol chromosome	carbon carbonate carbon dioxide catalyst cathode chemical chlorine chlorofluorocarbon chromatography colloid combustion compound covalent crystal crystallisation current	camera capacitor Celsius circuit compression concave condensation conduction conductor conservation constellation convection convex covalent
D	decompose diaphragm digestion	diffusion dilute dissolve distillation	density diffraction diode dispersion dynamic
E	ecosystem embryo enzymes evolution excretion extinct	electrolysis electrolyte electron element endothermic environment equation equilibrium erosion evaporation exothermic expansion	echo electromagnetic electron electrostatic energy equilibrium expansion

	Life and living processes (AT2)	Materials and their properties (AT3)	Physical processes (AT4)
F	faeces fermentation fertilization fertilizer foetus fossil fungus	filtration formula	fission frequency friction fuel fuse
G	gamete genes genetics germination	galena gas granite	galaxy galvanometer gravity
H	habitat herbivore homeostasis hormone hygiene	haemoglobin helium heterogenous homogenous hydrochloric acid hydrogen	harmonic hydraulic
I	immunity inhalation invertebrate	igneous indicator iodine ion isotope	induction inertia infrared insulation ionosphere
J			joule
K			kelvin kilogram kinetic
L	larva ligament lymph	liquid	
M	menstruation metabolism metamorphosis microscope mitosis mutation	magma magnesium metallic metamorphic mixture molecule	manometer mass metre (length) meter momentum
N	nucleus nutrient nitrition	neutral neutron nitrogen	newton nucleus
O	oesophagus omnivore organism osmosis ovary	oxidation oxide oxygen ozone	ohm oscillation
P	parasite penicillin	particle pollution	polarisation potential

	Life and living processes (AT2)	Materials and their properties (AT3)	Physical processes (AT4)
	peristalsis	potassium	pressure
	phloem	product	prism
	photosynthesis	protein	
	pituitary	proton	
	plasma		
	pollen		
	predator		
	prey		
	propagation		
	protein		
R	reproduction	reaction	radiation
	respiration	reactivity	radioactive
	retina	reduction	reflection
			refraction
			renewable
			resistance
			resistor
			resonance
			rheostat
S	saliva	salt	satellite
	sensitivity	sediment	solenoid
	skeleton	sodium	spectrum
	solvent	solid	symbol
	species	soluble	
	stomata	solute	
	symbiosis	solution	
		solvent	
		stratosphere	
		sublimation	
		sulphate	
		sulphuric acid	
		synthesis	
T	tendon	tectonics	temperature
	thyroid	troposphere	thermistor
	transpiration		thermometer
	tropism		torque
			transformer
			transistor
			transverse
U	urine		ultraviolet
V	vacuole		vapour
	vertebrate		velocity
		vitamin	vibration
			virtual
W			watt
			wavelength
			weight

Life and living processes (AT2)	Materials and their properties (AT3)	Physical processes (AT4)	
Z	zinc		

Scientific investigations (AT1)

accurate	evidence	measure	separate
conclusion	hypothesis	observation	theory
constant	inference	prediction	variable
control	mass	result	weight

records it and presents it graphically. Although these skills still need to be developed manually, the occasional use of data-logging systems can show the way, relieve the drudgery sometimes and also raise self-esteem for many pupils.

7 Using laminated cards to help and enrich reading

Science textbooks have certainly improved in the last decade, thanks partly to the research which showed that the language level of most common texts was far too high. But a page of text on science can still be a daunting prospect to many pupils. One practical strategy for making reading more active, more sociable, and less daunting is to use cards of various kinds to go with a piece of text. This can involve a lot of preparation and adaptation by the teacher but can pay off not just for pupils with 'special needs' but for all learners of the written word! The following examples should help to explain:

(a) *True/false cards:* Statements from the text are either transcribed straight onto laminated cards or adapted slightly so that they are false. Using the text, such as a page from a book, students have to sort the cards into two categories – true or false. They discuss these and then perhaps compare their results with another group or present them to the teacher.

(b) *Agree/disagree cards:* On a more value-laden, sensitive or controversial topic, statements from, for example, different pressure groups or parties can be made into cards and then, during group discussion, placed into disagree/agree/not sure categories.

(c) *Matching pairs:* A variety of activities can be done with cards that form matching pairs. The pairs might be:

- a part of a body and its function
- part of any device, such as a car, and its function
- types of teeth and the job they do
- a picture and a word
- a common name and its scientific name
- a material and a common use for it
- a chemical name and its symbol (elements or compounds)

There are many other possibilities in science. The activity can then involve lining the cards up as a group, or it could be done as a memory game often called 'pelmonism'. This involves placing all the cards face down on the table in two separate groups, such as name in one group, chemical symbol in another. By gradually uncovering cards, players form pairs which they then keep if they form a pair but replace (face down) if they don't.

(d) *Putting words or terms into groups:* Words can be placed onto cards, such as names of a range of animals, and then sorted into classes or groups with a heading on another card (underlined or in upper case) at the top of each group, for example mammals/non-mammals. This could be done with metals and non-metals; solids, liquids and gases; conductors and insulators; vertebrates and invertebrates, and so on.

(e) *Sequencing:* Sentence cards describing, for example, a process or an experiment are jumbled up. They are placed by groups into their version of the correct sequence.

There are many other examples of reading activities that can be done with cards, such as sorting the 'odd one out' and explaining why. They are all specific examples of DARTs (Directed Activities Related to Text), which are discussed further in Chapter 11.

And now to repeat the point made earlier: the guidelines and practical examples listed above allow for individual differences in teaching a group. But in truth, what is 'good practice' for some is good practice for all; the strategies are useful for all pupils. To sum up: ' . . . There is nothing special about teaching pupils with special needs. . . . Good teaching for them is simply good teaching.' (Postlethwaite, 1993: 39).

REFERENCES AND FURTHER READING

Assessment of Performance Unit (APU) (1988) *Science at Age 15: A Review of APU Findings*, London: HMSO.

—— (1989) *National Assessment: The APU Science Approach*, London: HMSO.

Ditchfield, C. (ed.) (1987) *Better Science for Young People with Special Educational Needs* (Secondary Science Curriculum Review Curriculum Guide 8), London/Hatfield: Heinemann/Association for Science Education.

Duerden, B., Fortune, D. and Johnson, M. (1992) 'Access and Progress in Science', *British Journal of Special Education*, 19 (12): 59–63.

Duerden, B. and Jury, A. (1993) 'Pupils with Special Needs in Mainstream Schools', in Hull, R. (ed.), *ASE Secondary Science Teachers' Handbook*, Hemel Hempstead: Simon & Schuster.

Dyson, A. (1991) 'Special Needs Teachers in Mainstream Schools', *Support for Learning*, 6 (2): 51–60.

Hoyle, P. (1993) 'Race, Equality and Science Teaching', in Hull, R. (ed.), *ASE Secondary Science Teachers' Handbook*, Hemel Hempstead: Simon & Schuster.

King, V. (1989) 'Support Teaching: The Practice Papers: 11', *Special Children*, October 1989.

National Curriculum Council (NCC) (1989) *A Curriculum for All-Special Needs in the National Curriculum* (NCC Curriculum Guidance 2), York: NCC.

—— (1992a) *The National Curriculum and Pupils with Severe Learning Difficulties* (NCC Curriculum Guidance 9), York: NCC.

—— (1992b) *Teaching Science to Pupils with Special Educational Needs* (NCC Curriculum Guidance 10), York: NCC.

Pask, G. (1975) *The Cybernetics of Human Learning and Performance*, London: Hutchinson.

Postlethwaite, K. (1993) *Differentiated Science Teaching*, Milton Keynes: Open University Press (The early pages of this chapter draw heavily from Postlethwaite – readers are strongly recommended to explore his book in full.).

Reid, D. J. and Hodson, D. (1987) *Science for All: Teaching Science in the Secondary School*, London: Cassell Education.

Robertson, J. (1990) *Effective Classroom Control*, London: Hodder & Stoughton.

Smail, B. (1993) 'Science for Girls and Boys', in Hull, R. (ed.), *ASE Secondary Science Teachers' Handbook*, Hemel Hempstead: Simon & Schuster.

Thorp, S. (ed.) (1991) *Race, Equality and Science Teaching*, Hatfield: ASE.

Tunnicliffe, S. D. (1987) 'Science Materials for Special Needs', *British Journal of Special Education,* 14 (2).

Widlake, P. (ed.) (1989) *Special Children's Handbook*, London: Hutchinson Education/Special Children.

Wood, K., Lapp, D. and Flood, J. (1992) *Guiding Readers Through Text: A Review of Study Guiders*, London: Delaware International Reading Association (a practical guide to ways of encouraging active, structured reading).

The National Association for Special Educational Needs (NASEN, Stafford ST17 4JX) produces a range of useful publications, including:

Barthorpe, T. and Visser, J. (1991) *Differentiation: Your Responsibility*.

The ASE manual, *Race, Equality and Science Teaching*, contains a number of ideas and activities for teaching science to pupils with different needs.

8   Practical work in science education

' . . . Teachers need to be aware of the goals, potential, merits and difficulties of the school laboratory.'

(Tamir, 1991: 20)

Practical work is one of the distinctive features of science teaching and one of the great expectations of pupil learning. How best should practical work be organised and conducted? What types of practical work can and should be done? Why do we do practical work at all in the science curriculum? These questions are all interwoven. We start with the most fundamental but least asked: Why do practical work?

WHY DO PRACTICAL WORK IN SCIENCE LESSONS?

An enormous amount of time and money is invested in making practical work an element of secondary school science. Schools employ lab technicians, consume consumables of all kinds and invest large sums in pieces of apparatus that most pupils have never seen elsewhere and are never likely to encounter again after school. In the post-1988 era of local management and devolved budgets, it is inevitable that the traditional expense of practical work will be questioned by someone running the school. Science teachers need to be able to justify the time and money spent on practical work not only for this reason, but also in order to answer the two further questions of 'what?' and 'how?'

In 1963, Kerr organised a survey of 701 science teachers from 151 schools in order to find out why they did practical work in school science. He suggested ten aims or purposes which those in the survey were asked to rank for importance in relation to three different age ranges: lower secondary, upper secondary and 'sixth form'. The aims presented to teachers are shown in table 8.1.

It is interesting to note that those aims are still largely relevant today, three decades on. Before reading further, consider each of those aims carefully and rank

Table 8.1 Ten possible aims of science practical work

1	To encourage accurate observation and careful recording.
2	To promote simple, common-sense, scientific methods of thought.
3	To develop manipulative skills.
4	To give training in problem-solving.
5	To fit the requirements of practical examinations.
6	To elucidate the theoretical work so as to aid comprehension.
7	To verify facts and principles already taught.
8	To be an integral part of the process of finding facts by investigation and arriving at principles.
9	To arouse and maintain interest in the subject.
10	To make biological, chemical and physical phenomena more real through actual experience.

Source: Used by Kerr, 1963.

them for yourself for different ages of pupils. Jot down your own ranking for: years 7, 8 and 9; years 10 and 11; years 12 and 13 (the 'sixth form').

The full analysis of results is well worth reading in full (Kerr, 1963). Here is my own potted summary of the responses:

- There was a change in emphasis in practical work as pupils move through the secondary school, for example, away from arousing interest towards careful recording.
- However, observation and scientific thinking were ranked highly throughout.
- Aim 9 was highest for years 7–9.
- Aim 1 was highest for years 12–13.

Taking all teachers and all age groups into account, the overall ranking of aims was:
   1 (first), 2 and 8 (joint second), 6, 10, 9, 7, 3, 4, 5 (last).
   How do these compare with your own ranking?

THE ROLE AND POTENTIAL OF PRACTICAL WORK

The place of practical work in science needs to be justified; fortunately, there are many useful discussions which help by giving us a framework for practical work by outlining its purpose and potential. These can be summarised only briefly here.

Woolnough and Allsop (1985), in an excellent discussion on practical science, suggest that in the past four types of aim have been given by teachers and curriculum developers for small-group practicals:

1   motivational, i.e. that practical science can motivate and interest pupils (cf Kerr, 1963)
2   the development of experimental skills and techniques, such as observation, measurement, handling apparatus, etc.
3   simulating the work of a real scientist – 'being a real scientist for the day' (a phrase from the early Nuffield days)

4   supporting theory, i.e. using practical to 'discover', elucidate or illuminate theory; and improving retention in line with the other catch-phrase of practical work: 'I hear and I forget, I see and I remember, I do and I understand.'

(Both the latter two groups of aims are wide open to criticism, as Woolnough and Allsop themselves point out, and their problems will be considered shortly.)

The authors go on to examine and discuss their own view of the purposes of practical work and then put forward their own three 'fundamental aims':

1   developing practical skills and techniques
2   being a problem-solving scientist
3   getting a feel for phenomena

The types of practical work in school science associated with these aims are discussed in detail by Woolnough and Allsop, who label the three types Exercises, Investigations and Experiences, respectively. Their full description of each type is well worth reading (Woolnough and Allsop, 1985: 47–59), but examples would include:

> *Exercises:* using a microscope, estimating, measuring, heating, manipulating, performing standard tests, such as food tests, setting up apparatus and equipment, such as a cathode ray oscilloscope, an electric circuit
> *Investigations:* often of the what, which or how variety, such as What causes rusting? Which material is best for X? How do shampoos affect hair strength? (investigations are given a whole section later)
> *Experiences:* studying, observing, handling, holding, exploring, watching, growing, such as plants, crystals; pushing and pulling, feeling. . . .

This is a useful classification for classroom teachers – it will not only enable them to plan practical work for range and variety, but also help them to consider *why* they are doing a practical.

In a later discussion, Millar (1991: 51) unpicks the idea of 'practical skills'. He divides the skills which he feels *can* be taught and improved into:

> *Practical techniques:* such as measuring temperature to within certain limits, separating by filtration or other 'standard' procedures
> *Inquiry tactics:* such as repeating measurements, tabulating data and drawing graphs in order to look for patterns, identifying variables to alter, control, etc.

By developing these skills, pupils will develop their 'procedural understanding' of science (in contrast to their conceptual understanding). Millar argues that pupils can progress in practical science by increasing their competence in a wider range of techniques and by enlarging and extending their 'toolkit' of tactics for investigational work. These are the dual aims of practical science.

We only have space to consider a third framework for practical work. This is the Predict-Observe-Explain (P-O-E) pattern suggested by Gunstone (1991: 69). He offers as a framework for demonstrations a constructivist approach to practical work which includes P-O-E tasks. I have adapted it as a possible scheme for small group work, too:

1   *Predict:* Students are shown a particular situation and asked to predict what they believe will happen. They are asked to give reasons for their prediction, preferably in writing.
2   *Observe:* The demo or class practical is then performed and all students write down what they observe.
3   The third (probably most difficult stage) is to consider the P and O stages and to attempt to explain, or reconcile, any conflict between prediction and observation.

The latter stage is, in my view, by far the most difficult stage to handle, especially if this framework were used for a class practical! Gunstone elaborates fully on this interesting approach and other strategies which he has suggested (Gunstone, 1991 and previous work cited there).

These frameworks for practical work are a selection of many offered on the

Table 8.2   The role of practical work in science

---

1 *To develop skills:*
- practical techniques
- procedures
- 'tactics'
- investigation strategies
- working with others
- communicating
- problem-solving

2 *To illuminate/illustrate ('first-hand' knowledge):*
- an event
- a phenomenon
- a concept
- a law
- a principle
- a theory

3 *To motivate/stimulate:*
- entertain
- arouse curiosity
- enhance attitudes
- develop interest
- fascinate

4 *To challenge/confront:*
for example 'What if . . . ?', Predict-Observe-Explain, 'Why . . . ?'

---

purpose of practical work. I offer my own summary of the reasons for practical science in table 8.2 – readers are invited to look critically and carefully at this table before we move on to the issue of organising practical activity.

TYPES OF PRACTICAL WORK AND HOW TO ORGANISE THEM

Different types of practical activity will be appropriate for the different aims shown in table 8.2. There are at least six possibilities for organising and carrying out practical work in the average school situation with its usual constraints:

1   Demonstrations
2   Class experiments, all on similar task, in small groups
3   A circus of experiments, i.e. small groups on different activities in a 'carousel', spread over chunks of a lesson or over several lessons
4   Simulations and role-play
5   Investigations
6   Problem-solving activities

The latter three are given special treatment in separate chapters. Aspects of the first three are considered briefly here.

Demonstrations

Why use demonstrations?

Demonstrations can be useful in aims 2, 3 and 4 of table 8.2. They can be used to illustrate events or phenomena, such as chemical reactions, especially if those events are too expensive, dangerous, difficult or time-consuming to be done by all. There is still a valuable place in science teaching at all levels for the interesting, sometimes unforgettable, demonstration that may form an important episode in a pupil's learning. Thus a good demo can excite, intrigue, fascinate and entertain – especially if it has the advantage of scale, i.e. bigger, better, more visible, clearer and with more impact than a class experiment.

How should demonstrations be used and carried out?

All good demonstrations need a framework so that pupils are active and can participate – in short, learners need to be occupied during a demo. Passive entertainment is not enough. The Gunstone framework of Predict-Observe-Explain is one excellent possibility, especially in achieving aim 3 of table 8.2. At a simpler level pupils could engage in just one of these stages, using a pencil and 'jotter'. They could be asked to record results and begin to tabulate them. In short, there needs to be an activity, preferably involving writing and recording, to structure every demo. This is essential not only on educational grounds but also for management and control. Finally, as said before, demonstrations need to go for impact. This means, to state the obvious, that every pupil needs to be able to see what is happening. Careful management of seating and/or standing is well worth the investment in time.

Whole-class practical work

Why?

The reasons for class activity in small groups relate closely to almost all the aims of table 8.2: to develop practical skills and techniques, to illuminate and illustrate, to give a feeling for sizes and orders of magnitude, to generate results for analysis, to entertain, and to challenge.

How?

There are several aspects to managing and organising whole-class practicals, most of which can only be learnt adequately from observation and experience. But there are certain key points to be remembered: apparatus needs to be carefully distributed around the lab if pupils are to fetch it themselves – this will avoid bottlenecks; the teacher is in a supervisory role at all times and needs to be in a position to see the whole room – discussing the finer points with a small group with back to the rest of the class is not good practice; always allow more than enough time for clearing away.

In planning for and structuring class practicals there are several important, necessary stages in addition to the actual activity:

- setting the scene, i.e. the pre-experiment discussion, discussing and giving instructions, arranging groups and managing the room
- gathering results: Are the pupils given a free hand or a set results table? Will the results of everyone be recorded centrally, such as on an OHP or blackboard? Or will they record individually or as a small group without sharing widely?
- discussing the experiment and its results
- interpreting and concluding: This is the most problematic and widely discussed aspect of practical work (see further reading on the problems of 'guided discovery' and the handling of pupil results).
- Should conclusions be elicited from pupils or given to them? Who should interpret their data – the pupil or the teacher? This element of practical work relates very closely, of course, to the initial aim of the activity.
- writing up and reporting: This is another area of science activity that has caused great debate (see Chapter 11). Indeed, should practicals always be written up? Can they not be recorded and stored for posterity in other ways – audio tape, video, photograph or picture? Using solely written work for reporting strongly disadvantages those who may be good at practical science but poor at writing (for whatever reason).

A circus of experiments

Why use this way of organising practical?

A circus can be useful in allowing hands-on activity for all when the number of certain pieces of apparatus or other resources, such as computers and software or specialised equipment is limited. By arranging a carousel, every pupil or group can see and use the resource in turn. It can also be valuable in providing a fairly quick, highly varied set of experiences relating to one topic, such as energy or forces. Thus circuses often fulfil the experiential aim of practical work.

How can a circus be organised?

Initially it requires a great deal more preparation from teacher and technician to provide a carousel of (say) ten different activities labelled A to J for a group of 25 children than planning a single task which all do at the same time. But this initial planning and organisation can pay dividends and save time in the long term. Additional preparation is needed to ensure:

- All work-places/activities are prepared, set out and labelled before children enter.
- Each activity occupies roughly the same amount of time.
- The change-over from one activity to the next is carefully planned and the sequence written down for all to see.
- Consumables can be re-stocked as time goes on.
- Instructions for each stage are clear and readable – a work card or sheet at each station will be invaluable.
- Each activity is self-contained, as the sequence through which pupils go through the carousel will be different for every group.
- Extension activities are given at each station to allow for time differences (between activities and children) and the ability range.

Simulation as part of practical science

Active work in science need not always involve the 'real thing' – indeed much of real science involves experiments with models and simulations of real events, for example, river flow in tanks, study of flight in wind tunnels. Pupils should therefore learn that in order to study and understand reality we often need to model it and simplify it. Thus the use of models, analogies and simulations is not only a valuable way of learning but also an important part of scientific exploration. Simulation can involve:

1 the use of IT, for example a computer simulation, an interactive videodisc (discussed fully in a later chapter)
2 physical models, for example a ripple tank, marbles in a tray, molecular models, an orrery, a planetarium, analogues of electric current (such as water flow)

3   secondary sources, for example tables of data, graphs and charts, news cuttings, scientific articles, video tape, photographs, images from remote sensing
4   role play, for example of processes such as melting and boiling or conduction, convection and radiation, molecular movement, etc.

These four types of simulation can achieve many of the aims outlined in table 8.2, such as illustrating phenomena, clarifying theory. Indeed they can often be more effective than the 'real thing' because of increased clarity and simplicity.

General rules

The usual rules for all practical work apply to all the types listed above:

- The activity must be safe. Use whatever is necessary to ensure safety, such as goggles for heating, a safety screen for some demos, etc.
- Always try out the class practical, circus, or demo in advance.
- Give a clear list of all requirements to technical/support staff well in advance.
- Manage any movement around the room carefully and safely.
- Give clear instructions for the activity, using different approaches. Possibilities are: oral (just telling from the start, or oral instructions arising from a class discussion); a worksheet; an overhead transparency; pupils rearranging a jumbled list of instructions into the correct order (which is then checked before starting!). A variety of approaches is needed both for reinforcement (to avoid the 'I've told them so now they know' syndrome) and to cater for all needs and styles in a mixed class.

Remember to count everything out and count it all back in again in as visible and systematic way as possible. Certain bits of science kit, like magnets and crocodile clips, have a habit of sticking to people!

PITFALLS AND PROBLEMS TO WATCH FOR

Practical work in science has enormous potential for exciting pupils, giving first-hand knowledge (almost unique to science as a curriculum subject) and supporting theory. However, I would like to finish with a summary of some of the pitfalls and problems of practical work, which is very brief simply because so much has been written on it elsewhere. Table 8.3 provides a summary – each issue is considered in turn with an indication of further reading.

First, science teachers may create problems for themselves if they suggest that pupils in school science are really behaving like 'real scientists'. Few scientists can make explicit the processes that they themselves are engaged in:

> 'Ask a scientist what he conceives the scientific method to be and he will adopt an expression that is at once solemn and shifty-eyed: solemn, because he feels that he ought to declare an opinion; shifty-eyed because he is considering how to conceal the fact that he has no opinion to declare.'
>
> (Medawar, 1969: 11)

What chance then do science teachers have of accurately mimicking or assessing the processes of scientists, even if such an aim were desirable? (see Driver, 1983, on the pupil as scientist; and a critique of the 1970s and 1980s enthusiasm for discovery learning in Wellington, 1981 and Atkinson and Delamont, 1977).

Secondly, it may be the case that practical work, especially if things go wrong, can actually confuse rather than illuminate laws and theories. This has led to the tweaking, fiddling and stage management that has become one of the unwritten skills of the science teacher.

This links to the third point – observation, like the truth, is rarely pure and never simple. Learners often need to be told what to look for, i.e. the framework precedes the practical. This is as true for looking down microscopes as it is for 'observing' magnetic fields or viewing convection currents in air or water. There are at least three points about observation that emerge from current views on the nature of science:

- Observations rarely form the starting point for a practising scientist.
- Observations are theory dependent, i.e. theory normally precedes observation.
- If more than one person (be it pupil or scientist) observes the same phenomenon, their observations may well be different, i. e. people see through their theories (see Hodson, 1986).

The practical point for teachers is that it makes little sense to either teach or assess observation in isolation.

The fourth point is that an insistence on practical work as an essential feature of school science can actually restrict the science curriculum: 'We won't teach that topic because we can't do practical work in it.' This has led to an often hidden reluctance amongst science teachers to include a topic in a scheme of work because they cannot find a way of including a traditional practical. Thus topics like cosmology, earth science and astronomy, and many of the controversial issues which involve science, have often been neglected. This has led in turn to the use of

Table 8.3 Pitfalls and problems with practical work in science

1	Can we mimic 'real science'?
	(a) Can scientific method be broken down into a set of discrete processes?
	(b) Can scientific processes be caught and taught?
	(c) Is 'discovery learning' a con?
2	Does practical work illuminate or confuse learning in science?
3	The observation problem: Which comes first – the theory or the practical? Can children observe without a framework?
4	Does an insistence on (and a pupil expectation of) practical work limit and restrict the range of topics covered in science and the teaching strategies used?
5	Group work: What are the consequences if we simply put pupils into small groups and let them get on with it?

a very restricted range of teaching strategies amongst science teachers (see Woolnough and Allsop, 1985).

The final problem considered here is the issue of group work. Teachers commonly place pupils in small groups and assume that the group will work. Close observation shows that this is often not the case, especially in groups of three or more. One pupil may dominate while others play little part, for example, in planning, predicting or carrying out a practical. Pupils may willingly adopt different roles, some of which may have nothing to do with the science, for example one member may simply record and tabulate results with no clue as to what they mean or where they came from. There are many other issues connected with group work – my general point here is that we cannot assume that groups are teams or that pupils share or rotate their roles in a group. In short, group work must be managed – it cannot be taken for granted.

REFERENCES AND FURTHER READING

General discussions on the aims and conduct of practical work

Bentley, D. and Watts, M. (eds) (1989) *Learning and Teaching in School Science*, Milton Keynes: Open University Press (pp. 21–41 especially).

Driver, R. (1983) *The Pupil as Scientist*, Milton Keynes: Open University Press.

Gunstone, R. F. (1991) 'Reconstructing theory for practical experience', in Woolnough, B. (ed.) (1991) *Practical Science*, Milton Keynes: Open University Press.

Kerr, J. (1963) *Practical Work in School Science*, Leicester: Leicester University Press (a classic enquiry into the nature and purpose of school science practical work, based on a study of 701 teachers in 151 schools).

Medawar, P. (1969) *Induction and Intuition in Scientific Thought*, London: Methuen.

Millar, R. (1991) 'A Means to an End: The Role of Processes in Science Education', in Woolnough, B. (ed.) (1991) *Practical Science*, Milton Keynes: Open University Press.

Solomon, J. (1980) *Teaching Children in the Laboratory*, London: Croom Helm.

Tamir, P. (1991) 'Practical Work in School Science: An Analysis of Current Practice', in Woolnough, B. (ed.) (1991) *Practical Science*, Milton Keynes: Open University Press.

Woolnough, B. and Allsop, T. (1985) *Practical Work in Science*, Cambridge: Cambridge University Press.

Woolnough, B. (ed.) (1991) *Practical Science*, Milton Keynes: Open University Press (a range of useful chapters on school practical work).

Safety aspects

ASE (1988) *Safeguards in the School Laboratory* (9th ed.), Hatfield: ASE.

Borrows, P. (1992) 'Safety in Secondary Schools', in Hull, R. (ed.), *ASE Secondary Science Teachers' Handbook*, Simon & Shuster (This highlights the common accidents in labs most of which involve chemicals in the eye or mouth or on the body; and describes five 'main danger areas' such as burns from alcohol fires and alkali metal explosions.).

Everett, K. and Jenkins, E. (1991) *A Safety Handbook for Science Teachers*, London: John Murray.

Critical comments on the value of school science practicals

Atkinson, P. and Delamont, S. (1977) 'Mock-ups and Cock-ups: the stage management of guided discovery instruction', in Woods, P. and Hammersley, M. (eds), *School Experience*, London: Croom Helm.

Hodson, D. (1986) 'The Nature of Scientific Observation', *School Science Review* 68 (242): 17–29.

—— (1990) 'A Critical Look at Practical Work in School Science', *School Science Review,* 71 (256): 33–9.

Millar, R. (1989) 'What Is Scientific Method and Can It Be Taught?' in Wellington, J. (ed.), *Skills and Processes in Science Education*, London: Routledge.

Wellington, J. (1981) 'What's Supposed to Happen Sir? : some problems with discovery learning', *School Science Review,* 63 (222): 167–73.

—— (1989) (ed.) *Skills and Processes in Science Education*, London: Routledge.

9   Investigations in science

Click, click, click (the school clock). We were supposed to be reading the instructions for an experiment we were going to perform in class that day. Now there's another stupid thing. Year after year, this same teacher makes his students perform the same experiments. Well, if the experiments have been done so many times before, how can they still be experiments? The teacher *knows* what is going to happen. I thought experimenting meant trying *new* things to see what would happen. We weren't experimenting at all. We were playacting.

(*Claudia and the Great Search*, by Ann Martin, New York: Scholastic)

What are 'investigations'? Are they the same as problem-solving? What types of investigations are there? How should they be carried out and organised? What help can we provide to pupils to guide them and to structure the investigation? Do they present any problems in the classroom? How do they fit into the National Curriculum? Can they really reflect the way that science and scientists work? These are the questions that this chapter raises.

WHAT ARE INVESTIGATIONS?

Examples of investigations

Below are listed some examples of investigations that I have either seen, used, read or heard about:

- How much rainfall do we get in each month throughout the year?
- What conditions do wood lice like best?
- Design an instrument to make the best spectrum.
- What are the best conditions for yeast growth?
- Which kind of paper is best for mopping up water?
- Design a machine for exercising a dog.
- Design a machine for weighing an elephant.

- Which ball is most bouncy?
- Which surface is best for bouncing a ball on?
- What makes sugar dissolve faster?
- Which factors affect the frequency of the note from a stretched string?
- Study the reaction times of different people.
- How do people's reaction times vary with different stimuli and conditions (for example, after drinking coffee, late in the day, etc.)?
- Which is the best detergent/washing powder?
- Investigate the composition, structure and strength of local soils.
- Which trainer sole is best?
- What factors determine how fast a car can travel?
- What happens to the boiling/melting point of water if you add solvents?
- Can people tell the difference between margarine and butter?
- Separate a mixture of iron filings, salt, sand, and polystyrene chips.
- Design and make a device for enabling an egg to fall three metres without breaking.
- Build a tower to a height of one metre, using drinking straws, which can support an egg/coin/marble.
- Which factors affect the speed at which different things dry?
- Which fuel (from a safe selection!) produces the most heat.
- Which insulating material is best for keeping hot water hot?
- Imagine a village is threatened by an erupting volcano. Devise ways of protecting it.

Different types of investigation

These are all investigations that have been suggested for, or tried in, the classroom. Varying degrees of structure and guidance will have been given. Some have a 'correct' answer; some don't. Some will take weeks or even months; some a few minutes. Some involve imaginary situations; most involve real situations. Some contexts are 'everyday'; some will be new to pupils. Some involve design-and-make skills (technological?); some do not. Some are 'problem-solving activities', but clearly not all investigations need be of a problem-solving kind. In an attempt to make some sense of the wide range of investigations now being used or suggested, I have tried a 'typology of investigations', which is shown in table 9.1.

This classification can be helpful in considering suggested ideas for investigations and published examples; it can also be useful in considering a department's policy and planning for investigational work.

Open and closed, pupil-led and teacher-led

A second framework for reflecting on the types of investigational work done in science lessons is given in figure 9.1.

The three axes shown are not independent, of course. The first, teacher-led to pupil-led, indicates a continuum from one extreme at which pupils pose the

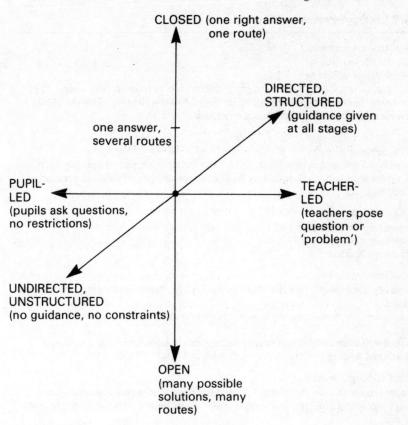

CLOSED (one right answer, one route)

DIRECTED, STRUCTURED (guidance given at all stages)

one answer, several routes

PUPIL-LED (pupils ask questions, no restrictions)

TEACHER-LED (teachers pose question or 'problem')

UNDIRECTED, UNSTRUCTURED (no guidance, no constraints)

OPEN (many possible solutions, many routes)

Figure 9.1   Dimensions of investigational work

questions to investigate to the other, in which all the questions are set, posed and restricted by the teacher. In practice, different work at different times will lie at different points along this axis – indeed, it must do if teachers are to meet the requirements of the National Curriculum (see later in this chapter).

The second axis, open to closed, shows a second continuum from one extreme in which an investigation or a problem-solving activity will have only one 'correct' answer and only one route for reaching it, to the other in which many possible solutions are equally acceptable, with many routes to them. In between these extremes lie many permutations and possibilities.

The third axis (obviously not independent of the others but still worth separating), is from undirected and unstructured to directed and structured. At one extreme, pupils will be given guidance, constraint and structure all along the way, i.e. in planning, designing, carrying out and evaluating. At the other no guidance, structure and restriction will be placed on them. Neither extreme is very likely to occur in practice.

The main purpose of this framework is to help teachers in planning for and

Table 9.1 A typology of investigations

'Which' type investigations
- Which factors affect X?
- Which *design* is best for . . . ?
- Which X is best for . . . ? (for example, insulator, sole of trainers, floor covering, paper-towel for absorbing, soil, washing-up liquid, hamster food. . . . This can often involve critically testing manufacturers' claims!).

'What' type investigations
- What happens if . . . ?
- What is the connection between X and Y? (for example, shape and strength, aperture of a pinhole camera and image, length of pendulum and period time, temperature and dissolving . . .).

'How do' investigations
- How do different Xs affect Y?
- How does X vary with Y?
- How does X affect Y?

General investigations
- A survey, for example historical (nuclear energy, the chemical elements); local (pond study).
- A long-term project, for example local stream pollution, air quality, soil or path erosion.
- (These will often involve secondary sources, such as books, the media, extensive research and reading.)

Problem-solving activities
- Design-and-make, for example a dog-exercising machine, a desalination device.
- Solve a practical problem, for example bridge a gap, build a structure, make an alarm system.
- Simulations (see Chapter 13).

---

reflecting on the type of investigational work they do in schools. It should help to increase variety and to clarify assessment.

Why do them?

There are many good reasons for using an investigational approach to science teaching, in addition to the pragmatic one of 'it's in the National Curriculum'. For many pupils it can be a great motivator, particularly if they really 'get into' a long-term investigation. Many pupils who are not successful in, and motivated by, other aspects of science work, such as learning content or written work, can sometimes be surprisingly successful at and therefore 'turned on by' investigational work. It can also be extremely enjoyable, perhaps leading more pupils to choose science once they reach the age of choice and consent. It can lead to teamwork and cooperation in science learning, which may be difficult to develop quite so actively in other ways. For many teachers of science, the introduction of investigational work can change entirely the way they approach the teaching of science generally, for example, the teaching of content (conceptual understanding) and process (procedural understanding) can be geared entirely towards an investigation as the end point or motivator. Certain critics of the investigational approach argue that it will leave 'less time for content', but this need not be the case – on the contrary, it could provide the motivation for learning content.

COPING IN THE CLASSROOM

Pitfalls and problems to watch for

We have already seen that investigational work can have a number of benefits in learning and teaching science. But there are, of course, a number of pitfalls and problems that teachers (and pupils) need to be aware of:

- *What is an investigation? :* There is little agreement or clarity in the use of words such as 'investigation', 'experiment', etc. amongst teachers. 'Investigation' and 'experiment' are best seen as lying on a continuum, rather than as separate activities. The framework and typology shown in figure 9.1 and table 9.1 respectively may help.
- *Who does what in a group? :* Group dynamics must be considered because most practical work is carried out collectively. What is the role of each team member? Do they contribute equally or do some assume minor subsidiary roles? Do they all learn equally or are some participating within a clerical role, with little or no understanding of the underlying principles? If plans are produced individually, whose plan is followed in a group investigation?
- *How should the 'process' of investigational work relate to learning 'theory' or content? :* Process skills interact closely with children's prior knowledge and understanding – they cannot be separated from them. This has implications for the type of investigation that children can be expected to carry out and is important in considering progression, assessment, and the linking of AT 1 with other ATs.
- *What is progression? :* Progression in investigation work is difficult to identify, observe and measure (see Chapter 10).
- *When and how should the teacher interfere? :* How much input should a teacher make in an investigation? When and how should she or he intervene – At the planning stage? At the interpretation stage? This will have implications for the accessibility of the investigation within the National Curriculum criteria.
- *'Right' and 'wrong' answers:* How should teachers deal with 'incorrect answers' (i.e. scientifically unacceptable) to a closed-ended investigation? (Pupils will often look for the 'right' answer to certain kinds of investigation.)
- *Planning:* The planning part of an investigation is one of the most difficult aspects for pupils.

Investigational work rarely reflects the 'true nature of science' (indeed, how could it possibly be expected to?). It may promote the 'data first, theory second' view of science, i.e. the 'Sherlock Holmes in a white coat' notion. In addition, assessment of investigations is (to put it mildly) not easy. A separate chapter has been devoted to the assessment of practical work, including investigations.

For pupils to carry out investigations successfully in the classroom, most teachers feel that they will need guidance and structure of some sort – the only difference of opinion is to what degree. The next section offers some practical possibilities that have been put forward.

Giving guidance and help

A summary of the 'Footsteps in Science' guidelines that were developed in Sheffield schools is given in figure 9.2. These are displayed in an attractive fashion (in the form of footsteps) for pupils to follow during investigational work.

Other schools and education authorities use structured sheets with questions for pupils to follow and fill in at different stages, for example:

My question or idea to investigate is _____

This is what I think will happen. _____

This is why. _____

This is what I am going to do. _____

What things will you keep the same during the investigation? _____

What will you change during the investigation? _____

How will you make sure it is a fair test? _____

What equipment will you need?_____

What will you measure, count or look for? _____

Another education authority (Wakefield) has produced an attractive leaflet for all pupils explaining the steps in investigation under a framework of Planning, Doing and Reporting. Here is a short excerpt:

Planning

- Think of the question you are trying to answer.
- What do you predict will happen?
- Have you a reason or hypothesis for your prediction?

Doing

- You must look closely (observe) what happens.

1 THINK
   1 What are you trying to find out?
   2 What do you think will happen?
   3 Why do you think this will happen?
     ↓

2 PLAN
   1 Draw a labelled diagram.
   2 Is there any other apparatus?
   3 What are you going to change and how?
   4 What are you going to measure and how?
   5 What are you going to keep the same to make it a fair test and how?
   6 Draw a Results Table.
     ↓

3 DO EXPERIMENT
   1 Follow your plan.
   2 Remember safety precautions.
   3 Record your results.
     ↓

4 PROCESS YOUR RESULTS
     ↓

5 CONCLUSIONS
   1 What have you found out?
   2 Why do you think this happens?
   3 Are there any patterns?
   4 Do your conclusions match your original idea? If not, why not?
     ↓

6 REVIEW
   1 Can you explain your results in any other way?
   2 What are the sources of error?
   3 If you were to repeat the investigation what would you do differently to improve it?

Figure 9.2 Investigations: steps to follow
Source: The Sheffield 'Footsteps in Science' Guidelines for Schools

- Make careful measurements using the right instruments.
- Say what you need to change and keep the same – the variables.

Reporting

- Say what your results mean.
- Try to explain or interpret them.
- Could you have done better?
- How might you change your plan?
- Evaluate your work.

Many other frameworks and guidelines for pupils have been produced – the above selections are a tiny sample. They will certainly help to overcome at least some of the pitfalls and problems outlined above. The main general feeling is that pupils will need guidance and structure for at least part of the time during their investigational work. What does seem to vary from one school to another is the amount of guidance given to pupils, which of course has implications for assessment.

Developing a model/structure for investigational work: three levels

One of the aims of doing investigational work in the classroom, of course, must be to develop in pupils some sort of understanding of science procedures as well as the more specific 'kitbag' of skills and techniques. The latter can be taught almost as rules of thumb and can quite rightly involve training as much as education. Thus pupils can be taught how to read a range of measuring instruments, how to set up data-logging equipment, how to record results manually, and how to set up certain common types of apparatus, such as for distillation. This is all part of basic practical science education, verging on training.

At a slightly higher level pupils can be taught the importance of accuracy, the limitations of certain measuring instruments and the need to repeat measurements, i.e. take lots of readings. They can also learn the ideas of identifying and controlling variables and therefore the notion of a 'fair test'.

Eventually, the aim must be to develop a general model of 'investigational work' which pupils can use and apply in a number of different situations. Several models have been offered in diagram form in publications from the Assessment of Performance Unit (APU) and in the non-statutory guidance, and are worth studying critically. The non-statutory guidance model is similar to the statutory model discussed shortly.

The ultimate aim in investigational work, therefore, must be to encourage (or even inculcate) a generalised pattern or model of such work. To develop this, pupils must be able to see each investigation task at some level of abstraction. They must be able to pay attention to the general, structural features of the task as well as its context-embedded, surface, specific features. This must be the justification or rationale for expecting thousands of pupils to spend thousands of hours on investigations in science, i.e. to develop a pattern or model for tackling investigations and problems. How else could we justify the time spent?

This has implications for teaching. As well as providing pupils with interesting investigations in exciting, often everyday contexts, teachers also need to spend time on the general features of each task. What are the pupils doing and why? What types of variable are they controlling? What is this idea of a 'fair test'? Why is it important to repeat measurements? What limits does their experiment and others like it have? Only by considering the general structural features of each specific task will the model develop – a model which might then be transferred to other contexts and other tasks, including perhaps those outside the science classroom. In this way pupils may also learn something about the nature, purpose and limitations of science itself.

INVESTIGATIONS IN THE NATIONAL CURRICULUM

The AT 1 model of investigations

A definite model or template for scientific investigations is now part of the statutory guidance for science in the National Curriculum – known commonly as Sc 1. This template, with its three strands and ten levels, is shown in table 9.2.

The model does have difficulties, some are discussed later. One worth mentioning at the outset is that the model as printed does imply a linear approach to investigation, i.e. question, prediction and hypothesis, then observation and measurement of manipulated variables, followed by interpretation and evaluation. In reality, of course, the situation is far more a cycle than a linear path, as figure 9.3 indicates.

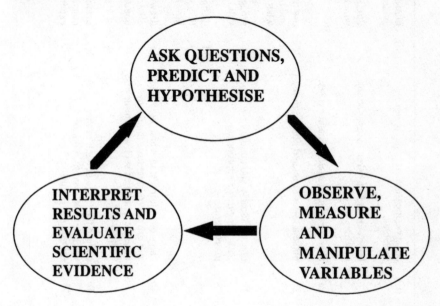

Figure 9.3   A cyclic view of Sc 1

This is more the world of 'real science' and in fact is also the way that many investigations in the classroom do and should proceed. I would suggest that this is the model that teachers should try to promote in the classroom, whilst not pretending that any model could reflect the complex, unpredictable and sometimes erratic ways in which real science actually has worked and still does.

Linking AT 1 to the other attainment targets

Work in Sc 1 must be related to the programmes of study and statements of attainment in the other three science areas. Unless this occurs, it will be very

Table 9.2 Scientific investigation

(i) ask questions, predict and hypothesise.	(ii) observe, measure and manipulate variables.	(iii) interpret results and evaluate scientific evidence.
Pupils should carry out investigations in which they:	Pupils should carry out investigations in which they:	Pupils should carry out investigations in which they:
	1a observe familiar materials and events.	
2a ask questions such as 'how ...?', 'why ...?' and 'what will happen if ...?', suggest ideas and make predictions.	2b make a series of related observations.	2c use their observations to support conclusions and compare what they have observed with what they expected.
3a suggest questions, ideas and predictions, based on everyday experience, which can be tested.	3b observe closely and quantify by measuring using appropriate instruments.	3c recognise that their conclusions may not be valid unless a fair test has been carried out.
		3d distinguish between a description of what they observed and a simple explanation of how and why it happened.
4a ask questions, suggest ideas and make predictions, based on some relevant prior knowledge, in a form which can be investigated.	4b carry out a fair test in which they select and use appropriate instruments to measure quantities such as volume and temperature.	4c draw conclusions which link patterns in observations or results to the original question, prediction or idea.
5a formulate hypotheses where the causal link is based on scientific knowledge, understanding or theory.	5b choose the range of each of the variables involved to produce meaningful results.	5c evaluate the validity of their conclusions by considering different interpretations of their experimental evidence.

6a use scientific knowledge, understanding or theory to predict relationships between continuous variables.	6b consider the range of factors involved, identify the key variables and those to be controlled and/or taken account of, and make qualitative or quantitative observations involving fine discrimination.	6c use their results to draw conclusions, explain the relationship between variables and refer to a model to explain the results.
7a use scientific knowledge, understanding or theory to predict the relative effect of a number of variables.	7b manipulate or take account of the relative effect of two or more independent variables.	7c use observations or results to draw conclusions which state the relative effects of the independent variables and explain the limitations of the evidence obtained.
8a use scientific knowledge, understanding or theory to generate quantitative predictions and a strategy for the investigation.	8b select and use measuring instruments which provide the degree of accuracy commensurate with the outcome they have predicted.	8c justify each aspect of the investigation in terms of the contribution to the overall conclusion.
9a use a scientific theory to make quantitative predictions and organise the collection of valid and reliable data.	9b systematically use a range of investigatory techniques to judge the relative effect of the factors involved.	9c analyse and interpret the data obtained, in terms of complex functions where appropriate, in a way which demonstrates an appreciation of the uncertainty of evidence and the tentative nature of conclusions.
10a use scientific knowledge and an understanding of laws, theories and models to develop hypotheses which seek to explain the behaviour of objects and events they have studied.	10b collect data which are sufficiently valid and reliable to enable them to make a critical evaluation of the law, theory or model.	10c use and analyse the data obtained to evaluate the law, theory or model in terms of the extent to which it can explain the observed behaviour.

Source: National Curriculum Council

difficult for pupils to reach the higher levels of Sc 1, particularly in strands (ii) and (iii), for example to make predictions based on scientific knowledge and theory; to refer to a model to explain results (level 6). The link between Sc 1 and the other ATs, however, is easier suggested than done. Here are just two concrete problems:

1   If teachers are to make a deliberate link between AT 1 and the 'content' ATs, then it becomes very difficult to allow pupils freedom in posing their own questions. If pupils did, it would be almost impossible for teachers to forge a link between 'practical' and 'theory' and thus meet many of the statutory requirements of Sc 1.
2   Work at one level in a 'content' AT may not correspond to the same level at Sc 1, i.e. there may be a discrepancy between levels in trying to link Sc 1 to the other areas.

There is also a danger if a school science department places one person 'in charge of' investigation work for a key stage – will that person coordinate and manage Sc 1 so that it fits in with work in other ATs? Would a better model for organisation be to spread the load around so that each teacher has some responsibility for Sc 1, ensuring that the content ATs are linked into investigations, which is thus built into schemes of work?

Difficulties with scientific investigation in Sc 1

There are several difficulties that teachers will face in putting the existing pattern for Sc 1 into practice:

- My own experience with the existing statements of AT 1 is that few people, myself included, understand them fully. Interpreting them and translating them into classroom practice is not an easy task.
- As yet, few teachers or advisers seem to have produced good, practical exemplars of investigations at KS 4. The standing joke amongst teachers is that level 8 is undergraduate work, level 9 is PhD and level 10 is post-doctoral research.
- The actual investigation given to or planned by pupils (and especially the equipment and measuring instruments provided) strictly limits the level which a group can reach in an investigation. For example, level 8 in strand (ii) can only be achieved if pupils are able to 'select and use' a satisfactory range of measuring instruments. Thus some investigations, with a limited range of materials, resources and measuring devices, could only reach a certain level, no matter how ingenious and creative the pupils, i.e. resources are often the limiting factor.
- For organisational reasons, such as to give the lab technician fair warning, and for other good reasons it is often best to totally separate the planning and predicting stage from the other two. Is this acceptable? Is it good practice?

According to the SEAC (1993) document on assessing: 'Each strand in Sc 1 is generally progressive so that, for example, statements in a strand at level 6 include the requirements of the statements in that strand at levels 1–5.' In practice, however, this is not the experience of teachers. Many are finding that in doing an investigation, pupils are able to satisfy a statement of attainment at a higher level without fulfilling a statement 'lower down'. Thus a pupil might be able to 'justify each aspect of an investigation in terms of the contribution to the overall conclusion' (level 8c), but be unable to 'evaluate the validity of their conclusions by considering different interpretations of their experimental evidence' (level 5c). Indeed, the latter statement seems to be one that teachers find especially difficult to make sense of and to put into practice – what is meant by the 'validity of a conclusion'?

There are several other difficult questions about assessment in Sc 1:

- Should teachers focus on just one strand when assessing?
- What evidence should be used in assessment – written work, observations of pupils?
- If assessment is based largely on written work, is this unfair to the 'good investigator' who is a poor writer?
- Should teachers lead up to an investigation by covering all the relevant theory needed – or is this unfair prompting and prodding in order to score more highly in strand (i)?

Assessment is considered more fully in a separate chapter.

Can pupils learn about the nature of science by doing investigations?

My answer is that they can, but the statements of attainment as currently laid down reflect only one view or model of science. It may be a reasonable mirror or representation of how some scientists actually work (although certain critics might not even admit this). However, it is certain that it could never be a model of scientific procedure, method or practice which mirrors 'real science' in all its forms – indeed, what model ever could be? Perhaps the answer is to allow several different models of scientific investigation which pupils in labs could follow for different types of work. This would certainly get round the following problem: the current statutory guidelines present only one view of science that teachers will inevitably adhere to; therefore, pupils will receive the message that this is 'the nature of science'. This is not a useful, let alone a truthful, message. Despite the complexity and controversy in all the current debates on the history, philosophy and sociology of science, one message is clear: Scientists have, do and will work in a variety of different ways at different times in different disciplines for different reasons. Sir Isaac Newton would probably not have reached level 1 in the present format; where would Einstein, who never controlled a lab variable in his life, have got to?

REFERENCES AND FURTHER READING

An excellent introduction is:
Qualter, A., Strang, J., Swatton, P. and Taylor, R. (1990) *Exploration – A Way of Learning Science*, Oxford: Basil Blackwell.
Documents from the National Curriculum Council (NCC), Department of Education and Science (DES), Assessment of Performance Unit (APU) and Secondary Assessment and

Examinations Council (SEAC) are all essential reading (if you can find the time), especially:

Department of Education and Science (DES) (1991) *Science in the National Curriculum: Non-statutory Guidance*, pp. D1 to D12, London: DES.

SEAC (1993) *Assessing Sc 1 – Scientific Investigation*, London: SEAC.

SEAC/APU (1991) *Planning and Carrying out Investigationa: A Booklet for Teachers*, London: SEAC.

The ATLAS (Active Teaching and Learning Approaches in Science) materials contain many valuable ideas and useful guidance for teachers in doing investigations and making sense of Sc 1 (from Collins Educational, London, W6 8JB).

For a more critical look at approaches to investigational work try:

Woolnough, B. (ed.) (1991) *Practical Science* (various chapters), Milton Keynes: Open University Press.

Woolnough, B. and Allsop, T. (1985) *Practical Work in Science*, Cambridge: Cambridge University Press.

Various publishers produce resources for the classroom on investigational work, for example: Stanley Thornes, Simon & Schuster.

Finally, keep your eyes wide open for new publications – this is certain to be a rapidly changing, hotly debated area.

A GLOSSARY OF TERMS AND VARIABLES

Conceptual understanding/knowledge: Concerned with the ideas and concepts of science, for example force, energy, magnetism, humidity, evolution, reaction.

Hypothesis: A reasoned explanation put forward for an observed event, or events. It should be testable (falsifiable) by investigation.

Procedural understanding/knowledge: Concerned with the procedures of experimental, investigational work, i.e. identifying variables and understanding their importance; planning and designing an investigation; understanding ideas of measurement such as accuracy, reliability and 'repeatability'; recording, displaying and interpreting data.

Qualitative approach: One that does not involve measurement, for example, using terms like quickly/slowly or large/small.

Quantitative approach: One that involves measurements to make observations more precise and put numbers against them.

VARIABLES

A variable is a quantity that can take different values. It can be categoric, discrete, continuous or derived.

Categoric: A categoric variable is a classification, such as colour (red, green, yellow, etc.); shape (square, oblong, round).

Continuous: A continuous variable can have any value, such as mass, weight, volume, length, temperature, time.

Control*:   Control variables are those that must be controlled and held constant by the investigator and which make the investigation a 'fair test'. (Sometimes the control variable is confused with 'the control' in an experiment, particularly in biology. A control, such as a plant which is not given any of the nutrients being tested, can be considered as one value of the independent variable.)

Dependent*:   The dependent variable is the effect or outcome of interest to the investigator. It is measured or judged in the investigation. In the example below it would be the length of the spring.

Derived: A derived variable has to be calculated from more than one measurement, for example speed from distance travelled and the time taken; acceleration; work.

Discrete: A discrete variable can only have an integer value, such as the number of layers of insulation or the number of germinated seeds.

Independent*: The independent variable is the one which the investigator chooses to change systematically. For example, in an investigation into how different springs stretch, the independent variable is the mass chosen to hang on the spring.

Interacting: Two independent variables whose effects on the dependent variable are not easily separated, such as the effect of water and air on rusting.

Key: Key variables define an investigation. They are the independent variable and the dependent variable.

* i.e. independent is 'the one you change'; dependent is 'the one you keep an eye on'; control is 'the one you keep the same'.

10 Assessing practical work in science

Stephen Knutton

This chapter is concerned with issues in the assessment of practical work. After a brief historical survey of practical assessment, it examines the advantages and limitations of various means of assessment – including skills assessment. A particular focus is the assessment of attainment target 1 [Sc 1] of the National Curriculum and its three strands for assessing investigations. The nature of the judgements that teachers are required to make are considered. Finally there is a discussion of some of the difficulties associated with the assessment of Sc 1.

PRACTICAL ASSESSMENT – HISTORICAL BACKGROUND

In the UK practical work has traditionally played a very significant role in school science education. In the early part of the twentieth century Armstrong promoted the heuristic approach to science teaching with its considerable reliance upon laboratory work. A survey by Beatty and Woolnough (1982) revealed that in 83 per cent of their sample of schools, between forty and eighty per cent of the time in 11–13 science classes was spent doing practical work. Teachers clearly thought of practical work as an important activity and yet paradoxically it contributed little to their science assessment.

The assessment of school practical science was largely confined to the practical examination until the curriculum developments of the 1960s. The practical examination relied upon the ability of examiners to set tasks that could be accomplished in a large number of laboratories which were not necessarily well equipped. This resulted in the setting of exercises that were capable of being carried out year after year in only slightly changed form – many will remember the four ion analysis and titrations in Advanced-level chemistry. The resulting practical examinations could only be assessed from the written accounts of candidates which may or may not give an accurate picture of their practical expertise (especially if the candidate had a bad day); they had a backwash effect upon the curriculum as teachers spent a lot of time preparing their candidates for the examination and pupils often experienced a restricted diet of practical work. This approach of practical examination was usually only practised at Advanced level, although such examinations were thought appropriate for some CSE courses and there were some optional practical tests for GCE Ordinary-level candidates, but these were never very popular.

The first major change occurred through the curriculum development initiated by the Nuffield Foundation in the 1960s. This involved the introduction of teacher assessment of practical skills in place of the practical examination over the two years of an Advanced-level course. Other examination boards offering more traditional syllabuses soon followed. The continuous assessment of practical work has a number of advantages, such as:

- the elimination of 'chance' failure in a 'one off' situation
- providing a richer and more varied experience of practical work
- enabling a wider range of skills to be assessed (such as attitudes)
- greater reliability (teachers are in the best position to assess students' practical skills because they see them over an extended period of time.)
- permitting theory and practice to be more closely linked
- becoming an integral part of the teaching and learning process (i.e. formative rather than just summative)

The teacher assessment of practical skills does raise some potential problems. There is a need for the moderation of the standards applied by different teachers and schools. It is also possible that the different role of the teacher might affect the nature of the teacher-pupil relationship.

Typically, students have been assessed on four or five criteria such as manipulative skills, observational and recording skills, interpretation, planning ability and attitude. For each of these skills teachers are usually provided with descriptors to help them in their assessment of students. In a number of schemes the rank order of students produced by the class teacher is not altered although in some cases there may be moderation of overall marks downwards in the case of identified leniency or vice versa.

During the early 1980s the skills approach was extensively researched in Scotland to provide the basis for the criterion-referenced assessment of practical skills; this work was published as Techniques for the Assessment of Practical Skills [TAPS] (Bryce *et al.*, 1983). The TAPS scheme initially identified six skill categories:

- observational skills
- recording skills
- measurement skills
- manipulative skills
- procedural skills
- following instructions

For each of these skill areas the researchers developed sequential sets of tasks with a high degree of structure. The tasks are accompanied by materials to enable teachers to observe pupils using a variety of approaches – although a 'stations' method is preferred for many activities – with pupils being assessed on a pass/fail basis. This can lead to a considerable recording burden for the teacher but provides a welcome motivational boost to pupils and gives valuable information for the record of achievement.

The major criticism of this approach to assessing practical skills is that it is *atomistic.* It is undoubtedly the case that breaking down complicated skills into smaller, more manageable sub-skills (i. e. the ability to read off the volume of liquid in a measuring cylinder to an accuracy of one scale division) is helpful to many pupils in making science more accessible. There are also inherent dangers; atomisation can lead to trivialisation of the subject matter and, in order to avoid ambiguity, skill statements may become unwieldy. Woolnough and Allsop (1985) argue that emphasising the mastery of a large number of small tasks may cause pupils to lose sight of the purpose of practical investigations in science. They advocate a *holistic* approach to the assessment of practical work.

General Certificate of Secondary Education (GCSE)

The introduction of the first GCSE examinations in 1988 represented a significant shift by necessitating the assessment of practical work for most pupils. This requirement for teachers to make assessments of the practical skills of all their pupils placed new demands upon them. Amongst the problems experienced by teachers were the shortages of apparatus for suitable experimental work and a dearth of well tried out experimental activities capable of yielding the necessary assessments of skills. Within a short time the ingenuity of science teachers produced a wealth of published resource materials. Problems still remained on the management aspects of making valid assessments of groups of up to thirty students. These logistical problems were a real concern for many teachers who were, not surprisingly, daunted at the thought of trying to assess the practical skills of such a large group on the same occasion. As time has progressed a range of strategies for coping with these situations has been devised; these have been described and evaluated by Edwards (1988). They include:

- devising exercises that leave a record
- making use of an additional assessor
- routinely checking during normal practical work
- adopting a 'stations' approach
- making use of teacher demonstrations
- using questions in written examinations

National Curriculum

The place of practical work in the science curriculum for all pupils up to year 11 was an integral part of the National Science Curriculum proposals. In the original form, with seventeen attainment targets, AT 1 entitled 'Exploration of Science' had a weighting of 25 per cent and required teachers to make assessments of the practical abilities of pupils throughout their school careers to age 16 and to report them at the end of each key stage. The 1991 revision of the National Science Curriculum made significant changes to the requirements for the assessment of the new Sc 1 'Scientific Investigation'.

The move towards the assessment of investigations partially reflects work carried out over a number of years by the Assessment of Performance Unit (APU) Science Team but places greater emphasis upon the higher levels of achievement implicit in the problem-solving model adopted by the APU.

ASSESSING SCIENCE INVESTIGATIONS

Throughout each of the key stages pupil attainment in Sc 1 is assessed by the teacher during normal lessons through investigations. The programmes of study set out a range of activities in which pupils should engage to promote their investigative skills. Any investigation requires a context and therefore the teacher needs to set the scene. This might take one or more lessons so as to provide pupils with the opportunity to formulate their own questions that they can subsequently test. The actual nature of the question posed can have a very significant influence upon the level of attainment pupils are able to demonstrate. In order to reach level 6 in strand (i) – the design or preparation stage – the investigation must involve the prediction of a relationship between continuous variables. Furthermore, an investigation needs to involve two or more independent variables before any of the strands of Sc 1 can be met at level 6.

The choice of investigation is therefore crucial if pupils are to be able to demonstrate their true capabilities. Questions posed by some pupils may well be of genuine interest to them but fail to provide access to the higher levels that they may be capable of demonstrating. Others may wish to tackle questions that are beyond their capability and are likely to be unsuccessful.

A number of important factors in determining the level of difficulty of an investigation have been identified:

- the *context* in which the investigation is set (from everyday to novel situations across the key stages)
- the *level of conceptual understanding* upon which the investigation is based (from concrete situations to ones involving abstract ideas)
- the *nature, number and complexity of the variables* involved (single or multiple independent variables, categoric or continuous variables, dependent variables)
- the *degree of complexity of the results* obtained

Figure 10.1 illustrates the progression in the characteristics of investigations through key stages 1 to 4.

Progression in design (concepts and variables)

As a first stage it is necessary for the teacher to gauge the range of levels over which

KEY STAGE ONE
Pupils should be encouraged to develop their investigative skills and understanding of science in the context of explorations and investigations largely of the 'Do ...', 'Describe which ...' and 'Find a way to ...' type, involving problems with **obvious key variables** which can be solved using a **qualitative approach** and which are set within the **everyday experience** of pupils.

KEY STAGE TWO
Pupils should be encouraged to develop their investigative skills and their understanding of science in activities which:
• are set within the **everyday experience** of pupils and provide opportunities to explore with increasing precision, where appropriate.
• require the deployment of an increasingly systematic approach involving the **identification and manipulation of obvious key variables**.
These activities should:
• involve problems that can be solved qualitatively, but which increasingly allow for some **quantification of the variables involved**.
• develop skills in using equipment and measurement, encouraging pupils **to make decisions about when, what and how to measure**.

KEY STAGE THREE
Pupils should be encouraged to develop their investigative skills and their understanding of science through systematic experimentation and investigations which:
• are set within the **everyday experience of pupils and in wider contexts**, and which require the deployment of previously encountered concepts and their investigative skills to solve practical problems.
• require that pupils plan and carry through investigations in which they may have to **identify, describe and vary more than one key variable and where the variable measured can be treated continuously.**
• require pupils to make strategic decisions about the **number, range and accuracy of measurements.**

KEY STAGE FOUR
Pupils should be encouraged to develop their investigative skills and their understanding of science in activities which:
• are set in the **everyday experience of pupils and in novel contexts**, involving **increasingly abstract concepts** and the application of knowledge, understanding and skills, where pupils need to make decisions about the degree of precision and safe working required.
• are increasingly complex because there are **derived and/or interacting variables**.

Figure 10.1   Characteristics of investigations for key stages 1–4; extracts from the programmes of study
Source: APU/SEAC Assessment Matters No. 6, p. 9

a particular class of children is operating so that the investigations can be pitched at an appropriate level. Teachers can then ask themselves a series of questions about the variables involved in the possible investigation:

- Is the independent variable categoric? This allows access up to only level 5 of strand (i).
- Is the independent variable continuous? Beyond level 5 becomes accessible.
- Are two (or more) independent variables involved? Access to level 7 and above is possible.

In order for an investigation to cover a range of levels there is a necessity for a degree of 'open endedness'.

Progression in interpretation (Results)

For an investigation to be satisfying for the pupils it should yield results which they can make sense of and interpret. However, investigations do not always yield suitable results and it would be wrong to penalise pupils in strand (iii) because of poor data. It is therefore acceptable for the results of group endeavour or from the teacher to be used to make this assessment. The data resulting from the investigation must, however, be sufficiently complex to allow pupils to demonstrate their interpretative and evaluative ability as required by the criteria. Thus to reach level 4 the data must allow recognition of trends or simple patterns in relation to the original question, whereas to reach level six there must be opportunities to explain results in terms of an appropriate model.

Creating assessment opportunities for Sc 1

The Secondary Assessment and Examinations Council (SEAC) (1993a) have identified five key points for teachers to consider when setting up assessment situations:

- In order that pupils might show their attainment in Sc 1 throughout the key stage it is necessary for teachers to plan so that pupils are able to show what they know, understand and can do for all three strands and in a range of contexts from Sc 2, 3 and 4. There are considerable dangers in limiting the opportunities for assessment to a few occasions because few investigations are likely to provide adequate opportunities to demonstrate performance in each of the three strands. Furthermore, opportunities of feedback will be reduced and pupils may be denied the information they need to help them tackle subsequent investigations more effectively.
- It is vitally important that investigations are appropriately targeted. An investigation must allow opportunities for pupils to demonstrate their achievement at a range of levels. All the students being assessed must be able to start the investigation which should not, because of its nature, impose an arbitrary limit upon their attainment. In a class with a wide spread of potential attainment this

means either setting up a series of related but differently targeted investigations or devising a common investigation which pupils can tackle at a level appropriate to their differing capabilities.

- Investigations should demand approximate parity between the knowledge and understanding in Sc 2, 3 or 4 and the level they are working at in Sc 1. If their level of knowledge and understanding is inadequate then pupils will be unable to make appropriate predictions or hypotheses (strand i) or make sensible interpretations (strand ii). As a result, pupils will be unable to demonstrate their full abilities.

- Pupils are better able to demonstrate what they can do if they have a clear understanding of what is required. This can be achieved by i) providing them with a suitable structure and ii) translating the statements of attainment into language they can more easily understand. This also makes it much easier to involve the pupils in evaluating their own work.

- The provision of support for pupils during investigations is permissible and does not necessarily prevent the demonstration of evidence of attainment. Investigations are part of the teaching process and it would be wrong to let a pupil struggle through a fatally flawed activity. Intervention by the teacher may not be able to rescue evidence of attainment in, for example, strand (ii) but it may still be possible to note attainment in strand (iii) and, possibly, strand (i). More importantly, the guidance given by the teacher may assist the pupil to be better able to demonstrate attainment in strand (ii) on a future occasion.

Assessing investigations for Sc 1 Strands

Strand (i)

This strand is concerned with asking questions, predicting and hypothesising in the context of whole investigations. Of crucial importance is the requirement that the questions posed must be those generated by the pupils themselves. Great care must therefore be taken to ensure that the teacher does not give too much guidance in any stimulus background material. Progression is evident in the different levels, with level 3 requiring predictions based on 'everyday experience', level 4 requiring linkage to relevant prior knowledge and level 5 demanding the formulation of a hypothesis rather than simply making a prediction.

Strand (ii)

This strand is about 'carrying out investigations' and is therefore concerned with the practical skills, procedures and strategies that pupils use in the carrying out of their investigations. The three most important features of this strand are (SEAC, 1993a):

- the need to make increasingly accurate observations and measurements using appropriate instruments
- the need to control variables

- the need to handle increasingly complex variables

At level 4 students are expected to be able to design a 'fair test' in order to test their prediction or hypothesis. Beyond this level they must demonstrate the ability to control variables in their investigations.

Strand (iii)

This strand is concerned with the interpretation of results and the evaluation of scientific evidence. Pupils need to demonstrate their ability to interpret results, to evaluate their validity and also to relate their findings to an appropriate level of scientific knowledge and understanding. Achievement in this strand is likely to be determined by the nature of prediction made in strand (i) and the complexity of data generated when carrying out the investigation, i.e. strand (ii).

In this strand only the lowest levels are accessible for simply summarising results. For level 3 and beyond there is a need for an explanation which may be in terms of patterns (level 4), alternative interpretations (level 5) or linkage to scientific models (level 6).

Whilst an investigation must cover all three strands, there are circumstances where a lesser number of strands might actually be assessed. Earlier in this chapter I gave the example of teacher assistance to allow a pupil to make progress on the other strands. There are other circumstances, such as group discussion being used to generate a common preparation stage for the investigation, which is then followed by individual work. This could make the assessment of individual pupil performance in strand (i) difficult to assess. In other investigations the teacher may have insufficient time to be able to assess strand (ii) for all the class. This does not render the assessments of the other two strands invalid. Another pupil may carry out the design stage satisfactorily but the results of the investigation may not be adequate to enable the pupil to demonstrate her or his capabilities in the other two strands. In these areas teacher judgements become crucially important.

MAKING KEY STAGE JUDGEMENTS

SEAC (1993a) have published guidance about the judgements to be made at the end of the key stage. Among the main points are:

- For Sc 1 no single investigation can provide a complete picture of pupils' attainment.
- For Sc 1 to accurately reflect a pupil's attainment it will be necessary for teachers to come to a decision about attainment in each strand before reviewing evidence across strands.
- In addition to written reports, it is likely that teachers will accumulate evidence of pupils' attainment through questioning pupils, observing pupils as they discuss their work with each other or when they are working practically or conducting an investigation (SEAC, 1991). This 'ephemeral evidence' will be

important when making decisions. Therefore the keeping of brief notes of discussions and annotating work will be of enormous value.

- Since Sc 1 is made up of closely related strands, simple rules for determining overall level, such as taking the mean or adopting the highest level reached in each strand are deemed to be inappropriate. For judgements to be secure it is crucial for the teacher to be able to demonstrate that they are based upon adequate evidence as well as in a range of different contexts.

Science teachers need to have a very clear idea when setting up a practical investigation just what it is that they are expecting of pupils in terms of outcomes. This means that there is a need to interpret the statements of attainment for Sc 1 (see Chapter 9) in terms of the specific outcomes for the investigation concerned. An example of the kind of outcomes a teacher might predict for an investigation into the strength of plastic bags, together with contextual material, is given in figure 10.2. Other examples can be found in materials to support the ATLAS project (Barnett and Green, 1992).

The publication by SEAC (1993b) of exemplar material in the form of four folders of individual pupils' work should help teachers in reaching judgements. The work in the folders contains a range of evidence for the attainment of each pupil and includes notes on ephemeral evidence where appropriate. Each piece of work is analysed in relation to the statements of attainment. The commentaries on how the evidence has been used to reach decisions about the pupil's overall level in Sc 1 should prove to be of particular value.

DIFFICULTIES WITH THE AT 1 MODEL OF ASSESSMENT

Tytler and Swatton (1992) have questioned the validity of the Sc 1 assessment model, which is based entirely upon pupil investigations. The Sc 1 approach is firmly rooted in the APU framework, which views scientific endeavour as primarily concerned with solving problems. This similarity is, however, only really true for the highest two levels: categories five and six, planning and performing investigations – with the latter category being seen as the *synthesis* of the other five assessment categories. These two categories were themselves underpinned by the skills necessary to perform successful investigations such as measurement, estimation and observation. As Woolnough (1989) points out, 'the whole is always greater than the sum of its parts'.

In the case of Sc 1 the assessment focus is *entirely* upon *whole* investigations. Whilst this need not necessarily imply that basic skills are not required, nor that their development should be ignored, it is the case that there is no credit for them in the assessment scheme nor incentive to promote them. As a result, Tytler and Swatton believe that in Sc 1 there is potential to constrain pupils and to underestimate their performance. By use of case studies of pupils involved in independent research projects they have attempted to 'critically evaluate whether Sc 1 provides a useful or adequate view of the process of student explorations and . . . of the processes of science itself'.

The nature of investigations

In Sc 1 it is implicit that investigative skills can be neatly divided into a series of component skills and furthermore that the structure of the statements of attainment is hierarchical. This, Tytler and Swatton believe, is an open invitation to teachers to adopt atomistic criteria rather than promote the involvement of pupils in real problems which generate interest and personal commitment from the pupils. The result could be sterile formula-driven and teacher-determined investigations rather than good science.

Design skills hierarchy

A major feature of Sc 1 is the idea that the ability to manipulate variables is one which becomes more and more sophisticated as the levels increase (see Chapter 9). Tytler and Swatton draw attention to the problems facing a criterion-referenced assessment in real problem-solving situations where it is difficult in advance to prescribe the method of attack – just as much a problem for the professional scientist as for the Sc 1 students. Woolnough (1991) argues that any simplistic model of progression is unacceptable because 'learning to be good at doing science follows more Bruner's roller coaster model of learning than a uniform climb up a flight of stairs'.

Level variation for component skills

The case studies of Tytler and Swatton reveal that a wide variation of skill levels were evident from the investigations undertaken. Furthermore, Tytler and Swatton formed the view that it was the needs of the particular investigation rather than factors concerning the developmental level of the student that determined the skill levels demonstrated. This relates, in part, to earlier work by the APU which showed the importance of *context* in determining pupil performance. The danger is that an overemphasis upon individual skill components might give a misleading picture of a student's overall performance.

Measurement-driven investigations

Within Sc 1 emphasis is placed upon the ability to select measuring instruments based upon decisions about the range and accuracy that is required by the variables. Is this selection-of-instruments process at a higher level of operation?

AT 1 and researchable questions

The whole philosophy of Sc 1 seems to be based upon the idea of selecting research 'questions' which will yield a definite answer. Does good science really operate like this? Investigations based around variable control and manipulation will satisfy the criteria of Sc 1 but because of their predictability there is little scope for

Teaching Context.	The area of study is related to the Properties and Uses of Materials. Students will have completed a study of the strength of materials under tension and have also investigated aspects of elasticity and density.

Scene Setting.	'A supermarket chain has decided to save money by using cheaper carrier bags. The staff are concerned that the new bags may not be strong enough to satisfy their customers.' What do you think the problems of using new bags might be? What do you think could affect how good the bags might be? Discuss your ideas with your group and when you have finished tell your teacher.

| The Task. | Individually decide what YOU think are the most important factors that will affect the choice of bag.

DESIGN an investigation to test what you think might happen What will you change, keep the same and measure? How will you make the tests fair?

CARRY OUT your investigation and then INTERPRET what you find out and present a report to the Supermarket Director. |
|---|---|

Figure 10.2   An investigation on testing plastics
Source: Based on INSET materials produced by the Northern Examinations and Assessment Board (1992) to support teachers of GCSE syllabuses at Key Stage 4

LEVEL	DESIGN	CARRY OUT	INTERPRET
3	–needs guidance on 'fair test'. –suggests what might happen e.g. thinner bags are weaker. –decides what to measure but is given equipment	–measures weight at which bag fails. OR –measures weight w.r.t. same deformation	–sees need for a 'fair test' i.e. similar bags, weight or objects etc. –describes what happens –gives his/her explanations (correct or not).
4	As for Level 3 but –designs fair test. –relates strength ot different bags, plastic, thickness. –decides what to measure and chooses equipment.	–completes fair test. –measures with enough accuracy to give sensible result.	–notes results e.g. bigger weight more stretch OR bigger weights break thin bags OR sharp objects cut thin plastic. –relates findings and explanation back to prediction.
5	As for Level 4 but –chooses number of bags, or different thicknesses, handle type. –chooses maximum load for bags and measures stretch or 'breaking point'. –comments on strength of materials in prediction	–measures a range of values (e.g. weights, thickness etc.)	–relates different thicknesses to stretch/break given same load. –comments on need to check results or whether –'bursting' is a good enough indicator.
6	As for Level 5 but –selects sample strips. –increases load and measures stretch to breaking point for different thicknesses, types. –refers to 'strength in tension' or breaking point etc.	Ditto	–relates 'stretch' and 'break' to weight/load OR thickness OR type of plastic. –includes 'Sci Theory' in explanation (e.g. Hooke's Law)
7–10	As for 6 but chooses two factors and includes reference to Law	Ditto	–notes two outcomes and comments on 'most' important.

ingenuity or surprise and they may prove to be less imaginative and satisfying. There is also a problem in communicating the philosophy of Sc 1 assessment to pupils who, rather than thinking at the age of 13 'Which question will get me the highest level?', may well be operating on the basis of questions that seem simply interesting or most worthwhile!

One feature of much problem-solving and investigative work is pupil collaboration with others, and yet this aspect does not appear in the Sc 1 statements. At Advanced level a number of internal assessment schemes have included student attitudes as an important component of their practical profile for many years. This is, of course, the most difficult 'area' to quantify and reach agreement upon, and this could well account for its omission.

In summing up their view of Sc 1 as a means of assessing explorations in science, Tytler and Swatton (1992) state:

> AT 1 gives us an instrumental view of what it means to be scientific; as if the essence of investigation lies in its component methodological processes. However the reality is altogether richer and more varied. Imposing a set of methodological rules on a process which is above all *creative,* can only serve to diminish its potential as a way of learning in science.

Investigations for levels 9 and 10

Many science teachers have been greatly exercised by the difficulty of producing suitable material to enable good students to access these higher levels. The previous chapter refers to the perceived difficulty of these levels for Sc 1. The absence of exemplar material is now a national debating point among science teachers. Some argue that its absence is indicative of its inaccessibility and therefore recommend reducing the ceiling for Sc 1 to the present level 8. A failure to do so might cause unacceptable distortion to 1994 GCSE science results with a consequential impact upon the take-up of science A-level courses. Others have pointed out that it is too early to reach conclusions. The first National Science Curriculum cohort has not yet reached the point where the highest standard of work would be expected. Furthermore, the situation may have been exacerbated by insufficient teaching of investigations!

REFERENCES AND FURTHER READING

Barnett, R. and Green, D. (1992) 'ATLAS Resources: Sc 1 Scientific Investigation', Sheffield: Centre for Science Education, Sheffield Hallam University.

Beatty, J. W. and Woolnough, B. E. (1982) 'Practical work in 11–13 science', *British Educational Research Journal*, 8: 23–30.

Bryce, T. G. K., McCall, J., MacGregor, J., Weston, R. A. J. and Robertson, I. J. (1983) *Techniques for the Assessment of Practical Skills in Foundation Science*, London: Heinemann.

Edwards, D. (1988) *Practical Assessment for GCSE: Chemistry*, London: Unwin-Hyman.

Northern Examinations and Assessment Board (NEAB) (June 1992), GCSE Science Framework 'Sample Investigations', Issue No. 1, Manchester: NEAB.

SEAC (1991) *KS 3 Teacher Assessment in Practice*, London: HMSO.

—— (1993a) *KS 3 Science School Assessment Folder*, 'Sample Test Questions', London: SEAC.

—— (1993b) *KS 3 Science*, 'Pupils' Work Assessed', London: SEAC.

Tytler, R. and Swatton, P. (1992) 'A critique of Attainment Target 1 based on case studies of students' investigations', *School Science Review* 74 (266): 21–35.

Woolnough, B, (1989) 'Towards a holistic view of processes in science education', in Wellington, J. J. (ed.), *Skills and Processes in Science Education: A Critical Analysis*, London: Routledge.

—— ed. (1991) *Practical Science*, Milton Keynes: Open University Press.

Woolnough, B. and Allsop, T. (1985) *Practical Work in Science*, Cambridge Science Education Series, Cambridge: Cambridge University Press.

11 Language in science education

Children solve practical tasks with the help of their speech as well as their eyes and hands.

(Vygotsky, 1978)

> Although science is a 'practical' subject, science teaching occurs extensively through the medium of language, both spoken and written. The purpose of this chapter is to focus on that language and the way that teachers, texts and children use it.

WATCH YOUR LANGUAGE: THE WORLD OF SECONDARY SCIENCE

In the school science lab pupils meet all sorts of strange objects and devices which they will never encounter elsewhere: they meet the world of the conical flask, the pestle and mortar, the bunsen burner, the evaporating dish, the gauze and the watch glass, not to mention the pipette and the burette. To enter the lab is akin to Alice's passage down the rabbit hole into a new world. This is equally true of pupils' strange encounters with a new world of discourse.

> Twas brillig and the slithy toves,
> Did gyre and gimble in the wabe;
> All mimsy were the borogoves,
> And the mome raths outgrabe.
> . . . Somehow it seems to fill my head with ideas – only I don't exactly know what they are!

(from *Through the Looking Glass*, by Lewis Carroll)

How many pupils, confronted by a science textbook or by a blackboard covered in scientific prose, are as confused as Alice was when she first read 'Jabberwocky'? Their heads may be full of ideas but they may not be quite sure what those ideas are, or where they came from. In many ways, the language of science resembles the language of Carroll's poem.

CLASSIFYING THE WORDS OF SCIENCE

Consider the random selection below of words used in science textbooks and by science teachers:

momentum	inertia	acceleration	power
photosynthesis	gene	speed	couple
fruit	wave	electric current	isotope
parasite	particle	critical angle	trachea
electron	substance	force	meniscus
neutron	material	pressure	mass
proton	photon	work	field
amoeba	velocity	energy	

Their only shared characteristic *could be* that each has a precision or 'fixedness' in its meaning. Science words *might be* considered to mean the same whatever the context and whoever the user. But do they? Certainly the 'fixed' meaning of science words is being questioned (Sutton, 1992).

But it is the *difference between* the words of science rather than their *shared* features that I would like to concentrate on here, for the words in the above list do vastly different jobs. Take 'trachea' and 'inertia', for example. The word 'trachea' simply *names* a real object or entity: a windpipe ('trachea', like many scientific words, is thus a synonym). It has meaning because it names or 'points to' a real entity. But how does a word like 'inertia' acquire meaning? It does not refer to an object or an entity. Surely then it must signify a *concept*. This concept is somehow derived from experience – the observation that 'heavy things tend to keep going', or a 'steam roller is hard to get started' or similar personal experiences.

Unfortunately, many concept words in science do not, and cannot, acquire meaning as easily as a word like 'trachea'. Take the word 'atom', for example. Your, and my, meaning for this word can never be derived from experience. The same is true for other so-called unobservable entities. There are even greater problems for the meaning of many terms used in physics: 'frictionless body,' 'point mass' and 'smooth surface', for example – not derived from experience, nor unobservable entities, but non-existent idealisations! The terms of Schrodinger's wave equation and De Broglie's statement of wave/particle duality present problems at an even higher level of abstraction. I find it impossible to conjure up even a vague mental image of a particle being a wave all at the same time.

This all indicates that it can be useful to divide the words of science into various types or categories. Through doing this, science teachers can become more aware of the language they use in classrooms. I have put forward a classification or 'Taxonomy' of the words of science in table 11.1.

Each category of words acquires meaning in a different way, and it is this complexity that teachers of science need to be aware of.

Table 11.1 A taxonomy of the words of science

Level 1 Naming words
1.1 Familiar objects, new names (synonyms)
1.2 New objects, new names
1.3 Names of chemical elements
1.4 Other nomenclature

Level 2 Process words
2.1 Capable of ostensive definition, i.e. being shown
2.2 Not capable of ostensive definition

Level 3 Concept words
3.1 Derived from experience (sensory concepts)
3.2 With dual meanings, i.e. everyday and scientific, for example, 'work'
3.3 Theoretical constructs (total abstractions, idealisations and postulated entities)

Level 4 Mathematical 'words' and symbols

- The first category can be called *naming words*. These are words that denote
  identifiable, observable, real objects or entities: words like 'trachea', 'oesophagus', 'tibia', 'fibula', 'fulcrum', 'meniscus', 'vertebra', 'pollen', 'saliva',
  'thorax', 'iris', 'larynx' and 'stigma'. Many of these are simply synonyms for
  everyday words already familiar to pupils, like 'windpipe', 'backbone', or 'spit'.
  Thus part of learning in science involves giving *familiar* objects new names. At
  a slightly higher level, some learning in science involves giving new names to
  unfamiliar objects, objects which pupils may never have seen before – perhaps
  because they cannot be seen with a naked eye (such as a cell) or because they
  belong to the world of school science laboratories, for example beaker, conical
  flask, bunsen burner, spatula, gauze, and splint.
- The second category of scientific words, at a new level of abstraction, can be
  called *process words*. These are words that denote processes that happen in
  science: words like 'evaporation', 'distillation', 'condensation', 'photosynthesis', 'crystallisation', 'fusion', 'vaporisation', 'combustion' and 'evolution'.
  Clearly, some of these process words acquire meaning for a pupil more easily
  than others. A teacher can point to a reaction on the front bench and say 'there,
  that's combustion', or demonstrate red ink losing its colour and say 'that's
  distillation'. Thus certain processes are in a sense visible, or at least 'showable'.
  Their meaning can be learnt by *ostensive definition* (from the Latin *ostendo*, 'I
  show'). Other processes belong to a higher level within this category. One
  cannot point to something happening and say 'That's evolution'. Through
  education and language development, 'evolution' may also become a concept
  (i. e. level 3.3).
- The third, and largest, category of words in science are *concept words*. These
  are words that denote concepts of various types: words like 'work', 'energy',
  'power', 'fruit', 'salt', 'pressure', 'force', 'volume', 'temperature', 'heat' and

so on. This area of learning in science is surely the one where most learning difficulties are encountered, for concept words denote ideas at gradually ascending levels of abstraction.

- We should also note that many words can start as a name but, through language development in science, gradually be used as a concept. For example, fuel may be a name for petrol or paraffin, but gradually it acquires a general, conceptual meaning, such as 'a flammable material yielding energy'. Similarly with the terms 'salt' and 'gas'.

At the lowest level, certain concepts are directly derived from experience. Like certain processes, they can be defined ostensively by pointing out examples where the concept pertains. Colour concepts, such as 'red', are almost certainly learnt in this way. These can be neatly termed *sensory concepts*. The next category contains words that have both a scientific and (perhaps unfortunately) an everyday meaning: examples include 'work', 'energy', 'power', 'fruit' and 'salt'. The existence of the two meanings causes pupils difficulties and confusion. It also explains the seemingly strange yet often perceptive conceptions (alternative frameworks) that pupils possess of 'heat', 'plant nutrition', 'pressure', 'energy', 'work' and so on. The same word is being used to denote two different ideas. In these cases the invention of totally new words (such as 'anode' and 'cathode' coined by Faraday) might have made life easier for generations of school science pupils. Finally, concept words belonging to a third level are used to denote what I will call *theoretical constructs*: words like 'element', 'mixture', 'compound', 'atom', 'electron', 'valency', 'mole', 'mass', 'frictionless body', 'smooth surface', 'field' and so on. Some of these theoretical constructs, such as atom and electron, people may prefer to call unobservable entities because in a sense they exist. Others are simply idealisations, or total abstractions, which cannot possibly exist, such as point masses or frictionless bodies, except in the language of mathematics.

The language of mathematics, its 'words' and symbols, can be placed at the fourth and highest level of abstraction in a hierarchy of scientific words. The mathematical language used in advanced physics is neither derived from, nor directly applicable to, experience. Its meaning is so detached as to become almost autonomous.

USING A TAXONOMY OF WORDS IN SCIENCE TEACHING

This hierarchy or classification is all very well, you might say, but of what possible use can it be to the science teacher? What implications does it have? I will suggest four areas where it might be applied:

1 Beware of meaning at the higher levels

Different scientific words *mean* in different ways. The word 'iris' *means* simply by labelling or pointing out an observable entity; similarly with many other words in level 1 of the taxonomy. But the meaning of words in higher levels is not as clear. At best they denote, or refer to, some mental image or abstract idea.

Words in the highest level of the taxonomy, such as 'electron', can *only* have meaning in a theoretical context. The meaning of 'electron' somehow belongs to a theoretical world of nuclei, atoms, electric fields, shells and orbits – an imaginary, almost make-believe world to pupils starting science. Yet 'electron' can acquire meaning, just as the words in a far-fetched fairy tale do.

The problem of meaning (or rather lack of it) at these higher levels of abstraction must be a major cause of failure in science education.

2 Are pupils 'ready'?

The lack of meaning for many pupils of scientific terms in level 3 of the taxonomy particularly may explain why many pupils fail to make sense of science. Perhaps they meet these words too soon – indeed the hierarchy in the taxonomy *could* be closely related to Piagetian stages of development. Is it possible, for example, for a pupil to acquire any meaning for a term denoting a theoretical construct before he or she has reached the formal-operational stage? (See Chapter 4.) More positively, can science teaching help achieve the required readiness and development?

3 Language development

A conscious awareness of gradually ascending development of meaning can often be useful to the science teacher in classroom teaching and lesson preparation. By developing word meanings for pupils – for example, from a word (say 'gas') being simply a name to becoming a concept – children's understanding, thought and language are enhanced. Word meanings can develop in a child's mind through both appropriate teaching and wider experiences.

4 Teaching for shared meaning

Science education must, to some extent, be initiation into new language. With naming words this can be quite simple. But the more abstract a term becomes the more it must be taught by analogy or by the use of models. If there is no *entity* which a term corresponds to, then clearly meaning becomes more difficult to communicate. But there are dangers.

Encouraging children to make the words of science meaningful *to them* should not imply encouraging them to develop *their own meanings* for scientific words. As Wittgenstein pointed out (1958), there can be no such thing as a private language. Languages are, by definition, public. In short, meanings in science need not be *impersonal* but they must be *interpersonal*. We need to teach for shared meaning (Edwards and Mercer, 1987).

These are just four areas where the taxonomy of table 11.1 has relevance to science teaching. The taxonomy also has important uses in considering teachers' written material and in assessing the readability of science texts. These are both considered in later sections.

TEACHER TALK

Science teachers spend a lot of their time talking. Her Majesty's Inspectorate reports in the past have shown that the dominant teaching style has been exposition from the teacher, and this is still common. It follows from this, and the discussion above on the complexity of scientific words, that teachers of science need to be especially careful of their spoken language.

One of the most valuable studies published on school language came from Barnes *et al.*, (1969). The study identified three types of language used by teachers:

- **specialist language presented:** words and forms of language unique to the subject which teachers are aware of as a potential problem and therefore present and explain to their students
- **specialist language not presented:** language special to the subject which is not deliberately presented either because it has been explained before or teachers are unaware that they are using it
- **the language of secondary education:** terms, words and forms of language used by teachers which pupils would not normally hear, see, or use except in the world of the school, i.e. not the language of the world outside

This an important classification and one of which all science teachers should be aware. It is invaluable as a framework for reflecting upon both teacher talk and (discussed shortly) teacher writing. Table 11.2 gives a summary of the categories, with examples from science; readers are invited to examine this table and see if they can add any further examples.

The right-hand column of the table, i.e. specialist language, can be further classified in terms of the taxonomy presented in table 11.1. Which of the specialist terms are naming words, which are process words and which are concept words? It would seem that, in watching their language, teachers should be especially wary of those in level 3.3 of my taxonomy.

Barnes and his colleagues went on to analyse some of the teacher and pupil talk that occurs in science lessons. Some of their extracts are superb; for brevity's sake I present just one below, said to be from a class for pupils who had recently moved into secondary education:

T: Now what we want is a method whereby we can take off this . . . um . . . green material . . . this green stuff off the grass and perhaps one or two of you can suggest how we might do this . . . yes?
P1: Boil it.
T: Boil it? What with?
P1: Some water in a beaker and . . .
T: Yes, there's that method . . . we could do it and . . . um . . . I think probably you could guess how we might be able to do it by what we've already got

Table 11.2 Watch your language

Can you add to the following lists?

The language of secondary education	Technical language/ specialist language
criterion	. . . regular . . .
. . . in terms of . . .	equilibrium
relatively	calibrate
factors	proportional to
specifically	uniform
complex	force
assumption	work
ideally . . .	energy
initially. . .	power
related to	moment
subject to	miscible
recap	random
determines	diverges
distinguish between	exert
effectively . . .	secrete
theoretically . . .	saturated
becomes apparent	mass
	trachea

---

out in the laboratory. How do you think we might do it? (Pestle and mortar are on bench.)

P2:   Could pound it . . .

T: Pound it up with water . . . and that's exactly what we're going to do.

T: We're going to cut the grass into small pieces and then we're going to put it into the . . . what we call a mortar . . . this is what we call a mortar . . . this bowl . . . and anyone know what we call the other thing which we're going to pound it in?

T: Now I don't know whether any of you could jump the gun a bit and tell me what actually is this green stuff which produces green colour . . .

P: Er . . . em . . . water.

T: No . . . have you heard of chlorophyll?

T: Put that into the distillation flask and then distil off and then we get thermometer recording the correct temperature which is the boiling point for acetone. Then we collect the acetone which came over as a distillate.

Look carefully at the talk here. Which words and terms can be classed as the language of secondary education? How is the specialist language being handled? It is also interesting to note the questioning going on here: is it closed or open? Is the teacher asking the pupil to 'guess what's in my head' (what Barnes calls a pseudo-question)?

The Barnes study contains many similar extracts and is thoroughly recommended; little has changed since its publication. It would be a valuable activity for any teacher to record his or her discourse with a class in the same way and then to analyse it using the frameworks above.

TEACHER WRITING FOR LEARNING AND UNDERSTANDING

One of the essential skills of the teacher is to present and explain the processes and the content of science in a palatable and interesting way. This is true of teacher talk but is equally applicable to teacher writing – whether it be on the blackboard, the OHP or a worksheet. All the above cautions and frameworks for care in language apply to the written word perhaps even more than to the spoken word. Writing is in some ways more permanent, more open to scrutiny and less flexible and interactive. The aim of this section is to offer guidelines on writing material for pupils. Teacher writing is worthy of long discussion (see further reading), but for brevity here I begin simply by offering guidelines for writing, aimed principally at worksheet writing although many of the points apply equally to (say) blackboard or assessment writing.

Table 11.3 Writing for learning in science: guidelines and checklist

Why write?
- To give experimental instructions
- To transmit information
- To structure a film, video, slides, etc.
- To ask questions, or to test (using, for example, all questions; information then questions; fill in the blanks; crosswords)
- To provide your audience with ready-made notes

Writing good material
- Write clearly and directly.
- Do not present *too much* information or *too little*.
- Try it out in rough first.
- Make the reader think!
- Use plenty of structure such as an appetiser; headings that stand out; summary/key points.
- Print neatly or type it – don't write.
- Use a ruler.
- Use graphs, diagrams and illustrations to break up the text where possible.
- *Do not* write to a Readability formula.

Watch your language
- Avoid long sentences (i.e. more than twenty words).
- Try to keep to one idea per sentence.
- Beware of technical terms which have not been introduced (such as 'mass', 'current', 'pressure', 'momentum', etc.).

Table 11.3 (Continued)

- Avoid the 'language of secondary education' (Barnes): terms like 'relationship with', 'recapitulate', 'exert', 'becomes apparent', 'derived from', etc.
- Avoid too many short, staccato sentences.
- Address the reader as 'you' (don't use the royal 'we').
- Keep language brief and concise (use a colleague as your editor).

Getting it right
- Have somebody from your target audience in mind as you write (for example, Jane Bloggs from Year 9).
- If possible, try it out on a member of your target audience first.
- Always ask a colleague or friend to check your writing before letting it loose (i.e. use a proofreader).
- Misspellings and poor grammar are not acceptable.

Readers are invited to look closely at these points – there may be guidelines here that you disagree with. If so, it is well worth drawing up your own list or adapting the one here – whichever guidelines you use, it is essential to have some pointers to clear and effective writing.

There is excellent further discussion of the use of writing in teaching and communicating science in Newton (1990), Sutton (1992) and Shortland and Gregory (1991).

THE LANGUAGE OF THE SCIENCE TEXTBOOK

In my view it is good practice for teachers to write some of their own material at least some of the time. It can help them, for example, to understand a topic more clearly themselves and to structure it and present it to pupils. Writing clear, readable material should be seen as one of the skills of a teacher. However, in the real world, teachers will commonly find themselves searching for, using and evaluating textual material written by others. The published scheme has proliferated and now is beginning to dominate – leading, unfortunately, to a reduced need for teachers to be able to write for pupils. The increased need now, however, is for teachers to be able to assess carefully, critically and to some extent objectively the texts they will be using and paying for. Many of the following features of science text can be assessed fairly quickly and intuitively:

- its 'appeal'
- its structure and layout
- the style of the writing
- the use of illustrations (photos and artwork)
- the use of colour where appropriate

Subjective, intuitive judgement is valuable in looking at science texts. There are, however, also a number of tried and tested formulae for assessing quantitatively the 'readability' of a piece of text. These should not be seen as alternatives to the intuition of (especially) an experienced teacher with a critical eye for text, but they can be useful extensions and checks of subjective judgement. They are well worth trying on a range of texts, from the *Sun* newspaper to the A-level science text. They first became well-known in a science context in the late 1970s and early 1980s (see Johnson, 1979) when the commonly used textbooks of the time, such as Abbot's O-level Physics and Mackean's Biology text, were shown to have reading ages of 18 and 19 respectively.

Table 11.4 How readable is text? Four measures to use

1 *The Flesch formula*
• Select at least three samples of 100 words.
• Count the average number of syllables in each 100-word sample (Y).
• Calculate the average length of the sentences in the samples (X).
• alculate the Reading Ease Score (RES) using the Flesch formula:
• Reading Ease Score = $206.835 - \{(X \times 1.015) + (Y \times 0.846)\}$
where   X = average sentence length in words
Y = average number of syllables per 100 words
Examples: RES 90+ : very easy, e.g. comics
60–70 : standard, e.g. mass non-fiction
30–50 : academic prose
• Change the Reading Ease Score to a US grade level using this table:

Reading ease score (RES)	Flesch grade level (FGL)
Over 70	$-((RES - 150)/10)$
Over 60	$-((RES - 110)/5)$
Over 50	$-((RES - 93)/3.33)$
Under 50	$-((RES - 140)/6.66)$

• Add 5 to the Flesch grade level to give the reading age of the text.

2 *THE FOG ('frequency of gobbledegook') TEST*
• Select sample passages of exactly 100 words.
• Calculate the average sentence length (S), i.e. the average number of words per sentence.
• Calculate the percentage of polysyllabic words (words of three syllables or more) in each sample and find the average (N).
• Calculate the US grade level using the formula:
  US grade level = $0.4 (S + N)$
• Find the reading age by adding 5 to the US grade level.

3 *The FRY readability graph*
• Select random samples of exactly 100 words (at least three samples and preferably more).
• Count the number of sentences in each sample. For a part sentence count the number of words and express as a fraction of the length of the last sentence, to the nearest one-tenth.
• Count the number of syllables in each 100-word sample. (For numerals and abbreviations count one syllable for each symbol, e.g. ASE is three.)
• Mark a dot on the graph (figure 11.4.1) where the average number of sentences and the average number of syllables in the samples intersects. The dot's position gives the US grade level.

• Add 5 to the US grade level to give the reading age.

From the Fry graph (figure 11.4.1) it is possible to tell the relative difficulty of vocabulary or sentence length. The curve of the Fry graph is meant to represent normal texts and therefore a point below the line (bottom left) will indicate material of greater than average sentence length and hence difficulties of sentence structure. Points above the line, top right, indicate higher than average vocabulary difficulty.

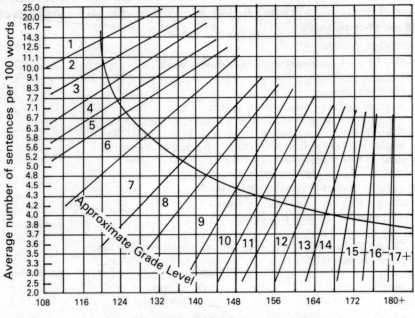

Average number of syllables per 100 words

Figure 11.4.1   Fry's extended readability graph

4 *The SMOG formula*

• Select three sample passages, each consisting of ten sentences – one from the beginning, one from the middle and one from the end of the text.
• Count the total number of words of three syllables or more in the thirty sentences selected.
• Find the square root of the total.
• Add 8 to give the reading age in years.

Note: Cloze Procedure

Teachers can also carry out a Cloze procedure test. A passage is selected from a text and words omitted regularly, such as every fifth or sixth word. The pupil has to read the passage and fill in the correct word (any word that makes complete sense):

60% success means the pupil could use the material independently
40–50% means the pupil could use the material with teacher support
below 40% indicates the 'frustration level', i.e. too difficult

This is a useful technique for matching pupil and text.

There are a number of readability measures with different features, all of which are discussed in full in Harrison (1980: 51–83). A summary of just four tests is given in alphabetical order; these have been chosen because they are fairly easy to apply, have reasonable validity and over the years have proved to be quite accurate. Generally, they look at sentence length and word length, judged by the number of syllables. The steps for applying each test are shown in table 11.4 as follows:

These are all tests of readability which can be easily applied by teachers and have been shown to be reasonably valid and accurate. However, as noted above, they should be seen as an addition to intuition, not a replacement for it. Furthermore, they do not help in assessing how difficult a science text is to understand. This is where the taxonomy suggested in table 11.1 can help.

Measurements of readability are largely preoccupied with counting syllables and sentence lengths and hunting for polysyllabic words. Is this the most accurate way of assessing the *difficulty* or 'transparency' of a text?

An excellent example of lack of transparency in a sentence is given by T. H. Savory (1953): 'If there are more cows in the world than there are hairs in the tail of any one cow, there must be some cows with the same number of hairs in their tails.' It is extremely difficult to see *through* these words to the objects and facts involved. The sentence is almost opaque. Similarly with many of the words and terms of the physical sciences. Yet the 'opacity' of certain words is not taken into account by any measure of readability.

Opacity is partly related to the taxonomy in table 11.1 (although not wholly, as Savory's example shows). Naming words are most transparent because they point directly to their referent, usually an observable entity. Words in the higher levels, meanwhile, are the most opaque; it is far more difficult to 'see through' these words to any clear meaning or referent.

Consider the word 'oesophagus'. With its five syllables it will be judged less readable than the words 'electron', 'valency' and especially 'mole' (indeed the word 'mole' has the same readability when used to refer to a little furry beast as it does when referring to the most difficult and discussed concept in chemistry). This is surely an unfair way of judging the difficulty or *understandability* of scientific prose.

Recent concentration on the readability of science textbooks has certainly done a useful job in making them more *readable*. But surely a measure of 'understandability' is also appropriate for the pupil? As this is clearly related to the taxonomy in table 11.1, some sort of weighting could be given to words depending on which level they belong to – the presence of a word in level 3.3, for example, could be given the added weighting of two extra syllables.

At present readability measures are unfair on biology textbooks (with their predominance of long naming words in level 1) yet give a deceptive underestimate of the difficulty of many physics texts (with their abundance of short words like 'work', 'energy', 'field', and 'mass' belonging to level 3.2).

READING FOR LEARNING IN SCIENCE

> Since reading is a major strategy for learning in virtually every aspect of education . . . it is the responsibility of every teacher to develop it.
>
> (Bullock, 1975)

Reading is by and large a neglected activity in science classes. Textbooks are often used to provide homework (if schools can afford such a luxury), to guide a practical, to keep pupils busy if they finish too soon or at worst to prop up a piece of apparatus. Traditionally science teachers have had little concern for text. This is unfortunate for many reasons: practising scientists spend a lot of their time reading; much science can be learnt more efficiently from reading than from (say) observing or listening; many pupils enjoy reading; and there is a wide range of reading on science available in children's books, magazines and newspapers.

The starting point in this section is that reading is an important but neglected activity in science education and that one of the responsibilities of science teachers is to teach pupils to read actively, critically and efficiently. This point is also followed up in a later chapter on using newspapers in education.

How can pupils be encouraged to read in science for longer periods? How can their reading become more active, reflective, critical and evaluative?

A project described in Lunzer, Gardner *et al.* (1984) suggested that passive reading occurs when reading tasks are vague and general, rather than specific; and when reading is solitary rather than shared. In contrast, active reading involves reading for specific purposes and the sharing of ideas and small-group work. The project therefore developed a number of strategies for use by teachers. These were called Directed Activities Related to Text, or DARTs (Lunzer, Gardner *et al.*, 1984; Davies and Greene, 1984).

Directed reading activities make pupils focus on important parts of the text and involve them in reflecting on its content. They involve the pupils in discussion, in sharing ideas, and in examining their interpretations of a text. DARTs fall into two broad categories.

1 Reconstruction (or completion) DARTs

These are essentially problem-solving activities that use modified text – the text or diagram has parts missing (words, phrases or labels deleted) or, alternatively, the text is broken into segments which have to be re-ordered into the 'correct' sequence. These activities are game-like and involve hunting for clues in order to complete the task. Pupils generally find them very enjoyable and the results can feed in to pupil writing.

2 Analysis DARTs

These use unmodified text and are more study-like. They are about finding targets in the text. The teacher decides what the 'information categories' of the text are and which of these to focus on. These are the targets which pupils are to search for; this

Table 11.5 DARTS table. A brief summary of directed activities related to text

Reconstruction darts
(Using modified text)

1 *Completing text, diagram or table*
   (a) *Text completion*
       Pupils predict and complete
       deleted words, phrases, or
       sentences (c.f. Cloze procedure).
   (b) *Diagram completion*
       Pupils predict and complete
       deleted labels and/or parts of
       diagrams using text and diagrams
       as sources of information.
   (c) *Table completion*
       Pupils use the text to complete a
       table using rows and columns
       provided by the teacher.

2 *Unscrambling and labelling*
   disordered and segmented text
   (a) Pupils predict logical order or
       time sequence of scrambled
       segments of text, e.g. a set of
       instructions, and re-arrange.
   (b) Pupils classify segments
       according to categories given by
       teacher.

3 *Predicting*
       Pupils predict and write next
       part(s) of text, e.g. an event or an
       instruction, with segments
       presented a section at a time.

Analysis Darts
(using unmodified text)

1 *Marking and labelling*
   (a) *Underlining/marking*
       Pupils search for specified targets
       in text, e.g. words or sentences,
       and mark them in some way.
   (b) *Labelling*
       Pupils label parts of the text,
       using labels provided for them.
   (c) *Segmenting*
       Pupils break the text down into
       segments, or units of information,
       and label these segments.

2 *Recording and constructing*
       Pupils construct diagrams
       showing content and flow of text
       using, for example: a flow
       diagram, a network, a branching
       tree, or a continuum.
   (b) *Table construction*
       Pupils construct and complete
       tables from information given in
       text, making up their own
       headings (rows and columns).
   (c) *Question answering and setting*
       (i) Teachers set questions;
           pupils study text to answer
           them.
       (ii) Pupils make up their own
           questions after studying text
           (either for the teacher to
           answer, or other pupils).
   (d) *Key points/summary*
       Pupils list the key points made by
       the text and/or summarise it.

involves the pupils in locating and categorising the information in the text. When the targets are found they are marked by underlining and/or labelling.

The search for targets can be followed by small-group and class discussion in which the merits of alternative markings are considered and pupils have a further opportunity to modify or revise their judgements.

In each case the text has to be prepared for pupils, or small groups of pupils, so that they can work with it. Many DARTs will involve marking or writing on the text itself. Table 11.5 shows a classification of the various DARTs that could be used with a piece of writing in science.

Put the heads (▶) on the arrows to show the correct direction for the cycle of decay.

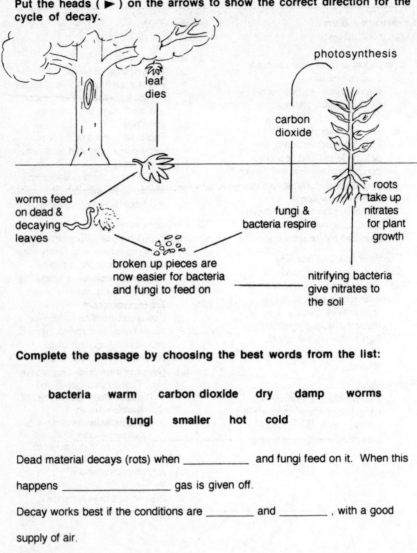

photosynthesis

leaf
dies

carbon
dioxide

worms feed
on dead &
decaying
leaves

fungi &
bacteria respire

roots
take up
nitrates
for plant
growth

broken up pieces are
now easier for bacteria
and fungi to feed on

nitrifying bacteria
give nitrates to
the soil

Complete the passage by choosing the best words from the list:

> **bacteria   warm   carbon dioxide   dry   damp   worms**
>
> **fungi   smaller   hot   cold**

Dead material decays (rots) when _____ and fungi feed on it. When this

happens _____ gas is given off.

Decay works best if the conditions are _____ and _____ , with a good

supply of air.

The decay process is helped by _____. They break the dead material into

smaller pieces so that bacteria and _____ can get into the material.

Figure 11.1 Cycle of Decay
Source: Based on Partridge, 1992: 78

Why is it important that dead animals and plants decay?

On your diagram, show two places where respiration is taking place (mark the spot with the following sign ' R----------->').

Sort this list out into things which can be broken down by bacteria and fungi and things which can't.   Put each object into the following table:

banana skin   **apple**   **tyre**   **leather shoe**

glass bottle   **wooden crate**   **cardboard box**

drink can   **polythene**

Things which can be broken down by bacteria	Things which can't be broken down by bacteria

Notice that the analysis DARTs can be done with the straight, unmodified text – by, for example, underlining certain types of work; labelling segments of the text; making up questions to ask about the text. Text from any source – government pamphlets, leaflets, the *Sun* or the *Daily Mirror* could be used for this purpose. The reconstruction DARTs require modification before use – by, for example, deleting key words from the text or labels from a diagram; chopping up a passage into segments which need re-sequencing to make sense.

THE PUPILS' WRITING

The debate on pupils' writing in science is as long and important as that on reading. We cannot do it justice here (see further reading), but the main questions concern the style in which pupils should write and the purpose of their writing in science education.

Reasons for writing

Until quite recently there seemed to be general agreement in science teaching that the main reasons for writing in science lessons were either to take notes on the content/knowledge required or to write up a piece of practical work (Sutton, 1989). On the latter there was also a consensus that it should follow the pattern: Aim . . . Method/procedure . . . Results . . . Conclusions. This consensus has lasted for at least three reasons:

1   Generations of pupils, some of whom become teachers, feel familiar and comfortable with it.
2   It provides a convenient structure for reporting the kind of practical work that has often been done in schools, i. e. verifying or proving a law, fact or principle.
3   It was believed to reflect the nature of science and the way that scientists actually proceed and write up.

The latter two assumptions are now wide open to question. Practical work (see Chapter 8) is less commonly of the 'To prove . . .' or 'To verify . . .' or 'To demonstrate that . . .' kind. For example, as a result of the National Curriculum, investigational work – which requires a completely different structure to write it up – is becoming more common, even if not every teacher is comfortable with it. Secondly, there have been a number of excellent, readable publications (see Chapter 9) to show this kind of write-up is a false reflection of the way that scientists actually work and report. In short, a theory or 'conclusion' does not actually follow an experiment and the collection of results. On the contrary, it precedes and shapes the experiment: observation is theory led. The reality is not a case of 'data first, theory later' (Sutton, 1989). Experienced scientists such as Medawar (1979) have shown that reports which portray science in this clean, logical, methodical, inductive way are simply a fraud.

Thus changing views on the role of practical work and the nature of science mean that teachers need to re-think the 'writing up' which pupils do. There is also growing recognition that pupils can actually learn science through writing and therefore that modes and styles of writing in science lessons should be tried other than either note taking or write-ups of practicals.

Styles of writing and alleged reasons for each

There is a strong case for widening the range of writing which pupils do in science lessons, beyond the traditional formal report style. Writing could be broadened first of all to allow (on some if not all occasions) subjective and creative reporting – asking for experiences and feelings. Writing could be further extended by asking for imaginative and creative work based on the pupils' learning in science, such as a letter to an MP or the PM/the police/a pressure group, a newspaper report, or any other writing which might involve written role play. Pupils should use their science knowledge and 'specialist science language' (see table 11.2) in this kind of writing, for example, with teachers offering them key words or scientific terms to be included.

In short, three styles of writing, each with a different purpose, are summarised below:

1 the impersonal, the third person, i.e. the formal report, objective and factual
2 the personal, the first person report, i.e. subjective, creative, interpretative reporting of, for example, observations, experiences, feelings, impressions
3 imaginative, expressive writing, for example 'a day in the life of . . .', 'a letter of complaint', 'how it feels to be . . .', 'a journey into . . .', 'shrunk to a millimetre . . .', which makes use of science knowledge and learning. This might also include imaginative drawing, as in Edward De Bono's well-known 'Design a dog-exercising machine/elephant-weighing machine' activity.

To encourage and stimulate different types of writing it will often be valuable to show pupils different models, such as writing from past scientists or past pupils, newspaper reports, science stories. Different types of reading will enhance different styles of writing (Sutton, 1989; Sheeran and Barnes, 1991).

There are so many other issues about pupil writing that cannot be covered here that we will finish with a brief mention of just four:

1 Writing has a range of purposes: it may be a way of keeping a record of content or practical work for future reference, such as revision; it may be used by a teacher to assist classroom control – pupils are almost as quiet when they write as when they eat; it may be a way, for pupils, of learning and clarifying; it can be a way of sharing, if pupils write in a small group. Teachers need to recognise these different purposes and use them.
2 The use of word-processors (on notepad, notebook, laptop or desktop) can be a great aid to some people's writing, whether they have special needs or not. IT can aid presentation, allow drafting and re-drafting, encourage people to get started, allow spell-checking and encourage collaborative writing. In short, the

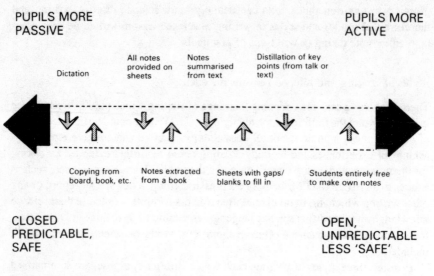

Figure 11.2   Ways of note-making and note-taking

use of IT can change writing and marking quite radically. This is discussed further in Chapter 12.

3   There are various methods of note-making and note-taking that pupils can follow, ranging from the totally passive (straight from the teacher's head to the pupil's notepaper) to the active. The continuum of possibilities is shown in figure 11.2.

Teachers should at least be aware of these different possibilities and examine the reasons why and when they might use them. For example, dictation might be a good means of classroom control but does it have any other value?

4   Why not *start* a lesson with some writing? This is an activity worth trying:

Give each pupil a small piece of blank rough paper as they walk in (small and rough because it is less daunting). Ask them to write on it one of the following:

- a summary of what they did last lesson (perhaps with comment)
- 'Everything you already know about . . .'
- their views on . . .
- what they would like to know about X – for example, food, health, magnetism, nuclear energy, etc.
- the answers to five questions that you pose, such as on the previous lesson
- the key words, say five, that you will use today
- the plan for the day's lesson

You could also give them a sheet of drawings or diagrams on which they are asked to write or comment – for example, illustrating situations where forces are being used and asking pupils to mark in and describe the forces.

Activities like this can be useful to start a lesson for a number of reasons: they are good for classroom control; they can help teachers to start 'from where the pupils are at'; they allow a recap and revision of the previous lesson; they can be a good source of feedback; they allow the use of open questions in a more manageable way than orally. They can also be enjoyable and amusing, especially if pupils write in twos. I thoroughly recommend it.

REFERENCES AND FURTHER READING

The Words of Science

Vygotsky, L. (1978) *Thought and Language*, Cambridge, Mass. : MIT Press.
Two excellent and influential pieces of research were carried out on pupils' understanding of non-technical words in science in the 1970s (words like 'pungent', 'significant', 'average', 'propagate', and 'valid'). They are still useful today.
Cassels, J. R. T. and Johnstone, A. H. (1978) *Understanding of Non-technical Words in Science*, London: Chemical Society Education Division.
Gardner, P. L. (1972) 'Words in Science', part of the Australian Science Education Project, Melbourne.
Clive Sutton's work in this area is excellent, ranging from:
Sutton, C. (1980) 'Science, Language and Meaning', *School Science Review*, 218 (62): 47–56.
to most recently:
Sutton, C. (1992) *Words, Science and Learning*, Milton Keynes: Open University Press.
One of the classics of twentieth-century philosophy which discusses the way language is used is:
Wittgenstein, L. (1958) *Philosophical Investigations*, Oxford: Blackwell.
In the science field, another classic from the same era is:
Savory, T. H. (1953) *The Language of Science*, London: Andre Deutsch.
The book which really opened up the language-in-education debate is:
Barnes, D., Britton, J., and Rosen, H. (1969) *Language, the Learner and the School*, Harmondsworth: Penguin.
Another important book is:
Stubbs, M. (1983) *Language, Schools and Classrooms* (2nd ed.), London: Routledge.
An excellent general book on classroom language and ritual, drawing on the work of Vygotsky, is:
Edwards, D. and Mercer, N. (1987) *Common Knowledge*, London: Methuen.
The ASE manual *Race, Equality and Science Teaching* (1991), Hatfield: ASE, gives a useful discussion on terms such as 'Third World', 'black', 'under-developed' and 'race' which are sometimes used thoughtlessly (see their Appendix 2, p. 176). It also contains activities for teachers on 'Language and Learning in Science' (pp. 85–8) and 'Children's Writing' (pp. 89–93).
Gill, D. and Levidow, L. (1987) *Anti-Racist Science Teaching*, London: Free Association, also contains practical discussions of racism in the language of science and pseudo-science.

Writing, and Teaching with, Text

Barlex, D. and Carre, C. (1985) *Visual Communication in Science*, Cambridge: Cambridge University Press (discussion and guidelines on using visual material in science teaching)
Chall, J. and Conard, S. (1991) *Should Textbooks Challenge Students?* , New York:

Teachers' College Press (argues that textbooks should not be so hard that students cannot read and understand them, nor so easy that students are un-challenged and bored by them).

Lloyd-Jones, R. (1985) *How to Produce Better Worksheets*, Cheltenham: Stanley Thornes (a useful guide on producing classroom material with examples that can be photocopied).

Newton, D. P. (1990) *Teaching with Text*, London: Kogan Page.

Partridge, T. (1992) *Starting Science: Book J*, Oxford: Oxford University Press.

Shortland, M. and Gregory, J. (1991) *Communicating Science: a Handbook*, Harlow: Longman.

Reading and Readability

Bullock, A. (1975) *A Language for Life*, London: HMSO.

Carrick, T. (1978) 'Problems for Assessing the Readability of Biology Textbooks for First Examinations', *Journal of Biological Education*, 12: 113–21.

Harrison, C. (1980) *Readability in the Classroom*, Cambridge: Cambridge University Press.

Johnson, K. (1979) 'Readability', *School Science Review* 60 (212): 562–8.

Knutton, S. (1983) 'Chemistry Textbooks: Are They Readable?' *Education in Chemistry* 20 (3): 100–5.

Long, R. (1991) 'Readability for Science', *School Science Review*, 262 (73): 21–33.

Zakaluk, B. and Samuels, J. (1988) *Readability: Its Past, Present and Future*, Newark, NJ: IRA.

Encouraging Active Reading

Three accounts of active reading containing discussion and valuable classroom ideas are:
Bulman, L. (1985) *Teaching Language and Study Skills in Secondary Science*, London: Heinemann (this also includes useful sections on readability, pupils' writing, teacher talk and writing worksheets).

Davies, F. and Greene, T. (1984) *Reading for Learning in the Sciences*, London: Oliver and Boyd.

Lunzer, E. and Gardner, P. L. (eds) (1984) *Learning from the Written Word*, London: Schools Council/Oliver and Boyd.

Pupils' Writing

Medawar, Sir Peter (1979) 'Is the Scientific Paper a Fraud?', reprinted in Brown, J., Cooper, A. *et al.* (1986) *Science in Schools*, Milton Keynes: Open University Press (a Nobel Prize winner tells us what scientific write-ups are really like. See also: Medawar, P. (1979) *Advice to a Young Scientist*, London: Harper & Row.).

Sheeran, Y. and Barnes, D. (1991) *School Writing*, Milton Keynes: Open University Press. (has an excellent chapter on 'Writing in Science').

Sutton, C. (1981) *Communicating in the Classroom*, London: Hodder & Stoughton (chapters 1 and 2 on writing).

—— (1989) 'Writing and Reading in Science', in Millar, R. (ed.), *Doing Science: Images of Science in Science Education*, pp.137–59, Lewes: Falmer Press.

Theme C
Enriching science teaching

12 Using IT in teaching and learning science

Information technology (IT) can be a valuable tool in learning and teaching both the processes and content of science. This chapter looks at different uses of IT in science education by examining their place in the curriculum, their benefits . . . and their drawbacks.

INTRODUCTION

Where does IT fit into the National Curriculum?

Information technology (IT) in the school curriculum is not only a 'cross-curricular skill', it is also a component of the technology curriculum (a foundation subject) and an element of the other subject pillars of the NC. In the science documents it appears in the programmes of study (PoS), largely as a tool but also as an object of study:

- At key stage (KS) 3 pupils should begin to 'use information and data accessed from a computer' (IT as a tool) and 'be able to identify the main features of an information transmission system and the ways in which data are coded, handled and transmitted' (IT as a subject of study).
- In the general introduction to KS 4 we read that pupils should use 'databases and spreadsheets in their work' (in reality, of course, many will have used them well before this stage).
- In the PoS for AT 1 pupils need to search for patterns in data and make predictions (here IT is an obvious tool); to use sensors such as temperature, moisture, light and pressure; to use computers to 'store, process and retrieve information'; and to 'control and collect data during experiments'.
- At KS 4, pupils will need to use IT for 'pattern searching in complex data' and to gather, record and present data in a 'full range of forms'. IT also has a role in accessing and organising data 'relevant to their study of science' and in using programmable systems to control external devices.

- IT appears explicitly in only one of the other attainment targets – AT 4. Here, the PoS require that pupils should use 'logic gates with input sensors and output devices' in decision making and control and, later (KS 4), they should 'consider the implications of information and control technology for everyday life'.

So much for the 'teaching contract' aspects of IT in the science curriculum. What about the 'assessment contract', i.e. the statements of attainment (SoAs)? Surprisingly, IT appears explicitly in only one of the SoAs: pupils should 'know how switches, relays, variable resistors, sensors and logic gates can be used to solve simple problems' (AT 4, level 5a).

These statements in the statutory guidance indicate clearly that the use of IT in science might well involve word-processing and desktop publishing; database and spreadsheet use; communications; data-logging; simulations and modelling; graphics; interactive media of any kind; and control hardware and software. The possibilities are summarised in table 12.1; the list will surely grow as IT itself progresses and becomes more cheaply available to schools. This chapter considers, albeit briefly, these various uses. But first, we need a framework for understanding why, how and when IT can be of value in science education.

Table 12.1 Uses and applications of IT indicated in the PoS for science, key stages 3

Word Processing/Desktop publishing e.g. in presenting data	*Control* e.g. controlling experiments; controlling external devices
Databases and spreadsheets e.g. in pattern searching; hypothesising; recording and presenting data; accessing and organising data	*Simulations and Modelling* e.g. predicting and searching for patterns
Communications e.g. identifying the features of a transmission system; data coding and handling	*Data-logging* e.g. using sensors; gathering and recording data
Interactive media (CD, Video-disc, etc.) e.g. accessing data; searching	*Graphics* e.g. presenting data

Why use IT in science education?

We can start to answer this by first listing some of the things that modern IT systems (hardware and software) are good at:

- collecting and storing large amounts of data
- performing complex calculations on stored data rapidly
- processing large amounts of data and displaying it in a variety of formats
- helping to present and communicate information

These capabilities all have direct relevance to the process of education, and at the same time raise important issues for education. One issue concerns the use of computers as labour-saving devices. As listed above, computers can collect data at a rapid rate and perform calculations on it extremely quickly. But the question arises: should the computer (in an *educational* context) be used to collect, process and display rather than the learner? In other words, does the use of a computer in saving labour take away an important educational experience for the learner? A similar issue appears in the use of computers and electronic calculators to perform complex calculations rapidly. This may be desirable in some learning situations, for example if the performance of a tedious calculation by human means actually impedes or 'clutters up' a learning process. But it can also be argued that the ability to perform complex calculations rapidly should be one of the *aims* of education, not something to be replaced by it.

The distinction between what counts as *authentic* (i.e. desirable and purposeful) and *inauthentic* (i.e. unnecessary and irrelevant) labour in the learning process is a central one in considering the use of IT in education. The notions of 'inauthentic' and 'authentic' labour will be revisited later.

It is also worth noting that computers do exactly what they are instructed to do, very quickly, as many times as they are told to do it. On the one hand, this means that they are not (or at least not yet) capable of making autonomous or independent judgements, or personal interpretations. However, it is also the case that they do not become tired, bored, hungry, irritable, angry or impatient, or liable to error. This may place them at an advantage in some situations as compared to teachers! It has been said that one of the reasons why children appear to enjoy learning with computers is precisely because of their impersonal, inhuman 'qualities'.

One final point on the 'abilities' of computers is worth stressing. Computers can, in a sense, speed up, or slow down, reality. As Kahn (1985) puts it: '[T]hey operate outside the viscous flow of time in which humans perform tasks.' This is an important point which will be elaborated upon and discussed when the use of computer simulations in education is considered. Computer simulations do, in some way, distort time – and perhaps reality.

Types of IT use in education

Now we look at IT from the learner's perspective. There are a number of ways of classifying IT use in education. The most useful classification dates back to 1977 and was produced by Kemmis, Atkin and Wright (Kemmis *et al.*, 1977). This seminal paper identified four 'paradigms' by which students learn through the use of IT (a paradigm is defined as a 'pattern, example or model' by the Oxford English dictionary). They are:

- the instructional paradigm
- the revelatory paradigm
- the conjectural paradigm
- the emancipatory paradigm

We will consider each one briefly in turn, but further reading is necessary to consider them fully and reflectively. (See, for example, Rushby, 1979; Blease, 1986; Wellington, 1985; Sewell, 1990.)

The Instructional Paradigm

The overall aim in this paradigm is to teach a learner a given piece of subject matter, or to impart a specific skill. It involves breaking a learning task into a series of sub-tasks, each with its own stated prerequisites and objectives. These separate tasks are then structured and sequenced to form a coherent whole.

Computer-assisted learning of this type is given names like 'skill and drill', 'drill and practice' and 'instructional dialogue'.

The Revelatory Paradigm

The second type of IT use involves guiding a student through a process of learning by discovery. The subject matter and its underlying model or theory are gradually 'revealed' to the student as he or she uses the program.

The revelatory paradigm is exemplified in educational programs by numerous simulations, of various types including: real (such as an industrial process), historical (for example, empathising with a historic event), theoretical (such as the particle theory of matter), or even imaginary (such as a city of the future).

The Conjectural Paradigm

This third category involves increasing control by the student over the computer by allowing students to manipulate and test their own ideas and hypotheses, for example by allowing modelling.

Modelling must be distinguished from *simulation*. Every simulation involves using a simplified representation, i.e. a model, of some situation, but in a simulation the model is ready-created by the programmer. The user can then alter and experiment with the external conditions and variables affecting the model, but cannot tamper with the model itself, i.e. internal conditions. In modelling, however, the user creates a model of the situation, and then may go on to test it, for example by seeing how well it represents and predicts reality.

For example, a model can be formed of some physical phenomenon, such as the expansion of a liquid or the motion of a projectile. The patterns predicted by the model could then be compared, say, with the results of an experiment.

The Emancipatory Paradigm

The fourth and final paradigm involves using a computer as a labour-saving device, a tool which relieves mental drudgery. As such, it can be used for calculating, for collecting and tabulating data, for statistical analysis, or even for drawing graphs. In this type of computer aided learning (CAL) the learner uses the computer as and when he or she wants to as an unintelligent, tedium-relieving slave in aiding his or her learning task. This relies on the distinction made earlier between authentic labour and inauthentic labour.

The four proposed paradigms are summarised in table 12.2. The focus (or locus)

Table 12.2 Types of learning in science with IT

Instructional	Revelatory (simulation)	Conjectural (modelling)	Emancipatory (labour-saving)
Drill-and-practice for example, structured Q&A dialogue in a definite sequence Learner is led by computer	*Of real situations:* Trying out an existing model Varying external conditions Discovering the nature of a model, i.e. guided discovery learning *Of imaginary situations:* Games of adventure, logic and skill Educational games	Making and testing a model of reality Testing ideas and hypotheses Drawing conclusions and discovering patterns from a set of data, for example using spreadsheets	Computer as a labour-saving device for, for example, calculating, drawing graphs, capturing data, retrieving information, word processing, storing data
COMPUTER IN CONTROL Subject-centred Content-laden	←	→	LEARNER IN CONTROL Learner-centred Content-free Open-ended

of control changes from the computer to the learner, as the type of IT use shifts along the paradigms. Each one is considered in turn in this chapter.
[There are other ways of classifying educational software and types of IT use in education. These are summarised in Scaife and Wellington (1993: 25–7).]

INSTRUCTIONAL USES OF IT

It is worth distinguishing between two types of 'instructional' uses of IT: drill-and-practice and tutorial use.

Drill-and-practice

This mode of learning has a long history associated with repetition, rote learning, drill, reinforcement and programmed learning. In CAL terms its basic purpose is to provide software that gives practice and repetition in the learning of either processes (skills) or content – most commonly content. This is often done through the use of a highly structured program, taking the user through a certain route, providing reinforcement and feedback along the way.

What advantages can it offer?

- Both learners and teachers who have an ambivalent attitude towards IT can soon become familiar with a drill-and-practice program. Simply loading the program and following screen instructions is often enough to get started. For many teachers it is a convenient starting point or launching pad to the further use of IT in the classroom.
- Drill-and-practice CAL can offer a non-threatening, individualised learning environment that suits certain learners. Students can proceed at their own pace, will not be subject to verbal rebuke or the body-language equivalent, and can (given the right software) choose their own path through material.
- Partly because of the above point, the use of CAL can be motivating. The use of rewards and reinforcement, if used carefully and thoughtfully, can increase motivation and attention.
- Finally, the use of drill-and-practice can lead to certain basic skills becoming automatic. This is a term used by Gagne (1985) who talks of the value of low-level skills, such as letter recognition or simple multiplication, becoming automatic. This 'automaticity' is a prerequisite for carrying out higher level, more complex activities. Through automaticity the learner is able to give more attention to the main tasks in science, or to higher level activities such as problem-solving.

Tutorial programs

A more sophisticated version of the instructional use of IT lies in the tutorial program. Again, its basic purpose is to teach a topic by interaction between computer and learner.

With drill software, if the learner makes a mistake the program does not identify the nature of the error and then go on to provide tuition to remedy it. However, with tutorial programs an increased number of options will 'respond' to learners and guide them along appropriate routes through the material.

In a sense, therefore, a good tutorial program (whether simply computer-based or using interactive video) is responsive and interactive. As Sewell (1990: 33) summarises it:

> . . . a good tutorial will have an internal model or representation not just of the material to be learned, but also of the likely learning strategies and ways in which learners are likely to respond to the material. In practice, few tutorials for school

use have achieved this level of sophistication, although progress is being made in the field of 'intelligent tutoring systems' which aim to satisfy the above requirements.

A small number of examples of instructional CAL which are being used in schools is given in table 12.3 merely to illustrate the type of skill-and-drill/tutorial software currently available.

Table 12.3 Some examples of instructional CAL in science

Structure and Bonding: Explains and tests atomic structure, electronic configuration and bonding using a random selection of elements and compounts from the first twenty elements of the Periodic Table.
Supplier: AVP

The Mole Concept: Using the technique of Computer Synchronised Audio (a voice-track combined with computer software), the concept of a mole is demonstrated and explained. Graphics and animation help to introduce the terms 'nucleus', 'proton', 'electron' and 'relative atomic mass'.
Supplier: BBC Publications

Uniformly Accelerated Motion: Also employs the tutorial technique of Computer Synchronised Audio. The essential theory of the subject is explained and illustrated not only by graphs but also by graphics animations. The program gives a thorough treatment of uniform velocity, uniform acceleration, the idea of terminal velocity and the acceleration due to gravity.
Supplier: BBC Software Publications

Balancing Equations: A revision and practice program in which pupils have to supply correct formulae for compounds in a chemical equation and balance the equation.
Supplier: Longman

The Human Skeleton: Gives a set of views of the skeleton, from front side and rear, with diagrams of the skull, vertebrae, ribs, girdles and limbs.
Supplier: AVP

The Four-Stroke Engine: The four-stroke cycle is demonstrated in stages for a single cylinder, including the valve action, the states of the gasses and the crank positions at each stage. The program illustrates two advantages over a traditional approach to teaching about the four-stroke cycle using posters; these are the animation facility and the option of referring back to the demonstrations as needed during a user's attempts at the tutorial questions.
Supplier: AVP

Electric Circuits: A package of four programs for teaching electrical components and symbols, AC/DC, Ohm's Law and simple circuits on a simulated circuit board.
Supplier: AVP

Animated Circuits for Education (ACE): A more sophisticated program using dynamic circuit diagrams to reach series and parallel, resistance, AC, diodes and rectification and transistor circuits.
Supplier: Bradford Technology

SIMULATION AND MODELLING

Types of simulation in science education

It is useful to make some fairly crude distinctions between types of simulation which should act as a rough guide:

1   direct copies of existing laboratory activities, such as titrations
2   simulations of industrial processes, such as the manufacture of sulphuric acid, bridge building
3   simulations of processes that are:

   - too dangerous
   - too slow, for example evolution, population growth, an ecosystem of any kind
   - too fast, for example collisions
   - too small, for example sub-atomic changes

   to be carried out in a school or college environment.
4   simulations involving non-existent entities, such as ideal gases, frictionless surfaces, perfectly elastic objects
5   simulation of models or theories, for example kinetic theory, the wave model of light

Why use computer simulations in science teaching?

The main advantages of using simulations can be summarised as follows:

- **Cost:** Money can be saved in directly copying some laboratory experiments, either by reducing outlay on consumables, such as chemicals and test-tubes, or by removing the need to buy increasingly costly equipment in the first place.
- **Time:** Using a computer simulation instead of a genuine practical activity may save time, although some teachers are finding that a good computer simulation in which pupils fully explore all the possibilities may take a great deal longer.
- **Safety:** Some activities simply cannot be carried out in a school setting because they are unsafe.
- **Motivation:** There is a feeling, though with little evidence to support it, that computer simulations motivate pupils in science education more than traditional practical work.
- **Control:** The use of a simulation allows ease of control of variables, which traditional school practical work does not. This may lead to unguided discovery learning by pupils who are encouraged to explore and hypothesise for themselves (i.e. the revelatory paradigm).
- **Management:** Last, but certainly not least, computer simulations offer far fewer management problems to teachers than do many traditional activities. Problems of handing out equipment, collecting it back again and guarding against damage and theft are removed at a stroke. Problems of supervision, timing and clearing

up virtually disappear. Indeed, who needs an expensive and noisy laboratory, it might be argued?

Dangers of simulation

So much for the supposed advantages of computer simulations. What of the dangers in using computer simulations in science education? The main dangers of using simulations lie in the hidden messages they convey, classified as follows:

- **Variables:** Simulations give pupils the impression that variables in a physical process can be easily, equally, and independently controlled. This message is conveyed by simulations of industrial processes, ecological systems, and laboratory experiments. In reality not all variables in a physical situation can be as easily, equally, and as independently controlled as certain simulations suggest.
- **Unquestioned models, facts and assumptions:** Every simulation is based on a certain model of reality. Users are only able to manipulate factors and variables within that model; they cannot tamper with that model itself. Moreover, they are neither encouraged nor able to question its validity. The model is hidden from the user. All simulations are based on certain assumptions. These are often embedded in the model itself. What are these assumptions? Are they ever revealed to the user? All simulations rely on certain facts, or data. Where do these facts come from? What sources have been used?
- **Caricatures of reality:** Any model is an idealisation of reality, i.e. it ignores certain features in order to concentrate on others. Some idealisations are worse than others. In some cases, a model may be used of a process not fully understood. Other models may be deceptive, misleading or downright inaccurate; they provide caricatures of reality, rather than representations of it.
- **Confusion with reality:** Pupils are almost certain to confound the programmer's model of reality with reality itself – such is the current power and potency of the computer, at least until its novelty as a learning aid wears off. Students may then be fooled into thinking that because they can use and understand a model of reality they can also understand the more complex real phenomena it represents or idealises. Perhaps more dangerously, the 'micro world' of the computer creates a reality of its own. The world of the micro, the keyboard and the VDU can assume its own reality in the mind of the user – a reality far more alluring and manageable than the complicated and messy world outside. The 'scientific world' presented in computer simulations may become as attractive and addictive as the micro worlds of arcade games as noted by Weizenbaum (1984) and Turkle (1984).
- **Double idealisations:** All the dangers and hidden messages discussed so far become increasingly important in a simulation which uses a computer model of a scientific model or scientific theory which itself is an idealisation of reality, i.e. the idealisation involved in modelling is doubly dangerous in simulations which involve a model of a model. A simulation of kinetic theory, for example, is itself based on a model of reality.

Safeguards in using simulations

Given that science teachers will continue to use simulations, what safeguards can be taken to reduce these dangers?

First, all teachers, and thereby pupils, must be fully conscious that the models they use in a computer simulation are personal, simplified and perhaps value-laden idealisations of reality. Models are made by humans. Students must be taught to examine and question these models.

Secondly, the facts, data, assumptions, and even the model itself which are used by the programmer must be made clear and available to the user. This can be done in a teacher's guide or in the documentation with the program. All sources of data should be stated and clearly referenced. Any student using a simulation can then be taught to examine and question the facts, assumptions and models underlying it.

By building these safeguards into the use of science simulations, this type of CAL in science may then move slightly towards the right of the continuum shown in table 12.2. Learners will be more in control of their own learning, rather than being controlled by the computer programmer.

Examples of simulation programs

A wide range of simulations is now available for school science, ranging from simulations of chemical collisions, the manufacture of ethanol or the siting of a blast furnace to the simulation of electric and magnetic fields, electricity use in the home, wave motion, floating and sinking, a 'Newtonian' world of frictionless movement and the construction of bridges. For the life sciences, simulations are available on pond life, the human eye, nerves, the life of the golden eagle and predator-prey relationships. Table 12.4 gives a small selection of examples.

MODELLING

In many ways, modelling in science education is a step up from simulation use. Every simulation involves using a simplified representation, i.e. a model, of some situation, but in a simulation the model is ready-created by the programmer. The user can then only alter and experiment with the external conditions and variables affecting the model but cannot tamper with the model itself, i.e. with internal conditions. In modelling, however, users create a model of the situation or a scientific process for themselves and then may go on to test it, for example by seeing how well it represents and predicts reality.

If a phenomenon, process, event or system can be described in terms of arithmetical, algebraic or statistical operations then it can be modelled. For example, a model can be formed of some physical phenomenon, such as the expansion of a liquid or the motion of a projectile. The patterns predicted by the model could then be compared with the results of an experiment. Clearly this involves far more control by the learner over the computer (see table 12.2).

Table 12.4 Some simulation programs for science

Gravity Pack: Contains three programs that simulate the motion of objects under the influence of gravity. The programs allow more control than is possible in laboratory experiments, so users can explore the characteristics of gravity and gravitational fields more effectively. A similar program is *Motion in Space*.
Supplier: Cambridge Micro Software

The World of Newton: Allows the user to investigate a microworld unfettered by the complications of the real world. The program uses a small, oblong object which can be moved around the screen according to Newton's Laws of Motion. The simulation illustrates the capacity of computer to model idealised situations.
Supplier: Longman

Predator-Prey relationships: How do the populations of predators and prey change over yearly periods? This program lets users investigate. The user supplies numbers, size, population, etc. The program predicts predator-prey relations over annual cycles.
Supplier: AVP

Population Pack: Programs on human population growth and on a Malthusian model of population, food and energy supplies.
Supplier: Longman

Bridge Building: Allows students to evaluate three different types of bridge (beam, Warren, arch). Pupils can choose different features of the bridge (such as material and arch depth) and evaluate the different factors important in bridge building.
Supplier: Longman

Make a Million: An educational game involving the industrial production of a variety of substances and electricity from basic raw materials. The processes involved are blasting, electrolysis, fractionating, generating electricity and making and adding acid.
Supplier: AVP

Watts in your Home: A simulation program showing energy/electricity use in a typical home. It provides an interesting way of comparing the costs of energy-consuming applicances in domestic use.
Supplier: Cambridge Micro Software (CUP)

Moving Molecules: A simulation based on the kinetic theory model which allows pupils to 'experiment' with particles inside a vessel by varying pressure, temperature or volume.
Supplier: CUP

Three Ecological Simulations:

1 *Ecology Foodwebs:* A three-stage package: an animated guide to foodwebs, an interactive section and a quiz. It uses games-style presentation.
2 *Lake Web* and *Bio-Wood:* Similar programs which challenge the user to survive in an environment. Survival depends on deciding what to eat, what to ignore and what to escape from.
3 *Golden Eagle:* Pupils can run a wildlife reserve with the aim of doubling the golden eagle population. It encourages systematic record keeping and learning from repeated attempts.
Supplier: AVP

Two Programs on Genetics and Evolution:

1 *The Blind Watchmaker:* Demonstrates that variations in organisms are due to

reproduction in which gene mutation occurs. The user plays the part of the environment, determining which organisms are adaptively favoured.

2　*Survival of the Fittest:* Investigates genetic principles underlying evolution. It includes a population division facility. Both programs offer an insight into the process of evolution, which would otherwise be extremely difficult to illustrate.

Supplier: SPA.

Encouraging pupils to create, use and test their own models in science will have great educational value, especially if good modelling programs are used which take care of the 'inauthentic labour' of programming, calculating and presenting, leaving the student free to devise, explore and test the model.

Several programs have been tried and tested in education. The *Cellular Modelling System* (Ogborn, 1986) is a good example of a spreadsheet (see later) modelling system. Other programs focus more on the outcome of a model than on the process – for example the *Dynamic Modelling System* (Ogborn, 1984). In the MEU/Cymru materials (Owen, Pritchard and Rowlands, 1992), modelling examples with the following programs are described: *Logicworks, Excel and Schema* (both spreadsheets), *Expert Builder, Stella, Hypercard* for the Apple.

Modelling may appear to be a high-level activity, beyond the ability of many pupils. But it seems that with increasingly user-friendly, icon driven software (see figure 12.1), a range of pupils can try modelling in science lessons. It is, after all, an essential part of 'real science' and scientific research in almost every discipline. It is also an important activity in industry and commerce. Finally, the use of modelling links closely with the skills and processes of Sc 1, scientific investigation, i.e. predicting, hypothesising, fair testing, and evaluating. In short, both modelling and simulation can develop the 'what happens if . . .?' approach which is the essence of science.

DATABASES

In its simplest form a database is nothing more than an organised collection of information. Thus an address book, a telephone directory, a card index, and a school register are all examples of databases. They all contain data, which can convey information to people and which is organised in a more or less systematic way, in alphabetical order. The advantage of organising data is partly for ease of use and access to information, but also depends on the fact that well-organised and structured data can be used to show patterns and trends and to allow people to make and test hypotheses or hunches. Therein lies the educational value of a database. Having an organised and clearly structured collection of data allows and even encourages people to derive information and knowledge from it.

The advantages of storing, organising and retrieving information from a computer system are worth considering briefly. First, using magnetic or optical media (floppy discs, 'laser discs', CD-ROM, etc.), huge amounts of data can be stored in a relatively compact form. Secondly, data can be retrieved from a computer

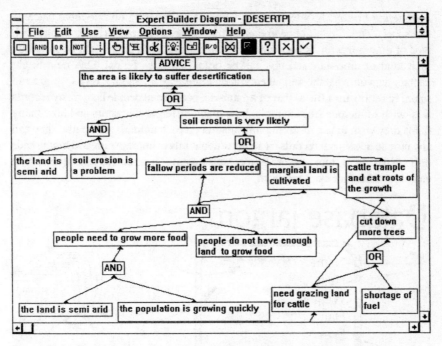

Figure 12.1 Studying desert formation using Expert Builder. This model was constructed by a pair of year 10 students who were studying how deserts are formed. They worked on a model that had been partially built by the teacher and modified it to incorporate a range of factors that had contributed to desertification. They then tested their model with reference to specific examples of desertification.
Source: Mary Webb, The Advisory Unit for Microtechnology in Education, Hertfordshire

database quickly. Thirdly, data retrieval from a computer database is relatively flexible. For example, to find a number in a paper-based telephone directory from a name and initials would be almost as quick as finding it from a computer-based directory. But consider the situation in reverse. How long would it take to find a person's name and initials with only their telephone number? With a suitable computer database this could be done as quickly as a search in the other direction. Fourthly, changes (editions, additions and subtractions) to a computer database can be made more easily and more painlessly than to, say, a card- or paper-based database – in a way similar to the use of word-processors in amending and re-drafting text.

The huge storage potential, speed, and flexibility of computer databases all have implications for their educational value.

Records, fields and files

Certain terms are generally used in connection with databases, and these are worth considering briefly. A 'file' is a collection of information on one topic (such as dinosaurs). This file might be organised into separate 'records' (for example, each type of dinosaur with its own name). Within each record data might be stored on each kind of dinosaur, and this can be organised into 'fields'. One field might contain data on what the animal eats, another on its size, another on its weight and so on. In setting up a file as part of a database, people can decide how many records they wish to include (for example, how many different dinosaurs and how many fields they wish to use in storing information on each animal). Of course, they can always add additional records (if we hear about more dinosaurs, or add more fields or if we decide to store new or more complex data). Thus records and fields can be added to, edited, or even removed.

Database jargon

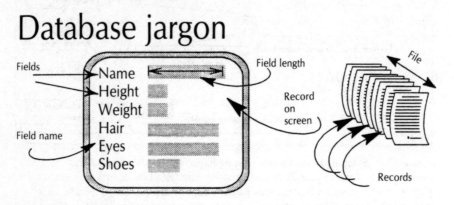

Figure 12.2 Database jargon
Source: Frost, R. 1991

Databases in science and technology education

What can databases be used for in the science and technology curriculum? A general framework would include the following:

1   For recording data collected during an investigation or an experiment: Data can be entered directly on to the database and stored on a computer-based medium (e.g., a disc).
2   In allowing students to sift or browse through their own or someone else's data using the computer. This kind of serendipitous learning (learning by browsing) can often be very valuable and is commonly underestimated.
3   Students can also explore data in a more systematic manner: They can:

   (a) look for patterns
   (b) put forward hunches
   (c) make predictions
   (d) suggest and test hypotheses

(e) draw and discuss interpretations

4 Better display: With suitable software the computer system can be used to display and present data so that it conveys information in an attractive and clear way (cf. spreadsheets).

The use of databases in science supports and enhances many of the so-called process skills in the science curriculum such as classifying, hypothesising and testing. This applies equally to textual and numerical data stored on the database.

Database programs and ideas for their use

Databases in use in UK schools include *Grass, Quest, Key, Dataease, Revolver, Clipboard, Find, DIY, Ourfacts* and *Excel*. The examples in table 12.5 illustrate some possible uses, with examples of data files.

SPREADSHEETS

A spreadsheet is, quite literally, a table for information which has rows and columns. A spreadsheet computer program allows you to present and manipulate that information for your own use. The rows are usually given numbers and the columns letters so that each particular box or cell on the sheet can be easily identified, for example A1, C7 (see figure 12.3).

Spreadsheet Jargon

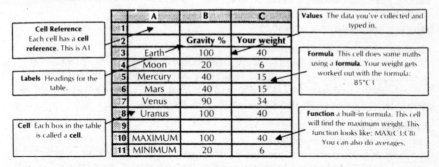

Figure 12.3 Spreadsheet jargon
Source: Frost, R. 1991

Numbers or text can be put into these cells and then different operations can be done on the numbers. These operations are decided by the user. For example, if column E shows distance travelled and column F shows time taken, then column G could be made to show speed, i.e. the number in column E divided by the number in column F is put into column G in every row.

Table 12.5 Some uses of databases and datafiles

Key

Key is a data-handling package that is ideal for school pupils and can be used with datafiles such as: Energy, Our Neighbours in Space, Rocks and Minerals, Acid Drops, Birds of Britain, Mammals, Materials, Minibeasts, Periodic Table, Weather and Climate, World Population. The datafile Life and Death of a River allows users to explore a case of river pollution and to see what can be done to clear it up. Weather and Climate is a datafile with data from eighty weather stations around the world. Pupils use this to analyse world weather patterns. Diet and fitness can be assessed using the datafile Fit to Eat. Users can analyse the food they eat and estimate fitness in terms of flexibility, strength, endurance and body fat.
Supplier: Anglia TV

Databases on Food

Pupils can investigate and analyse the nutritional content of foods with the databases *Micro-diet* (Longman Logotron), *Food* (Hutchinson Software), *Balance Your Diet* (Cambridge Micro Software), *The Food Problem* (ILECC),*Diets* (AVP).

Electricity in the UK

(interactive database on the use of energy and electricity in the United Kingdom)
Contains detailed information about the past and present use of energy and electricity in the UK. It also acts as a 'simulated' laboratory that allows users to estimate the likely future demand for these commodities and see how these demands might be met.
Supplier: UKAEA Education Service

BP Energy File

A database of world energy use, regularly updated using data from readily available sources. Pupils can use this program to study energy use in different places and of different fuels.
Supplier: BP Educational Resources

Chemdata and Periodic Properties

Chemdata (Longman) and *Periodic Properties* (Hodder & Stoughton, Sevenoaks) both allow students to 'discover' the relationships between the properties of the chemical elements. Both can display data in a table or in graphical form. Datafiles are provided on melting point, boiling point, density and many other properties.

Earth in Space

(database and teletype simulation)
The *Earth in Space* curriculum package includes two discs. One is a teletype simulation, which simulates information and beliefs related to the solar system (for example, Galileo's views compared with those of the Church). The other disc stores a database (DIY base) of facts on the solar system. The package contains a large number of activities and teachers' notes related to the two discs.

Pupils Constructing their Own Database

Any database program can be used here, for example, *Find, DIY, Key* and *Grass*, or any program which a school can acquire. Pupils can, for example, make their own databases of domestic electrical appliances. For each appliance, notes can be made of the name, its power rating (in watts) and the average time it is used. Other examples might be databases on: birds, animals, food, acids, elements, people, metals, famous bridges, materials, fuels . . . almost any area of science.

Thus spreadsheets in the classroom could be used for helping pupils to:

- record their results from an experiment
- sort the results out
- display the results neatly and, with some programs, attractively, for example as a pie chart, graph or scattergram
- do calculations on the results using the connections between rows and columns, for example multiplying or dividing one by another; adding two columns to produce a third
- looking for patterns in practical results or indeed data from any source

With more sophisticated spreadsheets, pupils can make more decisions about the way their data is entered, stored, manipulated and presented. Spreadsheets can be used for modelling by allowing students to test 'what happens if . . .?'. The effect of altering variables can be seen, as well as that of altering the connection between the variables. The spreadsheet takes away the drudgery of doing one calculation after another on a set of results so that more time can be spent in thinking about them and asking questions.

Some possible uses in the science classroom include:

- looking at the characteristics of people in the class and searching for patterns
- studying people's daily or weekly diet
- looking at the factors involved in heat loss from buildings and studying ways of minimising it
- tabulating and studying results from experiments involving (say) current voltage and resistance; length of pendulum and time for swing; suspended mass and length of a spring; force, mass and acceleration
- studying the power, time used and cost of different domestic electrical appliances.

Some examples of spreadsheets currently in use include: *Grasshopper*, *Excel*, *Logistix*, *Pipedream* (various versions) and *Eureka*.

DATA-LOGGING

Science students have been recording or 'logging' information with a paper and pencil for generations. The onset of cheap, portable IT in the classroom means that data-logging can now be done with the aid of computers. The basic elements of a data-logging system are shown in figure 12.4. The sensor responds to some property in the environment – this may be (say) a sound, temperature, humidity, pressure, position, oxygen level or light sensor. A message is then sent via an interface box to the computer, through one of its input ports. The computer, using appropriate software, will display the data and allow pupils to do things with it, such as draw graphs, do calculations, look at sections of a graph, plot different variables against each other, and so on.

Data-logging systems for schools have developed enormously since the early days in the 1980s, mainly in their user-friendliness and portability. A good system will now have a range of sensors that can be used at the same time; an interface that is battery driven and can be used away from the computer (remotely); and software that can do lots of different jobs (multi-tasking) and is easy to use, with icons and good graphics. There are many examples now in use, and different teachers and learners seem to favour different systems – new ones, as with most of IT, are developing all the time. Some common examples are:

1   *First Sense* and *DL-Plus* (Philip Harris): include software and can be used for the whole of the secondary age range, with a wide range of sensors
2   *Softlab* (NCET): software for data-logging that involves an approach, using icons and a Windows environment
3   *Sense and Control* (Educational Electronics): a data-logging interface that can accept a wide variety of sensors and can be used remotely. It can be used with a range of software, e.g. *Insight* (Longman Logotron).
4   *Log-IT:* a compact, very portable data-logger for remote use or when connected to a computer (reviewed in Scaife, 1991).
5   *The Motion Sensor:* dedicated to recording data about the position of objects in front of it, using a sonic beam. With its support material and software it is ideal for teaching about motion by allowing pupils to study their own movement (Barton and Rogers, 1991).

The questions that must be asked of any IT use in science education are: What advantages does it offer? and How can it extend and enrich science education?

There is some agreement on what computers can add to the process of data-logging:

- They can record data about events that take place very quickly – for example, a falling weight; the surge of current when a light is switched on; the discharge of some capacitors; a magnet falling through a coil.
- On the other hand, they can log events that take place very slowly, perhaps over many hours, days or weeks. Data-loggers do not need sleep, sustenance or toilet facilities (they do need a power supply, though).
- Resilience: Data-loggers do not worry about getting wet or cold, or being stuck up on a roof.
- Manipulation: With good software, data can be analysed and manipulated more quickly and with less drudgery for the student.
- Graphical displays of what is happening can be displayed on the screen there and then to pupils – for example, cooling due to evaporation; the 'clouding' of sodium thiosulphate solution as hydrochloric acid is added. Thus the graph is more immediately and closely associated with the event it represents – pupils don't have to spend a long time, or wait until the next lesson, before they can see a pattern.

In this way, time can be freed for discussion and interpretation of results that are perhaps the higher order skills of science. It can lead to a change of emphasis in school practical work away from the routine process of taking and writing down results to the use of closer observation, reflection, discussion and interpretation.

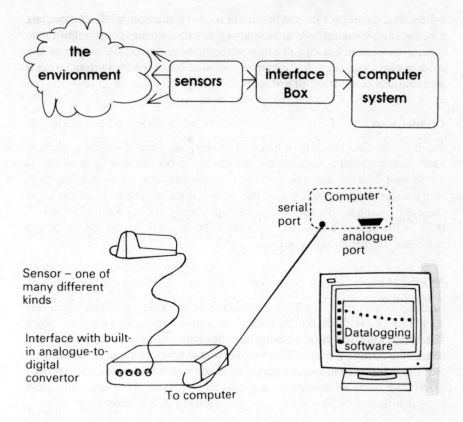

Figure 12.4 The basics of data-logging
Source: Frost, R. 1991

This can be of enormous benefit in investigational work and links in perfectly with the ideals of Sc 1.

WORD-PROCESSING AND DESKTOP PUBLISHING

Word-processing (WP)

The use of WP can provide the following enrichment and benefits in science education:

Drafting and Re-drafting

Pupils are given the opportunity to draft and re-draft their own work much more readily. This seems to affect different users in different ways. Some are much more inclined to actually make a start on a piece of writing (arguably the hardest part of the process), knowing full well that it can easily be changed or edited. Some are actually much more inclined to keep going, just to get their thoughts down onto paper or the screen, knowing that they can easily be re-drafted. This aspect of WP is often said to enhance the writing of so-called lower ability students – but it probably affects writers at all levels.

Collaboration

Pupils are able to collaborate (work cooperatively) on a piece of writing much more easily with a computer system than with pen and paper. Partnership in writing is encouraged. This occurs for perhaps two main reasons: first, the writing is up there on the screen for all partners to see. This enables them more easily to take an equal share in it. Secondly, the writing is actually physically done by a shared keyboard, there on the desk or bench. The keyboard often does not 'belong' to one person more than another as, say, a pen does.

Painless Marking

Marking of work done on a WP system can be so much more painless. Again, this applies equally at all levels of education and writing. Writers are far more inclined to seek feedback and critical comment if they know that alteration, addition and editing are relatively simple. This is again said to apply especially to those most likely to make spelling or grammatical mistakes, which is certainly true – the use of WP does remove the need for marks and corrections all over a script. But it can have an influence on people's writing attitudes and habits at all levels.

Better results

The final product of a piece of writing can be so much better through the use of WP and desktop publishing. This can produce a positive feedback loop, in turn influencing the earlier stages.

Better storage

Finally, writing done with a WP system can be easily stored and exchanged. Its positive effect is to allow a person or a group to stop writing at a convenient point and take it up again more easily later.

   Some common programs in use are: *Word* and *Word for Windows, Wordwise, Write, Writeon!, Prompt* and *Writer.*

Desktop Publishing (DTP)

DTP programs allow pupils to assemble pages with text, borders, boxes and pictures. DTP programs are more flexible than WP programs. DTP can allow pupils to use line drawings and sprites (pictures) as well as data from other programs. With DTP, pupils can design a newspaper format in columns, text flowing round graphics, attractive data displays such as a 3-D pie chart or text presentations with a variety of fonts, headings and borders.

In short, by using DTP and a good printer pupils can greatly improve their presentation of work, often through group work.

Some common programs include: *Pagemaker, Front Page Extra, Caxton, Newspaper, Quotation* and *Impression* (new version: Publisher).

INTERACTIVE MEDIA

Interactive Video (IV)

An interactive video-disc system may typically consist of a computer (including a disc drive and keyboard) which is linked to (or interfaced with) a video-disc player and a colour monitor. Often the system can be operated by a light pen, a mouse, a concept keyboard, a bar-code reader or a tracker ball, as well as the keyboard. People using IV can control or 'interact' with the system to choose their own sequence of video, sound, text, computer graphics or even still pictures.

IV can provide a combination of images, sounds and computer-generated text and diagrams which is perhaps unique in a learning situation. IV technology is evolving continually – readers can only keep abreast by studying weekly or monthly publications on, for example, systems that include CD-I (compact disc interactive) and DVI (digital video interactive).

Hardware is certain to change, but the educational principles underlying inter-action and interactive video are fairly constant.

The word 'interactive' has several implications which are worth spelling out:

1   Action/active learning: The user is involved in some action in using an interac-tive system. This may involve using a mouse or a light pen, pressing keys or using a tracker ball.
2   Choice: In an interactive situation the user has choice over the learning engaged in. The learner can decide which frame to go to, go forward or backwards through the frames one at a time, or freeze a frame.
3   Control: Learners have control over their own learning situation (for example, of the sequence, of the pace, of the level of difficulty, of the number of repetitions).
4   The onus or responsibility for learning rests with the user (largely as a conse-quence of points 1 to 3). The learner is involved in decision-making and the management of learning.

The educational potential of IV lies in the following capabilities:

- high storage capacity (for data, pictures, etc.)
- its highly interactive nature
- its motivating power and novelty value
- the possibility for a flexible branching structure

Interactive media in science education

Interactive media combine the possibility of all four paradigms of CAL being used with the same items of hardware and software. In line with the paradigms of Kemmis *et al.* (1977) (see table 12.2) we can say that interactive media can be used in the following modes:

Tutorial mode

It can be used in skills training, in teaching certain concepts, or in teaching a certain body of knowledge. Its training use is quite widespread in commerce and industry, for example banks, the car industry.

Database mode (revelatory or emancipatory paradigm)

IV can be used almost like an encyclopaedia to allow storage of and access to information. Unlike other databases discussed earlier however, we do not yet have available systems that allow learners to 'write' their own information onto discs – they will be in 'read only' situations.

Surrogate mode

This will occur when IV is used to simulate certain situations (cf. the revelatory paradigm). Interactive video is often said to provide surrogate experiences, for example surrogate walks, surrogate field trips or surrogate travel. It may even, in a science context, provide surrogate experiments of situations that are either too dangerous, too fast or too slow to carry out in real life (cf. computer simulations).

These modes of use will encourage the 'what if' questioning and other exploratory or revelatory learning present in database and simulation use generally.

This range of educational uses of IV, within different paradigms, means that it can be used in a variety of different learning and teaching situations. As Atkins (1989) points out, 'the medium does not impose or require a particular style of teaching'. It may lead equally to a whole-class approach or, at the other extreme, small-group or individualised learning.

Examples of interactive video

Here are three examples of IV material which is now available and being used (finance permitting) in schools and colleges:

1 *Volcanoes:* Like the well-known 'Domesday system', this system arose from BBC Enterprises (in conjunction with Oxford University Press). It can be used in the form of a superb database with information on volcanoes and plate tectonics allowing open-ended learning. Here are some suggestions of how the disc might be used with students:

- to look at a model of the earth's structure. Do they think the model is a good one? What evidence is there to support it?
- to find out about how movements inside the earth can lead to earthquakes and volcanoes
- to compare world maps of volcanic activity with the pattern of plates in the earth's crust. One piece of film shows the activity at the plate margins.

2 *Ecodisc:* This is the third disc that arose from BBC Enterprises, and like the previous two runs on the BBC advanced interactive video system. It is used largely in the surrogate mode, by placing the user in a nature reserve in Devon, England. The user can explore, investigate, manage the reserve, or simply take a surrogate walk around the lake and woods. Using *Ecodisc* will develop many of the important process skills in science education, including predicting, measuring, evaluating and handling data. A full account of the potential of the disc is provided by McCormick (1987).

3 *Motion: A Visual Database:* This is an IV disc presenting nearly 200 short film sequences of a wide range of examples of motion. It is an excellent resource for a range of abilities, allowing extremely detailed exploration of motion for older or more able pupils or more qualitative study and discussion of motion in earlier years – for example Why is it best for a car to 'crumple' when it collides with a wall? Why wear seat belts and crash helmets? A full review of this resource, which is much more than a straight database, is given in Scaife and Wellington (1989).

What about multimedia?

One of the much-heralded technical developments in the early 1990s has been multimedia, sometimes described as the 'collision of computing and television'. Multimedia systems allow the usual text and graphics of the computer to be combined with high-quality audio and video information. The combination obviously has huge potential for enriching and enhancing learning. The principal storage medium has been CD-ROM, partly because this format is well established in other markets. At present it is not unfair to say that multimedia is barely used in science education, perhaps for a number of reasons. Some CD-ROM material is available for science, such as *Electricity and Magnetism* and *The Living Body* (Bradford Technology) and *Plant Science* (NCET). The use of multimedia in science education is certain to develop in the near future, although just at present the much larger IV disc format is perhaps more useful – an interesting debate and an area to watch.

LOOKING TO THE FUTURE OF IT IN SCIENCE

There are several issues for the future which can only be mentioned briefly here (discussed more fully in Scaife and Wellington, 1993: 91–103).

First, the use of IT at school and at home raises a number of points about equal opportunities. Most research evidence (Hoyles, 1988; Harrison and Hay, 1991) indicates that boys are more likely to have a home computer, a positive attitude to IT, and a network of friends with computer-related interests. This imbalance or inequality with respect to IT applies not only to gender but also to economic status and home background. Thus teachers need to be sensitive and reflective in managing and encouraging IT use. For example, if computer work at home is suggested or even rewarded, is this fair and just? This will become a key issue in the future.

In school, the boys tend to 'take over' computers during break or study periods, volunteer to do things on the computer for the teacher, and secure a greater share of resources and attention than the girls. Teachers need to ask: If volunteers are sought to demonstrate IT equipment, is attention paid to all groups and both sexes? Are both sexes given equal access to IT resources? Should teachers practise positive discrimination in allocating IT resources? These and other questions need to be addressed by teachers, now and in the future. Information technology has great potential in narrowing the gap between pupils because of its enormous value in helping learners with special needs, with (for example) writing, spelling and data-logging. Teachers must beware, however, that IT does not open up new gaps where opportunities are unequal or denied.

A second issue for the future concerns, of course, the rapid developments constantly occurring in both software and hardware. These in turn will gradually change the roles of both teachers and learners in science. Software seems certain to become more open ended, exploratory, and more learner centred – it will undoubtedly become far more powerful and sophisticated. Hardware will not only become more powerful, but also cheaper and more plentiful (in homes and schools). It will also become more flexible, more portable and (with new software) involve more media. How effective will multimedia prove to be? When will all pupils have their own personal, portable computers, as they now do calculators? How will the teacher's role be changed by these developments? The most likely shift is from teaching to learning, as teachers have less and less control over the learning experiences available to pupils at school and at home. Can school organisation and management adapt to these changes?

This chapter has looked mainly at existing uses of IT in science involving types of program such as tutorial, spreadsheet, database and simulation. It has also looked at some of the teaching and learning made possible by the hardware and software for data-logging and interactive video which have been available for some time now. Despite these possibilities, the use of IT to enrich and extend science teaching is not yet widespread in schools (see NCET). This may be for a number of reasons, including a lack of resources or the need for in-service training of teachers to raise their awareness of IT and its teaching/learning potential. My own suspicion is that the main difficulty for the classroom teacher is the way that IT is managed and deployed within a school, within a science department, and within the classroom. Classroom management of IT which allows pupils to use computers as an integral part of their science work requires great skill and expertise. From the wider management context, schools need to recognise that science teachers cannot use IT if it is not there when and where they need it. Locking computers away in 'computer rooms' does not make for flexible, integrated use of IT in a subject area. The optimistic hope for the future is that IT will be plentiful enough, and managed flexibly enough, to allow its use to permeate science teaching and learning (of both process and content) as an integrated element rather than a bolt-on or a special kind of activity in the science curriculum.

REFERENCES AND FURTHER READING

General

Blease, D. (1986) *Evaluating Educational Software*, London: Croom Helm.
Bradley, R. (1992) *The IT Handbook for Teachers*, Hemel Hempstead: Simon & Schuster.
Cloke, C. (1988) 'Information Technology in Science', *Computer Education* 60: 25–6.
Frost, R. (1993) *The IT in Primary Science Book*, IT in Science, Association for Science Education Booksales, College Lane, Hatfield AL10 9AA.
Frost, R. (1993) *The IT in Science Book of Datalogging and Control*, IT in Science, Association for Science Education Booksales, College Lane. Hatfield AL10 9AA.
Gifford, C. (ed.) (1992) *Science Investigations and Information Technology: An INSET Pack for Teachers*, Coventry: NCET (guidance on using databases, spreadsheets, WP, DTP, etc., communicating and 'making graphs' – comes with two discs).
Harrison and Hay (1991) 'Hi-technique of manual skills', *The Guardian*, 7 February 1991.
Hoyles, C. (ed.) (1988) *Girls and Computers*, London: Bedford Way Papers.
Kahn, B. (1985) *Computers in Science*, Cambridge: Cambridge University Press.
Kemmis, S., Atkin, M., and Wright, S. (1977) 'How Do Students Learn?', Occasional Paper No. 5, Norwich: CARE, University of East Anglia.
NCET (1993) *Evaluation of IT in Science*, Coventry: NCET.
Owen, M., Pritchard, J. and Rowlands, M. (1992) *Information Technology in Science*, Bangor, Wales: MEU, Cymru (pack of ideas, information and case histories of IT use in science).
Rogers, L. (1990) 'IT in Science in the National Curriculum', *Journal of Computer Assisted Learning*, 6: 246–54.
Rushby, N. (1979) *An Introduction to Educational Computing*, London: Croom Helm.
Scaife, J. and Wellington, J. J. (1993) *IT in Science and Technology Education*, Milton Keynes: Open University Press.
Sewell, D. (1990) *New Tools For New Minds: A Cognitive Perspective on the Use of Computers with Young Children*, Hemel Hempstead: Harvester Wheatsheaf.
Turkle, S. (1984), *The Second Self: Computers and the Human Spirit,* London: Granada.
Underwood, J. and Underwood, G. (1990) *Computers and Learning*, Oxford: Basil Blackwell.
Weizenbaum, J. (1984) *Computer Power and Human Reason*, Harmondsworth: Penguin.
Wellington, J. J. (1985) *Children, Computers and the Curriculum*, London: Harper & Row.

Interactive video

Atkins, M. (1989) 'Visual Stimulus: the Exciting World of Interactive Video Lessons' *Times Educational Supplement*, 5 May 1989.
Atkins, M. and Blissett, G. (1989) 'Learning Activities and Interactive Videodisc: An Exploratory Study', *British Journal of Educational Technology* 20 (1): 47–56.
McCormick, S. (1987) 'Ecodisc: An Ecological Visual Simulation', *Journal of Biological Education*, 21 (3): 175–80.
Mashiter, J. (1988) 'Interactive Video in Science', *School Science Review* 69 (248): 446–50.

Scaife, J. and Wellington, J. J. (1989) 'Caught in Action: The Motion Video-disc', *Times Educational Supplement* 1 September 1989.
Wellington, J. J. (1990a) 'Right on Cue: the Newcastle Interactive "Video Project"', *Times Educational Supplement* 10 August 1990.

Data-logging

Barton, R. and Rogers, L. (1991) 'The Computer as an Aid to Practical Science – Studying Motion with a Computer', *Journal of Computer Assisted Learning,* 7: 104–12.
Scaife, J. (1991) 'Facts Fingered: Review of the Log-IT data-logger', *Times Educational Supplement* 7 June 1991, p. 53.

Databases

Smart, L. (1988) 'The Database as a Catalyst', *Journal of Computer Assisted Learning*, 4: 140–9.
Spavold, J. (1989) 'Children and Databases', *Journal of Computer Assisted Learning*, 5: 145–60.

Word-processing

Clough, D. (1987) 'Word Processing in the Classroom and Science Education', *Primary Science Review*, 5: 4–5.
NCET (1992) *Choosing and Using Portable Computers*, Coventry: NCET.
Peacock, M. (1988) 'Handwriting Versus Word Processed Print', *Journal of Computer Assisted Learning*, 4: 162–72.
Peacock, M. and Breese, C. (1990) 'Pupils with Portable Writing Machines', *Educational Review* 42 (1): 41–56.

CAL

Gagne, R. M. (1985) *The Conditions of Learning*, New York: Holt, Rinehart & Winston.

Spreadsheets

Goodfellow, T. (1990) 'Spreadsheets: Powerful Tools in Science Education', *School Science Review,* 71 (257): 47.

Modelling

Ogborn, J. (1984) *Dynamic Modelling System*, London: Longman Software.
—— (1986) *Cellular Modelling System*, London: Longman Software.
—— (1990) 'A Future for Modelling in Science Education', *Journal of Computer Assisted Learning,* 6: 103–12.

Finding Software

An extremely valuable guide for teachers is: *Educational Software: A directory of currently available software for schools and colleges* (produced by NCET; published by J. Whitaker & Sons Ltd, London WC1A 1DF; updated each year).

Also: *Interactive Technologies Courseware*, from Bruce Wright, 3, The Drive, Bishopsteighton, Devon TQ14 9SD.

Addresses for Information, Software and Data-logging

(a) Information

Microcomputer Users in Secondary Education (MUSE), PO Box 43, Houghton on the Hill, Leicestershire LE7 9GX. Tel: (0533) 433839.

National Council for Educational Technology (NCET), Science Park, University of Warwick, Coventry CV4 7JJ. Tel: (0203) 416994.

National Educational Resources Information Services (NERIS), Maryland College, Leighton Street, Woburn MK17 9JD. Tel: (0525) 290364.

(b) Software

Anglia TV, Anglia House, Norwich NR1 3JG.

AVP Computing, School Hill Centre, Chepstow, Gwent NP6 5PH. Tel: 0291 625439.

BBC Enterprises/Longman Logotron, 124 Cambridge Science Park, Milton Road, Cambridge CB4 4ZS. Tel: 0223 425558.

BP Educational Resources, Alton, Hants. GU3 4BR.

Bradford Technology Ltd., Bradford BD7 1BX.

Cambridge University Press, Cambridge CB2 2RU.

Hutchinson, Wellington St, Cheltenham GL50 1YD.

Longman Logotron, 124 Cambridge Science Park, Milton Road, Cambridge CB4 4ZS. (Much of the Longman software mentioned above is no longer available for purchase, but is still widely used in schools).

SPA, Tewkesbury, Glos, SL20 6AB.

UKAEA Education Service, Building 354 West, Harwell Laboratory, Oxfordshire, OX11 0RA.

(c) Data-logging

LogIT, **Griffin and George,** Bishop Meadow Road, Loughborough, Leicestershire LE11 0RG.

Sense and Control, Motion Sensor, **Educational Electronics,** 28 Lake Street, Leighton Buzzard, Beds LY7 8RX.

First Sense, **Philip Harris,** Educ., Lynn Lane, Shenstone, Lichfield, Staffs WS14 0EE.

Practical Science with Microcomputers (for use with *Sense and Control*), *Sensing Science, Insights, Softlab,* **NCET** (see above).

13 Problem-solving in school science

Vic Lally

Teacher: Here are two types of washing powder . . .
Pupil: Oh no, Sir! Not another one of your problems.

(Qualter, A. et al., 1990)

> This chapter answers some key questions about problem-solving:
>   What is problem-solving in school science?
>   How do you set up your own problem-solving lessons?
>   Why can problem-solving be useful?
>   How does problem-solving fit into the National Curriculum?

INTRODUCTION

It is not possible in a single chapter to cover the whole field of problem-solving in school science. There is now a considerable body of literature on the subject (see further reading) where you may explore some of the research issues and background ideas in more depth than could possibly be achieved here. What I would like to do is convince you that problem-solving can be fun. I would also like to show how it can be a meaningful learning experience for your pupils and yourself and fit into the National Curriculum! Remember that the National Curriculum is a minimum entitlement and not a limitation.

> Science Education is not limited by the order [revised Order for Science 1991]. Rather the order should support science education by stipulating a legally required minimum. The order provides a skeleton which requires the flesh of the real world and the life force of a teacher to bring it alive.

(Association for Science Education, 1992)

Whether you are already familiar with problem-solving in science as a teaching strategy or you are thinking of trying it for the first time, I hope you will be encouraged to try at least one of the examples suggested. Problem-solving, if properly planned and organised, can be a very effective means of promoting learning in the science laboratory or classroom. One of the keys to effective learning is organised and well-planned variety. Problem-solving can make a significant contribution. What is more, it can be a successful way of putting some of 'the flesh of the real world' on the 'skeleton' of the required minimum (the National Curriculum). But first we need to be clear about a few basic ideas and definitions.

WHAT IS PROBLEM-SOLVING?

The term 'problem-solving' has several connotations. It may be coping with 10T on Friday afternoon or doing the crossword at lunch time with colleagues. In fact any situation in which a person has a project, goal or aim which cannot be met or fulfilled without further work or activity presents a problem. Problem-solving, therefore, is the set of mental and physical strategies used to reach the goal or aim or to complete the project. It is a central element of human endeavour, and an essential component of much scientific activity. It would seem, then, that problem-solving may include a wide variety of activities in all sorts of contexts. Clearly these definitions are fine in general terms but far too vague and all embracing for the purposes of busy science teachers. Yet, without too much in the way of guidance or help, science teachers have been vaguely exhorted to use 'problem-solving' in their teaching.

For example, the government's policy statement *Science 5 to 16* (DES, 1985: 5) states: 'Science is a practical subject and should be taught at all stages in a way which emphasises practical, investigative and problem solving activity.' It also states:

> The key to success lies in flexibility and variety. In particular opportunities for pupils to contribute their own ideas to discussions . . . the opportunity to test their own ideas. . . . The balance in practical work should be more towards solving problems and less towards illustrating previously taught theory.
>
> (DES, 1985: 17)

According to this view, problem-solving is seen as central to science itself as well as to learning in science lessons. Based on these ideas the National Curriculum has, more recently, firmly embedded problem-solving in the science curriculum of every child in England and Wales (DES, 1991). Attainment target 1 (scientific investigation) embodies a model of problem-solving (NCC, 1989: D2) which is very similar to a generalised problem-solving model (figure 13.1).

The actual number of stages in problem-solving models may vary, depending on how many sub-tasks are included. However, the basic model (right-hand side of figure 13.1) has four distinct stages. The first stage of the process will obviously involve a definition of the problem task. During this stage the problem-solver relates the problem to previous ones with features of the type now presented. This may involve careful observation of the 'problem situation' leading to insights, ideas and possible solutions. These will often be in an undeveloped form at this point. From these ideas a plan for an investigation will be developed. This will then be carried out, data collected and the success of the problem-solving activity evaluated.

This is the simplest linear route through a basic problem-solving process. After one 'run' through the process a feedback cycle may be set up. Evaluation of the solution or results may lead to a modification of any of the earlier stages and the repeating of the problem-solving process with refinements, modifications or even a reframing of the problem.

An interesting further definition of problem-solving is provided by Watts (1991: 131–3). He suggests two distinct categories which he calls PS1 and PS2. Essentially PS1 is concerned with problem-solving as a purely intellectual activity. It is mainly in the context of solving quantitative problems of the type associated with traditional academic science education. It is used to develop an individual's solution routines for use in examinations and as an aid to teacher-centred learning (characterised by whole-class teaching, teacher-defined curriculum and passive pupil participation in learning).

PS2, on the other hand, is concerned with problem-solving as a task of implementation. In other words, it will have a practical outcome rather than just a paper-and-pencil solution. The solution will be largely qualitative and involve real-life contexts that fit into the curriculum of practically based school science. The task may not be well defined, and only an outline of relevant information may be provided for pupils. It will usually be a group task with a group solution. It supports the development of problem-solving strategies that have recognised manipulative and affective outcomes in addition to the cognitive ones. The teaching style is more pupil-centred. Watts suggests that since the late 1980s, PS2 has gradually replaced PS1 as the favoured model in school science.

Problem-solving, then, is a four-stage process which may be linear or cyclical. It is an essential component of scientific activity and endorsed by the DFE (formerly DES) and the NCC as a 'preferred' method of teaching and learning in school science. In practice it may take a variety of forms, but some recent approaches tend to be pupil-centred (characterised by group work, pupil involvement in curriculum planning and active participation in learning). They are also curriculum-focused and have real-life contexts with practical outcomes. It should be noted, however, that in the revised orders for science (DES, 1991) there is now a stronger emphasis on the development of cognitive skills. Some of these higher order skills of Sc 1 include:

- using a quantitative approach
- using theoretical models
- controlling variables
- defining parameters
- assessing the confidence limits of data

There is a clear requirement to balance pupils' acquisition of these skills with their need for meaningful contexts and the other elements of a PS2 style of working.

WHY PROBLEM-SOLVING?

There are several reasons why problem-solving is important in school science. The

Assessment of Performance Unit (APU), when looking at the performance of pupils in science, adopted a view of science as an experimental subject concerned fundamentally with problem-solving (Murphy and Gott, 1984: 4). As we have already seen, this view is also embedded in the National Curriculum and government policy documents. In this view it is essential that practical problem-solving is included in any science curriculum. Indeed the statements are themselves a recognition that a rigid PS1 style of teaching and learning is no longer adequate in a basic science education. The life skills aspect of scientific and technological problem-solving is also important. Not only do we live in a culture dominated by science and technology, but the information and knowledge it generates are too vast to be assimilated by pupils. Furthermore, they are increasing at an astonishing rate. Pupils will therefore need a wide range of learning skills to cope with this increase. The ability to recognise problems in a broad range of contexts, understand their nature, and plan, execute and evaluate solutions will be central to these skills and of vital importance for citizens of the twenty-first century. To this end transferability of skills from one context to another may well be important, as problem-solving ability in a single very highly (and increasingly) specialised area will not be sufficient (nor advisable in technological market economies). I will return to the transferability issue in the final section.

A number of recent curriculum development projects have focused on problem-solving in science. For example, *Teaching Strategies in Biotechnology, Problem-Solving with Industry* and *Active Teaching and Learning in Science* (see further reading) have all looked at the learning benefits of PS2–style problem-solving. Their findings indicate that this type of problem-solving, if carefully used and properly structured, may have several beneficial outcomes:

- Most important among these is that pupils' motivation can be significantly increased (Henderson *et al.*, 1987: E5–15; Henderson and Lally, 1988: 149; Centre for Science Education, 1990: s1–s2 of Teachers' Guide).
- Secondly, pupils have a variety of learning styles and preferences, but most pupils learn effectively by doing and being involved. That is, they learn most effectively by being actively engaged in interesting work. This is the style that many prefer in their personal hobbies and out-of-school pursuits where, for many children, their most effective learning takes place. PS2-style problem-solving can provide a suitable framework for this kind of active learning.
- Finally, but not least among these benefits, good active problem-solving can build confidence, generate enthusiasm and increase knowledge and understanding of the content of the National Curriculum (see Lally, *et al.*, 1992: 121–3).

Carefully structured and managed problem-solving, then, can help to deliver several desirable learning outcomes in science education. These may be affective (interest, motivation, confidence) and manipulative. The cognitive outcomes of knowledge and understanding are greatly enhanced by a problem-solving approach. Pupils' dominant learning style (informal, active, practically based) may be built upon and used effectively in problem-solving to assist in achieving these outcomes.

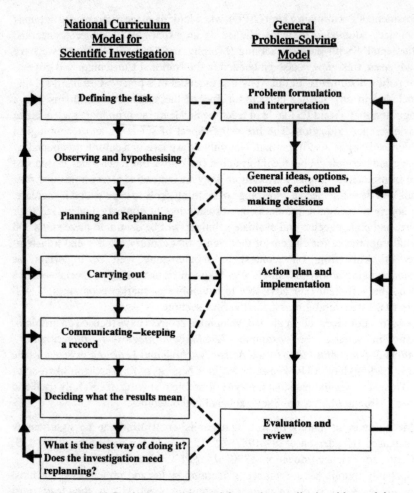

Figure 13.1 National Curriculum problem-solving and generalised problem-solving
models compared

PROBLEM-SOLVING AS A TEACHING STRATEGY

Introducing problem-solving as a 'strategy' into your repertoire of teaching skills
requires some thought and planning. One of the most important points to remember
is that pupils' expectations should not be overlooked. As with the learning of
concepts a constructivist approach may be appropriate. Start from the pupils'
understanding of what a science lesson is. If they are used to a particular style of
teaching then you may create problems if this is radically altered too quickly. It
takes time for pupils to adjust to new ways of working, especially if this requires
them to be more active and take greater personal responsibility for their own work.
Problems that require the rapid acquisition of a large number of new skills may

similarly create overload. The aim should be a balanced mixture of the new and the familiar so that pupils perceive the task as a 'do-able' challenge, yet see it as novel and interesting.

The choice of context for the problem is another important decision. This is particularly true if introducing problem-solving as a style of learning to pupils for the first time. Obviously problem-solving should be a natural extension of current work and not an isolated one-off. If it does not fit in to pupils' previous work they may become disoriented and lose motivation and interest. Contexts such as food and related products, because they are familiar, can provide excellent 'starter' activities and are of equal interest to both boys and girls. This will not always be possible, of course, but thinking about creating a graded introduction to this type of work, starting from a familiar context, is always a good idea. Clearly, also, the development of knowledge and understanding of the context must be built in to the planning of the activities from an early stage.

A further key element in this type of work is that pupils should feel encouraged to be creative, expressive and to think for themselves. This is easy to say but requires planning to achieve. Research by the Biotechnology in Schools Project (Henderson *et al.*, 1987), which involved extensive informal interviews with Y9 pupils (see, for example, section E, pp.9–15), showed that pupils' creative thinking in science was often overshadowed by the authority and expertise of the teacher. Many pupils said that they were often inhibited about expressing their thoughts aloud and worried about 'getting the wrong answer'. In other words, they did not feel a strong sense of owning the problem and its definition.

Table 13.1 summarises these and other key elements of problem-solving activities. Different types of activities combine these elements in a variety of ways. 'Egg races' (see British Association for the Advancement of Science, 1983 and 1985) may be very tightly defined at a macro and micro level. For example: 'Design a rubber band-powered vehicle that will transport an egg over a five-metre course.' This race framework is characteristically very competitive, which may compensate for lack of ownership. It is a fairly open-ended problem, but this will depend on the materials provided. The structure will generally be loose, with little guidance for pupils on design details or how to go through the problem-solving stages shown in figure 13.1.

This analysis is complicated a little by the interaction between elements. Context may affect ownership, for example, with pupils showing reluctance to take responsibility for organising their work if the context is very unfamiliar.

Simulations provide another framework for problem-solving activities. A simulation involves planning a clear structure for pupils' work so that they may proceed to the creative part of the work without the direct intervention of the teacher. Obviously the role of the teacher changes in this situation from that of lesson leader to lesson coordinator and activity facilitator. For the teacher this may take some getting used to, but the benefits in terms of increased pupil confidence, responsibility and creativity may be considerable. Of course, the teacher remains fully in control of the lesson by means of the simulation structure, but through its use

Table 13.1   Some key elements of classroom problem-solving

Element	Function
Context	The scene or situation in which a problem is set. Context-rich problem-solving adds reality and increases pupil involvement. Contexts should be familiar to pupils, particularly in early work.
Ownership of problem	Pupil ownership increases motivation. Ownership is increased by giving pupils responsibility for key aspects of the task.
Problem definition	Macro-definition will usually be determined by teacher or curriculum. Micro-definition by pupils enhances ownership (and therefore motivation).
Open-endedness	The number of possible solutions to a problem. For practical activities this may often be determined by the curriculum, time available and equipment limitations.
Framework	The style of the problem-solving, for example a simulation or an egg race.
Structure	The amount of guidance given to pupils for each stage of the problem-solving process.

provides pupils with a 'creative space' for their scientific thinking and imagination. The basis of the simulation is a three-stage framework:

1   the briefing
2   the action
3   the debriefing

Further details on designing and running simulations may be found in Jones (1980 and 1985). Before looking at some examples of classroom activities that illustrate these ideas, we need to look in a little more detail at the open-endedness element of problem-solving. Much is currently written about problems being 'open-ended' if they are also to be pupil-centred. The degree to which activities are open-ended will vary depending on a number of factors (see Lock, 1990, for some further ideas on this aspect). This in turn will affect the planning and preparation required of the teacher. Who defines the area of interest is probably one of the most significant factors. In National Curriculum work this will obviously be predetermined. However, within any topic pupils may still choose which investigation they pursue in a problem-solving activity. For example, it may be revealed in background or briefing information that several factors affect the performance of washing powders or the raising of bread doughs. Pupils may choose which one to investigate for themselves. Who does the planning and who decides the strategy to use are two further considerations here. Again, in the National Curriculum, the teacher will inevitably be involved in the major planning. There is no reason, however, why the micro-planning of the task cannot often be left to pupils. In summary, it is inevitable with the many curriculum constraints faced by teachers today that several of the key decisions about process and content of a problem-solving activity will not be taken by pupils. Yet, using problem-solving simulation frameworks (see above and illustrations below) and activities with alternative routes (such as Washday Biotechnology – see Ingleby *et al.*, 1987) pupils can still have a strong sense that they 'own' a problem and control its planning, execution, presentation and evaluation.

The two illustrations of problem-solving simulation classroom activities described below are both whole investigations taking two to three lessons' worth of time. The first (Dairy Biotechnology) is a highly structured activity in which pupils have a lot of control over the communicative aspects (the discussions, evidence analysis and presentation) but less over the basic problem definition. In the second (Vinegar Production), only an outline specification of the problem is provided and pupils can determine their own practical solution and evaluate it. They also have control over the communicative aspects, as in the first example.

In both investigations the three stages of the simulation framework are illustrated.

EXAMPLE 1: DAIRY BIOTECHNOLOGY

In this example, called 'Designing a New Yoghurt' from a unit called Dairy Biotechnology (Ingleby *et al.*, 1987, section 1), the National Curriculum context for the work is fermentation products in AT 3 (DES, 1991). Yoghurt is used because it is very suitable as a familiar fermentation product which is easy to work with. Pupils will have previously made yoghurt for themselves and be familiar with the manufacturing process from an earlier part of the unit. In addition, they will have conducted a simple consumer survey of commercial and home-made yoghurts, comparing them for price, flavour, texture and colour (see figure 13.2).

Briefing

At the start of the simulation, pupils are briefed and the scene is set for the work. First the teacher gives a short overview of the whole activity. The aim is for pupils to work in small groups as 'commercial' companies. The problem is to design a new yoghurt, including packaging and contents, and then produce a marketing campaign for the product. Companies of six pupils are formed and within this group each of three pairs receives a different role card for either (a) Customer Researchers, (b) Yoghurt Scientists or (c) Marketing Advisers (figure 13.3).

Action

During the first part of the action, each pair of pupils from the company then carries out the task assigned to it. The customer researchers use a systematic testing procedure of commercial and class-made yoghurts to find out which combination of price, packaging and ingredients is most popular. They record this information on a pro-forma which they can then take with them to the board meeting that follows. While they are engaged in this work, the yoghurt scientists are analysing the ingredients of yoghurt using information from a diet and health report (figure 13.4). At the same time the marketing advisers are engaged in an analysis of recent market trends in the yoghurt industry.

All of the support materials required by the pupil 'companies', including report pro-formas, are available in the laboratory. The teacher is not needed to direct the lesson and is free to act as a 'consultant' to the companies. He or she must take care, though, not to dominate pupils' discussions with directive questions or suggestions. It is the pupils, in the roles of company personnel, who are 'in charge' of the work. The teacher must take care to maintain this pupil-centred atmosphere during the work.

In the second stage of the action the pupil pairs convene as a company board, complete with an agenda (figure 13.5). Each company will have representatives from each of the three specialist activities, as described above.

The board meeting is a small group decision-making discussion. After the election of the chairperson and his or her opening comments, each pair in turn presents the evidence of its findings to the board. These presentations may well lead to conflicts of opinion within the group. For example, the customer researchers often find that sugar is popular as a yoghurt ingredient. The scientists, on the other hand, may sometimes suggest that this ingredient has damaging effects on health. When added to the findings of the market researchers, some heated and sophisticated discussions very often ensue. Once again the teacher must take care to do no more than 'eavesdrop' on these discussions.

In the final part of the action each group prepares a marketing strategy, including a rationale for its product profile. For example, a group may decide to market its yoghurt as a health food, use an alternative to sugar as a sweetener, and design its advertising to aim at this market. In doing so they may have decided on a compromise between the protestations of the scientists and the insistence of the marketing advisers. This is all wrapped up in presentations to the other companies (the rest of the class). These occasions are often fired with a friendly rivalry and reveal enormous involvement, imagination and command of relevant knowledge on the part of pupils. What might in another context be a rather timid and brief explanation by a group may, within the simulation framework, become a much anticipated and prepared-for 'event'.

Debriefing

In the debrief that follows, the teacher's role reverts to that of director. During the action he or she will have made note of any misunderstandings or issues that arose. In this last part of the simulation the pupils also return to their more usual roles. A whole class discussion will then be used to address the points noted. For example, if a group did not use a fair test in its customer survey this might be raised as a general point. Another group might have marketed a yoghurt with high sugar content as healthy. This might be challenged on the basis of the evidence provided to the yoghurt scientists (not all the pupils will have seen this information during the action).

The simulation, when used with Y10 pupils, takes about two hours to complete. Of course, not all problem-solving activities need take this long. However, as a whole investigation it includes National Curriculum content in AT 3 and investigative processes in AT 1 (for the yoghurt making and testing). Equally importantly, and this should be true of any active problem-solving investigation, it creates opportunities for pupils to communicate and cooperate. Pupils are put into a setting where they are encouraged to take full responsibility for their work, and are motivated to do so. Moreover, the observed motivation level is often high for most pupils.

There are several general points about problem-solving arising from Dairy Biotechnology. There is no single 'correct answer' to the product-design part of the problem so there is room for pupils' creativity. However, the yoghurt production and testing which precedes it is highly structured. Teacher direction decreases through the unit as pupils gain in confidence. All sections have plenty of guidance so that pupils cannot easily get lost or lose their focus on the task. This is particularly important for starter activities in problem-solving. Table 13.2 shows how 'Designing a New Yoghurt' fits into the generalised problem-solving model (see figure 13.2).

Table 13.2 A match of the generalised problem-solving model stages and 'Designing a New Yoghurt' problem-solving components

General problem-solving stage	*'Designing a new Yoghurt' component*
Problem formulation and interpretation	Formulation supplied by teacher as overview, through role cards and board meeting agenda. Further interpretation by pairs and company board
Generating ideas, options, courses of action and decisions	Pupils generate ideas and make decisions in discussion (pairs and board), which is structured by role cards and board meeting agenda.
Action plan and implementation	Generated by pupils within framework provided by the teacher
Evaluation and review	Provided by pupil peers in company presentations to class and by teacher in debriefing which follows the action.

Designing and Marketing Foods

- Activity 1   How yoghurt is manufactured – explores the details of yoghurt making

- Activity 2   Making a natural yoghurt – students make their own low fat yoghurt

- Activity 3   Making a nice yoghurt – a systematic investigation of preferences

- Activity 4   Designing a new yoghurt – exploring the interaction of interests in designing a new food product through analysis and discussion

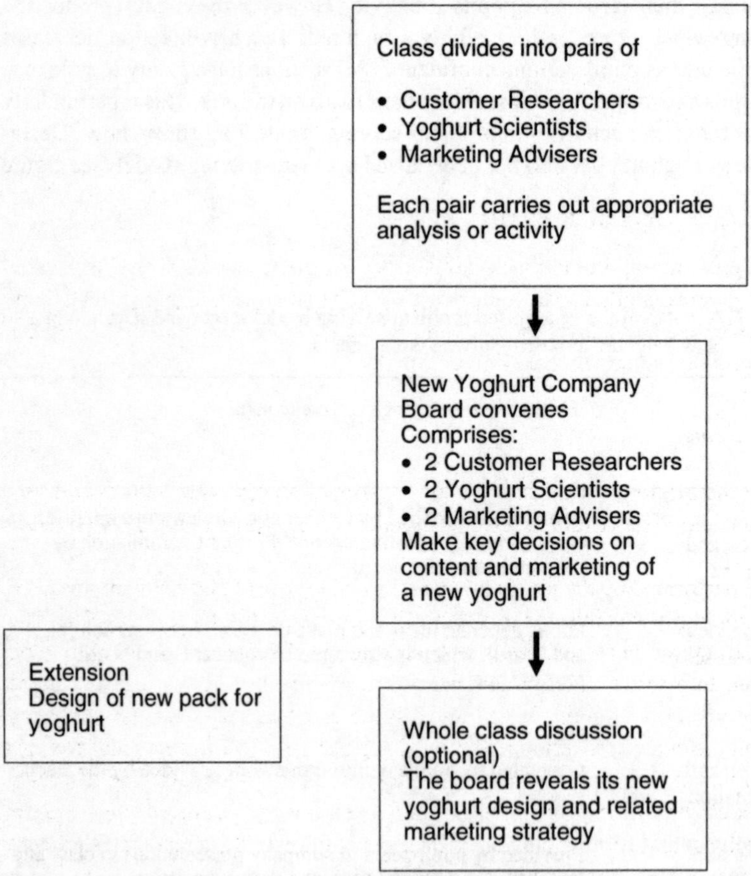

Class divides into pairs of

- Customer Researchers
- Yoghurt Scientists
- Marketing Advisers

Each pair carries out appropriate analysis or activity

New Yoghurt Company Board convenes
Comprises:
- 2 Customer Researchers
- 2 Yoghurt Scientists
- 2 Marketing Advisers
Make key decisions on content and marketing of a new yoghurt

Extension
Design of new pack for yoghurt

Whole class discussion (optional)
The board reveals its new yoghurt design and related marketing strategy

Figure 13.2   An overview of the Dairy Biotechnology Unit

Instructions for the Yoghurt Scientists

You are the scientists employed by the yoghurt company. Recent scientific findings have suggested that our health is closely connected with what we eat. Your job as scientists is to interpret these findings for the yoghurt company board. At the moment the public is worried about chemicals added to food and their effect on health. People are also concerned that the quantities of the different nutrients we eat may affect our health.

How to interpret the scientific findings

(a)   Collect one copy of each of the sheets labelled Scientific Evidence 1, Scientific Evidence 2 and Scientific Report.

(b)   Use Scientific Evidence 1 to complete Table 1 on the Scientific Report.

(c)   Read Scientific Evidence 2.

(d)   Using only the evidence provided, complete Table 2 on the Scientific Report.

Figure 13.3   The Yoghurt Scientists' role card
Source: Ingleby, *et al.*, (1987)

EXAMPLE 2: VINEGAR PRODUCTION

This problem-solving simulation is based on the work of Cullen (1987). Once again, pupils are given a familiar food context with which to work. First, pupils form small companies with a fixed development budget. Each has to design a working vinegar tower to produce some vinegar (figure 13.6).

Briefing

This time the briefing for the simulation consists of an overview introduction by the teacher and a short (about twenty minutes) lively drama called 'Acid Test' (figure 13.7).

This is performed by the pupils as a very effective way of getting them involved and is particularly suitable for mixed-ability groups of 13- to 16-year-olds. The script is structured and simple yet provides plenty of scope for imagination and expression. In a series of short acts pupils get involved in tracing the history of vinegar production from ancient times to the present day. Embedded within the play are all the clues needed for an outline design of a vinegar tower. This provides the principles of the design without revealing any practical details. The play may be enacted all the way through in one sitting. Alternatively, pupils may pause at the end of each act and fill in a play analysis sheet (figure 13.8), which helps them to focus on the key information points in the drama.

Scientific Evidence 1

(a) Diet and health – some recent findings

EATING TOO MUCH		PART OF BODY AFFECTED	NOT EATING ENOUGH	
Food*	Disease		Disease	Food*
Fat, *Salt*	Stroke		Allergies	Various foods
Fat, Sugar	Acne			
Sugar	Tooth decay			
Fat, Sugar	Overweight		Asthma	Various foods
Fat, Sugar, Salt	Cancers			
Fat	Breast cancer		Appendicitis	Fibre
Fat, Sugar	Heart disease		Constipation	Fibre
Fat? *Salt*	High blood pressure		Colo-rectal cancer	Fat? Fibre
Sugar?	Kidney stones		Piles	Fibre
Fat? Sugar?	Adult onset diabetes		Brittle bones	Vitamins and minerals
Fat? Sugar?	Ulcers			

Eating wholefoods, high in fibre and starch protect against eating too much of these foods*

Certain foods* missing from the diet can cause these diseases

? = cause not firmly established. *Fat* = major cause

Figure 13.4   The diet and health report summary diagram
Source: Ingleby, *et al.*, (1987)

Action

After the play, each pupil company designs, builds and evaluates its own vinegar tower. Additional advice and support for pupils is provided in two ways:

Stage 2 Meeting of the New Yoghurt Company Board

Present at the meeting

2 Customer Researchers
2 Yoghurt Scientists
2 Marketing Advisers
1 Chairperson

Agenda

1   Electing Chairperson
2   Chairperson's remarks
3   Customer Researchers' answers ⎫
4   Yoghurt Scientists' answers   ⎬   to the Chairperson's questions
5   Marketing Advisers' answers   ⎭
6   Board discussion and filing in columns 1 and 2 of discussion table
7   Decision of Board and filling in column 3 of discussion table.

Chairperson's remarks

Yoghurt sales in the UK continue to rise steadily. At least £145 million worth is now sold every year. But competition between us and other yoghurt making companies is very strong. We must be careful to make sure that we can give our customers what they want. There are signs of changing tastes.

I would like each of you to give your answers to these questions.

Question	1 Problems if we do this	2 *Advantages if we do this*	3 *Decisions of Board*
Should we add whole milk or cream?			
Should we add stabilizer?			
Should we add preservative?			
Should we add sugar?			
Should we advertise yoghurt as a healthy food?			

Figure 13.5   The agenda for the Yoghurt Company board meeting
Source: Ingleby, et al., 1987

Flow diagram of the work

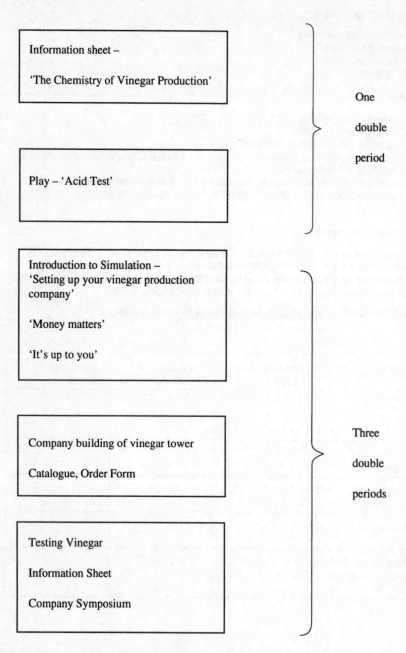

Information sheet –

'The Chemistry of Vinegar Production'

One

double

period

Play – 'Acid Test'

Introduction to Simulation –
'Setting up your vinegar production
company'

'Money matters'

'It's up to you'

Company building of vinegar tower

Catalogue, Order Form

Three

double

periods

Testing Vinegar

Information Sheet

Company Symposium

Figure 13.6   An overview of the Vinegar Production Unit
Source: Henderson, *et al.* (eds.), 1987

Ham:	(*Looking sternly at Harry*) Well I think a firm hand is needed. You know what they say 'spare the rod and spoil the child'. Anyway, onto business, let's have a look at this vinegar production of yours.
Wormwood:	Yes, of course, we've wasted enough time already. The beer is turned into vinegar inside these two kegs. (*Points to two big barrels*) They are both filled with beechwood shavings. Some vinegar, or should I say 'alegar' makers use twigs, bits of wood or even coke, but I think that beechwood shavings are best. One barrel is filled to the top with beer ... and a bit of old vinegar to get things going. The other is only half full. Now then Harry, show Mr. Ham what we do next.
Harry:	(*Proudly*) First I puts a big jug under this tap. (*He bends down and puts his mug under the tap of the full barrel*) Then I fills it up and pours it into this barrel. (*He lifts the mug and pretends to pour it into the half full barrel*) I keep doing this until this barrel is full.
Wormwood:	The brew trickles down over the shavings and mixes with the air you see. Air is very important. Without air ... no vinegar.
Ham:	Mm, yes, very interesting, and how often do you do this boy?
Harry:	Every day Mester, sometimes twice a day when it's hot weather.
Ham:	Well it certainly isn't hot today. (*Rubbing his arms*) I think, Mr. Wormwood, that we might speed up the process if we took a steam pipe from the boiler back there (*points behind him*) and brought it to warm up the kegs here.
Harry:	(*Muttering*) Then I'll have to do it twice every day!
Wormwood:	(*Clips Harry around the ear*) That's right lad now stop your muttering.
	Harry rubs his ear unhappily.
Ham:	(*Laughs*) Not necessarily Harry. I think, Mr. Wormwood, that it would be a lot simpler if we fitted a pump at the bottom of this barrel here and pumped the brew to a sprinkler at the top of the same barrel. Then it would trickle over the shavings constantly. You could do the whole process in a single barrel and Harry here wouldn't need to break his back. *Harry smiles –* Wormwood scowls.
Wormwood:	Mm, perhaps it is a good idea. (*Suddenly smiles*) Maybe I could get rid of this lad altogether then? *Harry stops smiling –* Wormwood chuckles
Ham:	I can think of an extra couple of features which might help.

Figure 13.7 A sample page from the Acid Test Drama
Source: Henderson, et al. (eds), 1987

Play Analysis Sheet

At the end of each act the Acid Test play record your answers to the following questions:

Act 1
- How was the wine made from date palms?
- What happened when the seal cracked on the last flask?

Act 2
- How was the vinegar used by Hannibal's soldiers?

Act 3
- Why was Mr. Ham famous?
- What was the raw material for vinegar?
- Using the information given draw the vinegar making apparatus used by Mr. Ham.
- What extra features did Mr. Ham and Wormwood discuss? How do they help the vinegar making process?

Figure 13.8 A play analysis sheet

1 Three company information sheets

These give background on the following:

- microbiology of vinegar
- testing the effectiveness of a vinegar tower using a pH meter
  keeping accounts (because the design must be built within budget)
- ordering materials and equipment and using the catalogue

The last point requires a little clarification. Although pupils are free to design and build a vinegar tower to any specification they wish, some limitations are necessarily imposed. All available materials and components are listed and illustrated in a 'Vinegar Parts' catalogue, together with their detailed specifications and prices (figure 13.9).

Each component is available to a company on a sale-or-return basis and must be ordered in advance (for example, during the previous lesson). This emphasises to pupils the need to plan carefully and bear in mind limiting factors such as cost. It also serves to reduce the burden on technical support by limiting the requirements for equipment.

2 Teacher Help

The teacher is available to 'help', but only in the role of 'consultant' to each

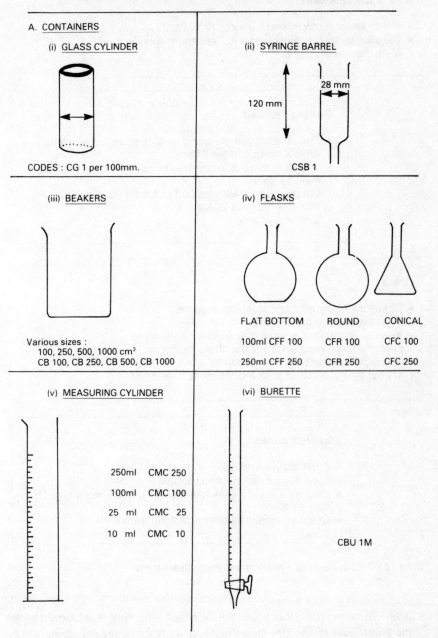

CATALOGUE OF EQUIPMENT WHICH MAY BE USED IN VINEGAR PLANT

A. CONTAINERS

   (i) GLASS CYLINDER

CODES : CG 1 per 100mm.

   (ii) SYRINGE BARREL

120 mm

28 mm

CSB 1

   (iii) BEAKERS

Various sizes :
100, 250, 500, 1000 cm³
CB 100, CB 250, CB 500, CB 1000

   (iv) FLASKS

FLAT BOTTOM	ROUND	CONICAL
100ml CFF 100	CFR 100	CFC 100
250ml CFF 250	CFR 250	CFC 250

   (v) MEASURING CYLINDER

250ml	CMC 250
100ml	CMC 100
25 ml	CMC 25
10 ml	CMC 10

   (vi) BURETTE

CBU 1M

Figure 13.9   A page from the Vinegar Parts Catalogue
Source: Henderson, et al. (eds), 1987

What's the problem?

- What idea or problem are you trying to test?
- Tell your partner or group about it. Take turns at doing this.
- Write it down or draw it.

Getting Planned

- Decide what you are going to do to solve the problem.
- Write it down or draw it here.
- If there is more than one way to solve the problem write them all down.
  List the good points and bad points for each method and decide which one to use.
- Is your plan safe?

Doing it!

- Get all the equipment and materials together.
- You may need to order these!
- Keep a record! Decide what to write down before you start. You may want to take some photographs.
- If your plan doesn't work when you try it find out why.
- Try out your plan again, with modifications if needed.

What Happened?

- What did you find out?
- Look at your records and pictures.
- Discuss what you think has happened with your group. Do they all agree?
- Could you make it better next time? How?

Figure 13.10 An example of a problem-solving guidance sheet

company. His or her consultancy time will be added to the final development costs for the tower! This really does makes pupils think twice before exhorting 'Miss, we can't do it!'

Further optional support may be given in the form of a four-part problem-solving guidance sheet (figure 13.10).

This breaks down the problem-solving process into the four main sections (see figure 13.1) for pupils. Within each section of the work, appropriate questions are asked to guide thinking and help pupils to articulate their ideas.

In the conclusion of the action part of this problem-solving simulation pupil companies present their working vinegar towers to the competitor companies (their peers). Features of each design and costings are evaluated, explained and discussed.

Debriefing

As with the previous simulation, the debriefing will take the form of a teacher-led whole class discussion. In this points of accuracy and issues arising may be raised, and pupils are given an opportunity to ask further questions.

You might try to carry out a tabulated analysis on 'Vinegar Production' similar to that for 'Designing a New Yoghurt' in table 13.2. This will help to check which aspects of the problem-solving process have been included and when they occur. It will also serve as a means of clarifying your objectives for the activity.

CONCLUDING COMMENTS

In this chapter I have outlined some approaches to problem-solving as a teaching and learning strategy by means of two simulation case studies. Hopefully I have given you a flavour of the exciting and active ways in which they can be used with pupils. Their design and use are based on a number of assumptions about real learning in real classrooms: that high levels of pupil motivation and interest are not always present; that ability, aptitude and favoured learning style vary quite widely (even within streamed classes); and that the curriculum imposes quite narrow limits on what might be tackled in terms of time and subject content. The examples I have described are available in full classroom versions (see further reading). They are intended as exemplars which you might wish to try without modification. But better still, they hopefully embody general elements of good practice which you may employ in designing and running your own problem-solving simulations. You will not wish every problem-solving task to be a whole investigation of this type. In some tasks you may require pupils to work at one or two elements of the problem-solving process, whether it is formulation, design or evaluation. Whole investigation tasks, however, help pupils to integrate these skills and provide an overall sense of achievement and purpose which is all too often lacking from too much practising of problem-solving sub-tasks.

In general, problem-solving tasks should convey a sense of ownership by allowing pupils to make some of the decisions necessary for the task. They should transfer some responsibility to pupils to take an active part in their own learning. However, this must be supported by the teacher through the use of materials that make the problem-solving process explicit to pupils. This is perhaps best done through context-specific help (as suggested in the case studies), but general support through the use of a problem-solving guidance sheet can help pupils to see the common elements in these tasks and may be a key to the growth of skill transferability.

The problem-solving simulations I have described are based on realistic scientific and technological contexts. This will be true for many of the 'relevant' contexts that you devise for yourself. As a consequence you will find that a considerable element of economic and industrial understanding (EIU) may easily be introduced as part of the basic scientific work. EIU is one of the cross-curricular themes that is particularly easy to address as an aim within scientific problem-solving (NCC, 1990). Environmental education and health education are two further examples of cross-curricular themes that are addressable within scientific 'PS2 style' problem-solving (see 'Preventing Heart Disease' in the Problem Solving with Industry series [Centre for Science Education, 1990] and 'The Limestone Enquiry' in SATIS volume 6 [ASE, 1986]).

Of course, problem-solving simulations are not the only form which active problem-solving may take. In the further reading section I have indicated other types and sources. I do not wish to advocate the use of problem-solving as a panacea for all the challenges of the National Curriculum. But I would like to recommend it to you as a valuable asset in the science teacher's repertoire. I hope that the suggestions and ideas for problem-solving found here, together with your own enthusiasm, will help you to put some of the flesh of the real world on the skeleton of the National Curriculum.

REFERENCES AND FURTHER READING

Association for Science Education (ASE) (1986) *Science and Technology in Society* (SATIS), Hatfield: ASE (these volumes contain many excellent context-rich problem-solving activities).
—— (1992) *Moving Targets*, Hatfield: ASE.
British Association for the Advancement of Science (1983) *Ideas for Egg Races and Other Practical Problem-Solving Activities*, London: British Association for the Advancement of Science.
—— (1985) *More Ideas for Egg Races*, London: British Association for the Advancement of Science.
Centre for Science Education, Sheffield City Polytechnic (now Sheffield Hallam University) (1990) *Problem-Solving with Industry Starter Pack – Teachers' Guide*, Sheffield: Centre for Science Education, Sheffield City Polytechnic (together with companion volumes two and three this series focuses on industrial contexts for active problem-solving. Problems include 'Why Did the Rope Break?', 'A Hair Raising Problem' and 'Preventing Heart Disease'.).
—— (1992) *Active Teaching and Learning in Science* (ATLAS), London: Collins (a lively volume of resources and practical ideas for science teaching. It includes a section on problem-solving and games and simulations).
Cullen, R. (1987) 'Problem-Solving: Vinegar Production' in Henderson, J., and Lally, V. E. and Cullen, R. (eds) *Teaching Strategies in Biotechnology*, Sheffield: University of Sheffield, Division of Education.
Department of Education and Science (DES) (1985) *Science 5 to 16: A Statement of Policy*, London: HMSO.
—— (1991) *Science in the National Curriculum*, London: HMSO

Henderson, J., and Lally, V. E. (1988) 'Problem-Solving and Controversial Issues in Biotechnology', *Journal of Biological Education*, 22 (2): 144–50.

Henderson, J., Lally, V. E. and Cullen, R. (eds) (1987) *Teaching Strategies in Biotechnology*, Sheffield: University of Sheffield, Division of Education (contains teaching materials for active problem-solving using biotechnology contexts).

Ingleby, D., Winspear, L., Lally, V. E. and Phipps, R. (eds) (1987) *Biotech*, Hatfield: ASE.

Jones, K. (1980) *Simulations: A Handbook for Teachers*, London: Kogan Page.

—— (1985) *Designing Your Own Simulations*, London: Methuen.

Lally, V. E., Knutton, S., Windale, M., and Henderson, J. (1992) 'A Collaborative Teacher-centred Model of In-service Education', *Educational Review* 44 (2): 111–26.

Lock, R. (1990) 'Open-ended Problem-Solving Investigations: What Do We Mean and How Can We Use Them?', *School Science Review*, 71 (256): 63–72.

Murphy, P. and Gott, R. (1984) *Science: Assessment Framework Age 13 & 15* (Science reports for teachers series), London: Assessment of Performance Unit.

National Curriculum Council (NCC) (1989) *Science: Non-Statutory Guidance*, York: NCC.

—— (1990) *Curriculum Guidance Four: Education for Economic and Industrial Understanding*, York: NCC.

Qualter, A., Strang, J., Swatton, P. and Taylor, R. (1990) *Exploration – A Way of Learning Science*, Oxford: Blackwell.

Watts, M. (1991) *The Science of Problem-Solving*, London: Cassell (a very up-to-date and comprehensive account of practical problem-solving including research issues, the National Curriculum and problem-solving. It contains much useful advice on setting up PS2–style activities.).

EQUIPMENT

A catalogue kit of simple vinegar tower parts may be assembled in about half a day. It should be sufficient for a whole class (approximately thirty pupils) and may be reused many times for this simulation. In 1992 the cost was about £40 excluding a storage trolley.

14 Teaching sensitive issues in science: the case of sex education

Jenny Henderson

Why teach sensitive issues in science education? How should they be approached? If learning is discussion-based, what problems are presented for the science classroom? This chapter shows how sensitive issues can be tackled in the science curriculum by presenting examples from the area of sex education. Many of the ideas, strategies and teaching points can be generalised to other areas which are also sensitive or controversial.

INTRODUCTION: TEACHING ABOUT SENSITIVE ISSUES

Much school science is about acquiring knowledge and skills. Concerned as it is with facts and principles, it has failed to engage many pupils and has had little meaning for the lives of the majority outside school (Henderson and Knutton, 1990; Claxton, 1991). It has failed to help pupils to develop an independence of mind and has not prepared them for the society in which they live. Many pupils will encounter science through the media in the form of the issues it raises, but they will also encounter it directly in the way it shapes their social and economic lives. They must acquire the skills to recognise science in its applications to economic, sociological and political issues. When they leave school they will be faced with opposing views. It is necessary for them to learn to explore their own views and those of others in order to develop an independent way of thinking. As a result of finding out more about themselves they will become more self-confident. They will acquire an understanding of bias and partiality of evidence and be willing to consider and be sensitive to the opinions of others.

Science is often presented to pupils in a way that makes it seem unproblematic. The science teacher 'knows' all the answers. By discussing sensitive controversial issues in science we are helping to modify the students' image of science towards a more realistic understanding.

There are many ways of approaching the teaching of sensitive issues, but if one is to guard against indoctrination, certain pedagogies would not be considered. A didactic style, for example, would be quite inappropriate. The approach should foster autonomy and critical awareness. It should renounce the authority of the teacher as the 'expert' capable of solving value issues. The teacher should refrain from supporting any side of a controversy and instead act as neutral chairperson who facilitates the pupils' exploration of the issue.

Information is acquired by considering evidence which should provide insights into other people's points of view and perspectives on life. The evidence may be presented as television broadcasts, video recordings, interviews or printed materials. Discussion, with pupils working in groups, is the ideal pedagogy. However, if we are to aim for active pupil participation some structuring will be required. This will encourage pupil involvement, provide an opportunity to practise the social skills of communicating and collaborating and help to develop cooperative group work skills.

PROBLEMS AND DIFFICULTIES OF DISCUSSION-BASED LEARNING

Introducing discussion-based work into the science classroom will not be without its problems. Some of these are summarised below:

- **Previous experience:** Students, particularly the older students, who have not experienced discussion-based activities may find this approach to learning threatening. It is certainly an effective approach in promoting the development of skills appropriate to handling controversial issues in the classroom, and is now supported by the National Curriculum. The following note is from the non-statutory guidance: '2.2 "Communication skills are firmly embedded in the attainment targets for science. The programmes of study for each key stage describe the range of communication skills the pupils will experience".'
- **The learning environment:** Traditional laboratories do not lend themselves to discussion-based activities. Where it is possible the room should be informal, carpeted and provided with comfortable chairs. It should be light, well ventilated, with ample room for movement. It should provide a private and safe environment.
- **The constitution of the group:** When teaching about sensitive issues it is preferable to have as small a group as possible as this will promote intimacy and sharing. With some topics, for example sex education, it may be more appropriate to teach in single-sex groups as the students may feel more relaxed and more likely to be open and honest during discussion. Group work should involve students working in pairs and in small groups as this will be more likely to overcome shyness and encourage contributions.
- **Teaching strategies:** It has already been said that a didactic style is inappropriate when teaching about controversial issues. Many strategies are far more successful in promoting discussion. These include simulation, games, case studies, role play, problem-solving exercises, open-ended questions and sentences, surveys and group work.
- **Assessment:** The skills fostered by discussion-based learning and cooperative group work are not easily assessed by traditional methods, but various possibili-

ties exist. Interviews, questionnaires and student self-assessment sheets could all contribute to a record of achievement.

- **Relationships between pupils and teachers:** Discussion in the classroom may be difficult because of the authority relationship between teacher and students where the teacher is dominant. Discussion-based work requires a reconsideration of the respective roles of teachers and students if it is to be successful. The teacher must help students develop their own ideas and respect the views of others. It may seem worrying for teachers to deliberately put themselves in a situation where they do not have direct control of what is learned and how the students interact. When controversial issues are discussed in the classroom, the techniques of control used by the teacher should help to foster independence and the development of critical insight by students.

- **Interventions:** Avoiding the temptation to interfere may prove difficult for teachers attempting discussion-based activities for the first time. Equally, when discussing controversial and sensitive issues, it is difficult to know when it is advisable to intervene. Teachers should learn not to be afraid of silences. If they intervene because they feel uncomfortable with the silence, they may stop someone who was about to make a point. Open-ended questions help to stimulate discussion – for example, 'What do other people in the group think?' or 'Would anyone like to add to that?'

- **Confronting prejudice:** Working with sensitive issues inevitably means working with prejudice. It is important to find ways of confronting the prejudice when it is voiced in ways that do not create bad feeling and which do not get in the way of the learning process. The group must agree which prejudices they are prepared to confront and then share the responsibility for challenging these prejudices in themselves and in other participants. The teachers' role is to facilitate this process. It may not be possible to stop a person's prejudice but it is possible to stop them using language and behaving in a way that the group finds offensive. It helps in this situation to confront the prejudice rather than the person.

TEACHING A SENSITIVE AND CONTROVERSIAL ISSUE: SEX AND HEALTH EDUCATION

In this chapter we will look at teaching approaches and practical activities that might be used when teaching sex and health education. The Education Act (no. 2) 1986 gives power to school governors to decide whether sex education shall be taught in school, but it is included in the National Science Curriculum and cross-curricular themes and also cannot be isolated from the rest of the curriculum. A separate written statement of the school's sex education policy must be available and kept up-to-date. Parents must be informed of the policy agreed with governors. Good practice is that which not only *informs* parents but also *involves* parents. Influences such as the family, community, peer group, media, legislation and the culture and religious backgrounds of students should be recognised.

Sex and health education in the National Science Curriculum

In attainment target 2: Life and living processes, at key stage 3, level 3, pupils should know 'the basic life processes common to humans', identifying processes such as 'reproducing'. At level 7 pupils should understand the life processes of 'reproduction'. The programmes of study state:

> Pupils should extend their study of the ways in which the healthy functioning of the human body may be affected by . . . viruses (including Human Immuno-deficiency Virus (HIV)), the abuse of solvents, alcohol, tobacco and other drugs, and how the body's natural defences may be enhanced by immunisation and medicines. They should study the human life cycle, including the physical and emotional changes that take place during adolescence, the physical and emotional factors necessary for the well-being of human beings in the early stages of the development, and understand the need to have a responsible attitude to sexual behaviour.

At key stage 4, an additional note appears in the programme of study:

> Pupils should consider how hormones can be used to control and promote fertility, growth and development in plants and animals, and be aware of the implications of their use. Pupils should have opportunities to consider the effects of solvents, alcohol, tobacco and other drugs on the way the human body functions.

Sex and health education as a cross-curricular theme

Health education is one of the five cross-curricular themes in the National Curriculum. There are nine components for a health education curriculum 5–16:

1 Substance use and misuse
2 Sex education
3 Family life education
4 Safety
5 Health-related exercise
6 Food and nutrition
7 Personal hygiene
8 Environmental aspects of health education
9 Psychological aspects of health education

The Guidance Document (NCC, 1990) suggests ways in which the health education curriculum may be implemented and outlines the advantages and disadvantages of each approach. The following approaches are thought to be most appropriate for secondary schools: permeating the whole curriculum; as a separately timetabled subject; as part of a PSE course/programme; or as part of a pastoral/tutorial programme. The document suggests the following programme at key stage 3 and key stage 4:

Key Stage 3 – Sex education

- recognise the importance of personal choice in managing relationships so that they do not present risks, for example to health or personal safety
- understand that organisms (including HIV) can be transmitted in many ways, in some cases sexually
- discuss moral values and explore those held by different cultures and groups
- understand the concept of stereotyping and identify its various forms
- be aware of the range of sexual attitudes and behaviours in present-day society
- understand that people have the right not to be sexually active; recognise that parenthood is a matter of choice; know in broad outline the biological and social factors that influence sexual behaviour and their consequences

Key Stage 4 – Sex education

- understand aspects of Britain's legislation relating to sexual behaviour
- understand the biological aspects of reproduction
- consider the advantages and disadvantages of various methods of family planning in terms of personal preference and social implications
- recognise and be able to discuss sensitive and controversial issues such as conception, birth, HIV/AIDS, child-rearing, abortion and technological developments which involve consideration of attitudes, values, beliefs and morality
- be aware of the need for preventative health care and know what this involves
- be aware of the availability of statutory and voluntary organisations that offer support in human relationships, e.g. Relate
- be aware that feeling positive about sexuality and sexual activity is important in relationships; understand the changing nature of sexuality over time and its impact on lifestyles, e.g. the menopause
- be aware of partnerships, marriage and divorce and the impact of loss, separation and bereavement
- be able to discuss issues such as sexual harassment in terms of their effects on individuals

SEX EDUCATION, HIV AND AIDS: PRACTICAL EXAMPLES OF ACTIVITIES AND TEACHING APPROACHES THAT ARE INTENDED TO PROMOTE FRANK AND OPEN DISCUSSION

In many schools sex education is taught as part of the personal and social education (PSE) programme. One of the main advantages is that it has the potential to be taught by a specialist team of teachers. If the staff are also personal tutors it has the added and very important advantage of being taught by those who have close relationships with their students. Yet surprisingly, sex education is still often the responsibility of the science department where it may focus on the cognitive and medical aspects and fail to tackle the work relating to attitudes and behaviour. In other schools, the science department is responsible for teaching the 'plumbing' and work on relationships and attitudes is left to PSE. This arrangement may well be regarded as unsatisfactory by both groups of teachers.

In an ideal world any teachers asked to teach sex education should themselves receive training. Work on HIV, sex and sexuality is more about the teacher than the student. How do you go about it? How might you approach it? If teachers do not feel comfortable, it is they who are the problem, not the children. It is therefore important to think through your own attitudes to sex and sexuality, to give consistent messages to the young people, to make the learning experience positive, enjoyable and informal.

Consider the diversity of the group, their cultural background, their differing ages and maturity, and make no assumptions about their sexual experience. This section offers some practical ideas and examples for the classroom.

Starters and ice-breakers

If you are teaching about a controversial issue to a group you do not know, it is a good idea to start with an activity to relax the participants and make them feel comfortable. Ice-breakers are intended to encourage members of a group to relax. They can be light-hearted, amusing and result in the exchange of information about themselves with the rest of the group.

ACTIVITY: 'If you weren't here, where would you like to be, money no object?

ACTIVITY: 'What did you want to be when you were little?'

Getting to know the group

One would hope that teachers would be teaching sex education to students they knew well. If not, it is important for members of the group to get to know each other as quickly as possible. There are many games for learning names.

ACTIVITY: Each member of the group writes her or his name on a large sheet of paper in the centre of the room. In turn each person tells a story or says something about the origin of her or his name.

Feelings and anxieties

Students may feel anxious and apprehensive before such a course, and it helps them to relax if they have an opportunity to share their feelings and discuss their anxieties.

ACTIVITY: In pairs, share one hope and one anxiety.

Setting a contract and agreeing ground rules

ACTIVITY: This activity would be very appropriate for a form tutor to use with his or her form when building relationships at the start of a school year.

Once these relationships have developed, there are few problems in tackling the teaching of a sensitive issue. When teaching such an issue to a group with whom one is not familiar, it is equally necessary to agree certain ground rules. Laying down the ground rules is important with any personal issue. HIV, for example, is a very important issue as it may be related to death and friends and family; it has, for example, to do with sex and sexuality and AIDS. Also important, however, is the way of working. Students will be working in groups, talking. There may be more than one person wishing to talk. It is therefore important for the group to determine basic rules – for example, confidentiality within the group, how to cope with disagreement, how to support each other, how to encourage participation, how to prevent assumptions being made about sex or sexuality, how to agree an anti-sexist/anti-racist policy. In groups of three or four brainstorm ground rules. Feed these back to the whole group. The group must all agree to each rule. The rules may be displayed and can be referred to when necessary.

Introducing HIV and AIDS

It is important at this stage to begin with students' feelings, anxieties, attitudes and prejudices towards AIDS/HIV.

ACTIVITY: My greatest fear
Each person writes his or her greatest personal fear on a card. The cards are shuffled and distributed randomly. Each person reads out, without comment, what is on the card he or she has been given. In pairs participants are asked to spend five minutes each way to share their own fear and their feelings about those of the group as a whole.

ACTIVITY: What do you know and what do you want to know about HIV and AIDS? or What do you want to know about sex/sexuality/sex education?

ACTIVITY: My expectation is . . .
It is important to find out from the group what they want out of the sessions. This may be done by discussion in pairs feeding back to the group or by a brainstorm from the whole group to find which are the issues and concerns they wish to address.
In sex education sessions these might include: the symptoms of HIV and AIDS, statistics/facts, transmission of the virus, clause 28, strategies for teaching sex education, etc.

Information

At this stage it is necessary to give the group information about the controversial issue, in this case about HIV and AIDS.

PRESENTATION: Information on HIV and AIDS/Transmission of HIV
This should be a short session confined to basic factual information with

opportunity for students to exchange and test the accuracy of the information they already have. Since a lot of information on HIV and AIDS is based on assumptions and prejudice, it is important that confusion about the risks of transmission are sorted out, especially if the information given challenges the assumptions and prejudices of the students. Thus, the basic information may be given in a short didactic session covering:

- what HIV and AIDS stand for
- the effect of the virus on the immune system
- the main diseases that constitute the syndrome
- the bodily fluids through which the virus can be transmitted
- the means by which the virus is transmitted
- testing the virus (see further reading)

Clarification

It is now important for students to apply the information they have acquired in order to exchange it for their own information and ask questions and clarify things for themselves. They should come to own the information, feel comfortable with it and, by the end of the session, feel they have shifted their perception of risk from people to practices.

The following activities may be used to enable students to apply the information:
ACTIVITY ONE: AIDS Questionnaire (from Harvey and Reiss, 1990)
1   What do the initials AIDS stand for?
2   What is AIDS?
3   What is HIV infection and what is the link between it and AIDS?
4   By the end of September 1989, how many cases of AIDS had been recorded in the UK? Tick one number:

                649   1149   1649   2649   4649   6469

5   How many carriers of the virus were there thought to be in the UK by the end of September 1989? Tick one number:

        1,000–2,500   2,500–5,000   5,000–10,000
        10,000–25,000   25,000–50,000   50,000–100,000

6   Which of the following are proven ways of transmitting the AIDS virus? Tick the appropriate ones:
By vaginal intercourse
Blood transfusion
By shared cups and glasses
In mother's milk
By oral sex
Use of shared sex toys
By anal intercourse
By kissing
In swimming pools
Across the placenta

Using shared hypodermic needles
By shaking hands
7   For each of the following statements write whether you think it is true or false.
   a)   Women cannot develop AIDS.
   b)   AIDS in the UK is mainly confined to homosexual men.
   c)   There is no known cure for AIDS.
   d)   AIDS is a problem mainly confined to Europe and North Africa.
   e)   Acting as a blood donor in the UK carries a risk of getting AIDS.
   f)   Using a condom guarantees protection against contracting HIV.
   g)   The test for HIV antibodies in the blood will tell a person whether or not
         they have become infected with HIV virus.
8   From where have you obtained most of your information on AIDS?
9   Have you discussed AIDS with:
   Parents?
   Friends of the same sex?
   Friends of the opposite sex?
   Boyfriend/girlfriend
10 Do you think that AIDS will cause people to change their sexual habits? Give
     your reasons.
11 Do you think that AIDS *should* cause people to change their sexual habits? Give
     your reasons.
12 Write two or three sentences which sum up what you feel about AIDS.

The answers to these questions are provided in *Aidsfacts* (Harvey and Reiss, 1990).

ACTIVITY TWO: Quiz on HIV/AIDS (from Dixon and Gordon, 1990)
1   Is it true that you can catch AIDS?
2   HIV came from:
   a)   Central Africa
   b)   North Africa
   c)   CIA
   d)   KGB
   e)   nobody knows
3   HIV has been SHOWN to be transmitted through:
   blood
   saliva
   semen
   sweat
   vaginal fluids
   breast milk
   skin
   vomit
   faeces
   urine
   tears
4   HIV can be transmitted by:

kissing
razors
blood transfusion
hugging
unprotected sexual intercourse
using drugs
oral sex
masturbation
insect bites
prostitutes
sexual intercourse using a condom

5   If you are HIV antibody positive:
   a)   you've got AIDS
   b)   you'll be dead in 5 years
   c)   you're infectious to other people

6   If you are antibody negative:
   a)   you're immune to HIV
   b)   you need not change your sexual behaviour
   c)   you have not come into contact with HIV

7   An antibody positive pregnant woman:
   a)   will transmit the virus to her unborn child
   b)   should have an abortion if she becomes pregnant

8   If you were HIV antibody positive, should you tell:
   a)   your GP?
   b)   your life insurer?
   c)   your sexual partners?
   d)   your employer?
   e)   your dentist?

9   The following are high risk groups:
   a)   homosexuals
   b)   heterosexuals
   c)   bisexuals
   d)   haemophiliacs
   e)   drug users
   f)   Africans
   g)   prostitutes
   h)   all of these
   i)   none of these

In *Working with Uncertainty* (Dixon and Gordon, 1990) the issues which these questions raise are listed.

ACTIVITY THREE: What do we know? (from Dixon and Gordon, 1990).
Prepare sufficient statement cards for each member of the group to have two each. Ask the group to imagine a continuum of risk on the floor. Sit the group in a circle and give the cards out to each person. Explain that in each case the risk assumes

the activity involves an infected person. Invite each person to read out what is on her or his card and place it on the continuum where he or she thinks it belongs, explaining why it has been put there. Other members of the group can challenge with extra information and suggestions and the owner of the card may change her or his minds. Continue until all the cards are laid out. Identify and remove cards about which there has been no disagreement. Focusing on those which have raised questions or disagreement, provide the factual information necessary for the group to make a decision.

Suggestions for Statement Cards:

> Kissing on cheeks
> Having lots of different sexual partners
> Injecting drugs for the first time
> Vaginal sex if you are on the pill
> Oral sex
> Having sex with your husband
> Having a blood transfusion in the UK
> Swimming in a public pool
> Using someone else's toothbrush
> Mouth to mouth resuscitation
> Deep kissing
> Having your ears pierced
> Sleeping with someone who has AIDS
> Having sex with a drug user
> Anal sex using a condom
> Sharing a drinking glass
> Hugging someone who has HIV
> Having casual sex abroad
> Injecting drugs using a shared needle
> Anal sex
> Caring for someone with AIDS

Plus:

> High Risk
> Low Risk
> No Risk
> Don't know

ACTIVITY FOUR: Condom use: Show the group how to put them on. Let them try using a model.

Attitudes towards sexuality and HIV

Working with issues surrounding HIV and AIDS inevitably means working with prejudice. It is important that these prejudices are recognised and challenged as they create confusion around information. The activity used at this point should encourage students to explore their own feelings and attitudes, their values and prejudices.

ACTIVITY: Car Park (from Dixon and Gordon, 1990)
In a large room ask students to line up and give each a card on which is written one
of the following roles. They are not to disclose their role until the end of the exercise.

A gay man who is HIV antibody positive

A gay man with AIDS

A 34-year-old white wealthy male who is an occasional cocaine user

A 32-year-old white female prostitute who is HIV antibody positive

A heterosexual married man

A heterosexual married woman

A 24-year-old black female prostitute

A lesbian

A pregnant HIV antibody positive woman

A pregnant woman

An HIV antibody positive bisexual married man

A single woman with AIDS

When they are lined up and in role, read out each of the following questions. If they
can answer 'yes' to that question they are to take one step forward; if 'no' they are
to remain where they are. They must answer 'yes' or 'no'.
Suggested questions:
Are you able to:

Join BUPA

Become a JP

Obtain life insurance

Expect sympathy from your GP when you are ill

Lead an active social life

Adopt a child

Go abroad on holiday

Work abroad

Obtain a mortgage

Work in a children's nursery

Have the sex you want when you want it

Kiss your lover in public

Plan 20 years ahead

Get medical help when you need it

Feel safe walking the streets after dark

Get support from society

Get free condoms if you want them

Have a home help if you need them

Expect sympathy from your family

Be honest with your colleagues

Have security in your employment

Plan a family

Get dental care when you want it

Marry your partner

Expect to be helped by the DHSS AIDS campaign

Expect to die where and as you would like

One by one ask participants to disclose the role they have assumed. De-role, asking the group to discuss the restrictions imposed on them by the roles defined in terms of sexual orientation and HIV infection.

ACTIVITY: Agree/Disagree

Designate an area of the floor 'agree' and 'disagree'. Give all participants a statement and ask them to place their statement saying whether they agree or disagree. Discuss each statement.

Examples of statements:

Lesbianism is an agreed and accepted form of sexuality

Lesbians don't catch HIV

Children are the innocent victims of HIV

In schools we should positively promote safer sex alternatives to sexual intercourse

The aim of sex education is to encourage people to enjoy their sexuality

All partners of people with HIV have the right to know

Definition of sex/sexuality and the language of sex

It is a good idea to agree a definition of sexuality within the group. There are important distinctions to be made between sexual choice, sexual orientation, sexual practice and sexual gender. Sexuality involves our relationships with ourselves, our partners, those around us and the society in which we live, whether we identify ourselves as homosexual, heterosexual, lesbian, bisexual or celibate.

It is also wise to establish a language that is acceptable to the group and with which the group feels comfortable and to provide the group with information on 'official' terms and when it is appropriate to use these terms.

ACTIVITY: Sexual language

Divide into six groups and give each group a large sheet of paper headed:

Female genital organs

Male genital organs

Vaginal intercourse

Anal intercourse

Oral sex

Masturbation

Tell the groups to not censor the language and to brainstorm all the words they know for the topic on their sheet. After ten minutes either pin the sheets up or ask the class to walk round the sheets adding words which are not already there. As a large group, go through the list making sure everyone realises the significance of each word, deciding which are and which are not acceptable for use in discussing sexual issues. The activity provides opportunity for discussion of the type of language which is used to describe sexual practices.

ACTIVITY: Sexual prejudice

This activity examines the prejudices that are held against sexually active groups. In small groups brainstorm the words used to describe:

    Young men
    Young women
    Gay men
    Lesbians
    Differently abled people
    Older people

Pin up the sheets and add words not already used. Discuss what the lists tell us about which people are allowed to be sexually active.

Issues and concerns

At this stage in a programme of sex education the students should feel sufficiently confident and relaxed to discuss their own experiences of the education they have received and their personal concerns and worries. One such concern is the apprehension they feel or will feel at the start of a sexual relationship. It is important for them to discuss these fears with their partners, and this is made much easier if they have been encouraged to think about the act and the implications of it before the time actually comes.

ACTIVITY: Concerns when contemplating your first sexual encounter

In a class it is important to assume there will be some young people who have not had a sexual encounter. Equally, depending on the age of the pupils, there are likely to be many who are sexually active. There may also be those who have been involved in a sexual experience which was not wanted, such as incest or abuse. In groups ask the class to brainstorm any concerns, thoughts, fears and worries they would have if they were contemplating their first sexual encounter. Phrasing it in this way means no member of the group has to admit whether or not they have had personal experience. The teacher may prefer to suggest single-gender groups for this activity. With some groups the teacher may decide it is less threatening to ask the students to hand in their concerns on a piece of paper. Collect the responses on a flip chart and with the whole group go through the list, discussing the issues that arise.

It may be appropriate to extend this activity to analyse the concerns. Ask the group to consider each statement and, marking with different colours of pen, decide into which of the following categories each fits:

    Self-concept
    Self-esteem
    Relationships (peers/parents/teachers)
    Values (what is right and wrong)
    Information
    Assertiveness
    Anything else

The concerns are more about self-esteem than anything else. Most young people are more concerned about their own body image and what their partners will think about them than about using contraceptives and catching HIV. Very few concerns are about obtaining information (for example, where do I get condoms from?).

Our own sex education

It is important at this stage to open the discussion about the sex education which they have already received and what they would have liked in terms of that education.

ACTIVITY: What education did you receive about sex and sexuality from school, parents, peers, medical literature?
Brainstorm together on a flip chart, discussing the issues as they arise. Discuss where the early messages about sexual behaviour came from, what was helpful, what helped them to talk to adults and what hindered them. Who should teach sex education? Where should it be taught? Should you have received more than you did?

ACTIVITY: What education did you need?
Brainstorm what would have helped young people to talk to adults about sex. What hinders this discussion?

Why have sex

It may help at this stage to consider the reasons why people have sex. For most young people loneliness is their greatest fear, and that is why they have sex.

ACTIVITY: Why do we have sex?
Brainstorm in a large group and discuss the issues. The group may decide that some of the reasons put forward could be provided for elsewhere.

Learning to be assertive

For the majority of young people, learning that they are able to say 'no' is an essential part of their education. There are many exercises that help to develop assertiveness skills.

Before starting an exercise, it is a good idea to consider the skills it is necessary to develop in order to be assertive. It may also be advisable to discuss with the students the difference between assertiveness and aggressiveness.

Assertiveness skills:

1 Be clear/direct/specific.
2 Use 'I' statements.
3 Don't apologise/justify/explain.
4 Be repetitive.
5 Make eye contact – shows you are confident and you mean what you say.
6 Keep your facial expressions consistent with what you are saying.

7 Posture should be upright and relaxed.
8 Use appropriate gestures.
9 Consider tone of voice/volume/inflection.
10 Choose an appropriate time and place.
   Remind the group to be aware of these skills and practise them to try and improve their performance.

ACTIVITY: A carousel
Arrange the chairs in an inner and an outer circle facing each other. Explain to the group that in the first instance the outer circle will try to assert their rights while the inner circle will argue and disagree. Each person in the outer circle is given a statement and told they have one minute to describe the context to their partner. The group are then told that at a signal from the teacher the pair will negotiate the statement for three minutes. They will then be given two minutes for debriefing. The statement is left on the chair whilst the people in the outer circle will move one place to the right and the inner circle move one place to the left. In this way each person will have a different statement to negotiate and a different partner for the negotiation. After an appropriate length of time, change roles so that those in the inner circle receive the statement and have the opportunity to assert their rights.
At the end of the activity, using a flip chart, debrief the whole group, discussing what they had learnt, what had helped and what had hindered them in their discussions.

Suggestions for statements:

   I want to use a condom.
   I want you to use a condom.
   I don't want penetrative sex.
   Even though I'm on the pill, I still want to use condoms.
   I'm not ready to have sex.
   I want to show I care but I don't want to have intercourse.
   I don't want to have anal sex.
   I think we should use a condom when having oral sex.
   I want to have more varied sex.
   I want my sexual needs satisfied.
   I don't want you to do that, it hurts.
   I'll come in for a cup of coffee but that's it.
   I just want you to stroke my back tonight.
   I want us to go to the youth clinic to sort out contraception.
   I don't want to go on the pill.
   I want to wait until we are married.
   I'm too young to have sex.
   I think we should go for HIV tests.
   I really love you so we don't need to worry about the virus.

A closing round

It may be that the course on HIV and AIDS has taken place over a short, concentrated period of time, two or three days, for example. In this case, at the end of any session that involves the discussion of sensitive issues, it is a good idea to finish with a light-hearted closing round. This will depend on the maturity of the group.

ACTIVITY: Negotiating safer sex
In pairs choose a situation, for example a one-night stand. Allow ten minutes for each pair to attempt to negotiate safer sex in the context of the relationship.
Creative safer sex: brainstorm within the group to consider alternative methods of safer sex.

ACTIVITY: 'Personal memo'
Ask the group to complete the following sentence.
'As a result of the sex education/HIV and AIDS training/drug education I am going to . . .'

ACTIVITY: Go round the group asking each one to say one thing that they will take away with them.

CONCLUSIONS

This chapter discusses some of the issues and problems that arise when teaching young people about sensitive and controversial areas of the curriculum. It uses sex education as its example. The chapter contains teaching approaches and activities that might be used in teaching sex education. Many of these could be adapted and used in any area of the science curriculum containing controversy and requiring sensitivity.

Sex education is controversial for many reasons. For instance, there are a number of areas of confusion. In the Education Act (no. 2) 1986, school governors were given the power to decide whether sex education should be a curricular component and, if so, what should be taught. It is also part of the National Curriculum. Clause 28 of the Local Government Act (1986) forbids presenting homosexual/lesbian partnerships as normal. The clause was intended to prevent the presentation of homosexual partnerships as a viable family alternative to heterosexual ones. There is nothing in the Education Act (no. 2) to prevent discussing homosexual/lesbian lifestyles.

Sex education is a sensitive subject to teach. Teachers may be required by their school to teach the subject when they do not feel comfortable or equipped to do so. In this case, the problem will not lie with the pupils but with the teacher. And yet so many relationships break down because people do not know how to discuss sensitive issues with each other. Surely, we are failing as teachers if we do not help young people to talk to each other about these delicate and yet vitally important issues which will affect them for the rest of their lives.

REFERENCES AND FURTHER READING

Learning about sex education, HIV and AIDS

Adler, M. W. (1991) *ABC of AIDS*, 2nd ed., London: British Medical Journal.

British Red Cross (1991) *Your Choice or Mine? Personal Relationships Fact File*, Dublin: Folens Limited, on behalf of The British Red Cross Society.

Department of Education and Science (DES) (1989) *Science in the National Curriculum*, London: HMSO.

Lee, C. (1983) *The Ostrich Position: Sex Schooling and Mystification*, London: Unwin.

Massey, D. (1988a) *School Sex Education: Why, What and How – A Guide for Teachers*, London: FPA Education and Training Department.

—— (1988b) *Teaching about AIDS*, London: HEA.

—— (1991) *Sex Education: Why, When and How,* London: FPA.

Morgan, D. R. (1990) *AIDS: A Challenge in Education*, London: Institute of Biology.

National Curriculum Council (NCC) (1990) *Curriculum Guidance 5,* London: HMSO.

Rogers, R. (1989) *HIV and AIDS: What Every Tutor Needs to Know*, London: Longman Tutorial Resources.

Ideas, activities and teaching strategies

Aggleton, P., Warwick, I., Horsley, C. and Wilton, T. (1990) *Aids: Working with Young People,* Horsham: AVERT, PO Box 91, Horsham, West Sussex, RH13 7YR.

Brandes, D. and Phillips, H. (1977) *Gamesters' Handbook. 140 Games for Teachers and Group Leaders*, Cheltenham: Stanley Thornes.

Dixon, H. and Gordon, P. (2nd ed. 1990) *Working with Uncertainty: A Handbook for Those Involved in Training on HIV and AIDS*, London: Family Planning Association.

Dixon, H. and Mullinar, G. (1985) *Taught not Caught: Strategies for Sex Education*, Wisbech: LDA, Duke Street, Wisbech, Cambs PE13 2AE.

Harvey, I. and Reiss, M. (1990) *Aidsfacts*, Cambridge: Cambridge Resource Packs, Cambridge Place, Cambridge CB2 1NS.

Handling Controversial Issues

Claxton, G. (1991) *Educating the Inquiring Mind: The Challenge for School Science*, London: Harvester Wheatsheaf.

Henderson, J. and Knutton, S. (1990) *Biotechnology in Schools: A Handbook for Teachers*, Milton Keynes: Open University Press.

Sheffield City Polytechnic (1992) *Active Teaching and Learning Approaches in Science*, London: Collins Educational.

Stradling, R., Noctor, M. and Baines, B. (1984) *Teaching Controversial Issues*, London: Edward Arnold.

Wellington, J. J. (1986a) *Controversial Issues in the Curriculum*, Oxford: Basil Blackwell.

—— (1986b) *The Nuclear Issue*, Oxford: Basil Blackwell.

15 Practical approaches to teaching and learning about the nature of science

Mick Nott

The nature of science is a challenge for science teachers. This chapter focuses on practical approaches to teaching the nature of science in secondary school science education. The purpose is to discuss how curriculum rhetoric can be turned into classroom actions, not to discuss the politics and logistics of the implementation of assessment. The focus is on activities that concentrate on the teaching and learning of the nature of science.

BACKGROUND: THE PROGRAMMES OF STUDY, NON-STATUTORY GUIDANCE AND ATTAINMENT TARGET 1

The programmes of study

There are sound educational reasons for teaching the nature of science, as well as legal and coercive reasons. Children are entitled to the National Curriculum; therefore, it is the duty of the science teacher to ensure that children have access to the PoS. When classrooms and departments are inspected it will be expected that the practice and schemes of work follow the PoS. The attainment targets (ATs) are solely the assessment 'contract'. The PoS are the teaching 'contract'.

In the general introduction to the PoS for children aged 11 to 14 the NC states: 'To communicate, to apply and to investigate scientific and technological knowledge and ideas, and to understand the history of scientific ideas, are essential elements of a developing experience of science.' It goes on to state: 'Pupils should be given opportunities to develop knowledge and understanding of how scientific ideas change through time. They should study the development of some important ideas in science.'

Later, in the general introduction to the PoS for children aged 14 to 16, the NC includes the statement:

Pupils should develop their knowledge and understanding of the ways in which scientific ideas change through time and how the nature of these ideas and the uses to which they are put are affected by the social, moral, spiritual and cultural contexts in which they are developed. In doing so, they should begin to recognise that, while science is an important way of thinking about experience, it is not the only way.

These general statements indicate that these are areas which teachers have to teach and which children are expected to experience, but they will not be part of the national assessment programme.

Non-statutory guidance: two domains for the nature of science

The PoS provides little help for classroom action. However, the non-statutory guidance (NSG) is very definite on two aspects or domains for the nature of science:

1 The first-hand experience: How and what are the children learning about science with practical experiences?
2 The second-hand experience: How and what are the children learning about science from stories about scientists and scientific ideas?

First, the NSG states:

It is important . . . that teachers . . . take time to draw their pupils' attention to how they are learning science. It is at this point [the nature of science] comes in, encouraging pupils to reflect on their own experience in order to develop their understanding of the nature of science.

The important part for classroom practice is the idea that children should reflect on their own experience. This could involve the children in considering questions at different stages of practical work that the teacher may ask, such as: 'What do you think will happen and why?' 'What is in this set of results which convinces you that . . .?' 'Can you explain why . . .?' 'Why do you think this experiment was a test of this theory?'

Secondly, the NSG states:

There is another strand to the nature of science which is less easy for pupils to develop from direct experience.

This includes how scientific ideas have developed in response to different needs both through time and within different cultures.

1 Attainment target (AT 1)

The strand of second-hand experience is *not* assessed, whereas the strand of first-hand experience is. Examples of statements that involve the nature of science and that will be assessed are given in figure 15.1. These statements are all included in AT 1, 'Scientific Investigations'.

So children should move from first-(or second-)hand experience into constructing and maybe altering their scientific models of the world and then back again (see figure 15.2). This pedagogic model fits closely with a particular view of the epistemology of science (Hesse, 1973).

The nature of science

At each level, students should be able to ...

Level 3 ... distinguish between a description of what they observed and a simple explanation of how and why it happened.

Level 4 ... draw conclusions which link patterns in observations or results to the original question, prediction or idea.

Level 5 ... formulate hypotheses where the causal link is based on scientific knowledge, understanding or theory.... evaluate the validity of their conclusions by considering different interpretations of their experimental evidence.

Level 6 ... use their results to draw conclusions, explain the relationship between variables and refer to a model to explain the results.

Level 7 ... Explain the limitations of the evidence obtained from their own investigations.

Level 8 ... use scientific knowledge, understanding or theory to generate quantitative predictions and a strategy for the investigation.

Level 9 ... use a scientific theory to make quantitative predictions and organise the collection of valid and reliable data.

Level 10 ... use and analyse the data obtained to evaluate the law, theory or model in terms of the extent to which it can explain the observed behaviour.

Figure 15.1 Examples of statements on the nature of science

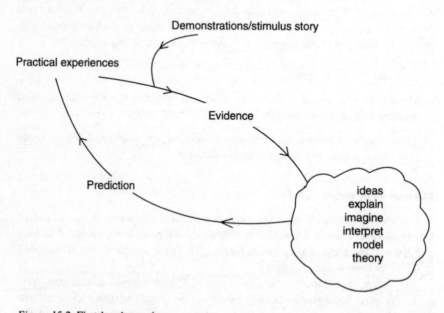

Figure 15.2 First-hand experience
Source: Solomon, 1991

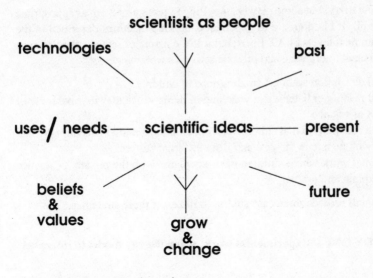

Figure 15.3   Second-hand experience
Source: Solomon, 1991

An example of this is the lessons that a science teacher would organise around the practical experience that copper goes black when heated in a flame (see Nuffield, 1971). The initial experience would be organised by the teacher; after all, children are hardly going to be spontaneously putting copper foil into bunsen flames. But the subsequent interpretations, resultant predictions and consequent practical experiences would be a matter of negotiation between the children themselves and the children and the teacher.

The strand of second-hand experience is the one that links the scientific ideas to culture and time, as represented in figure 15.3. This is linked with the model in figure 15.2.

For example, a science teacher may be developing the germ theory and do some demonstration work analogous to Pasteur's experiments with broth and swan-necked flasks. This would be an ideal time to highlight that the school demonstrations are analogous replicas of previous experiments. The story of Pasteur could be used for background reading, DART activities or stimulating practical work with the children (Solomon, 1991; Futtock, 1991).

CLASSROOM STRATEGIES FOR THE NATURE OF SCIENCE

School science in England and Wales is dominated by practical work. Although the value of this work has been questioned (see, for example, Hodson, 1990), science teachers are used to organising demonstrations and practicals and to setting written work based on them and the theories they are meant to illustrate. However, the nature of science sets new challenges that few science teachers have tried: some may be willing to try, but some may be unwilling to recognise them as appropriate to science at all. If children are to experience the kind of things described in the separate attainment levels of AT 1 pertaining to the nature of science, then science teachers will need to organise and provide activities which include:

- structured discussion amongst small groups of children
- structured reading or listening or watching of items which may involve some of the stories of science
- drama and role play so that children can develop the qualities of sympathy and empathy with people in the past and from different cultures
- experimental work where children have to engage with the models of science both to explain and predict

This chapter will provide three case studies to illustrate these strategies.

CASE STUDY ONE – Experimental work: using the ray model to interpret and predict

Attainment levels 6 and 7 in 'Scientific Investigations' expect that children will be able to use models to explain and predict experimental evidence. The following example illustrates how the history of science could provide ideas to structure classroom activities. This may also satisfy the need to introduce children to the history of scientific ideas as described in the PoS. Children are expected in school science to use and understand the ray model of light. Research (Driver *et al.*, 1985) has shown that this model is difficult to assimilate. My own experience of school teaching convinced me of the difficulty children had in drawing ray diagrams because they did not understand the model. The children I taught had not latched on to the idea of the infinite extension of the ray. Figure 15.4 shows a difference between children's science and scientists' science.

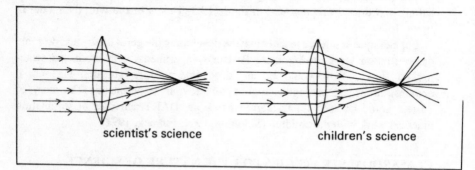

Figure 15.4 Children's science, scientists' science

Another 'standard' diagram that children find problematic is the pinhole camera. Figure 15.5 shows a standard diagram. Every item in the diagram is represented by lines on paper. Some lines have arrowheads drawn on them, but in my experience children often didn't notice them. The *real* object, the *theoretical* rays, the *real* camera and the *ethereal* image are all represented by lines of the same status. It is my hunch that this lack of differentiation may create comprehension problems. The diagram only makes sense if you understand the model already.

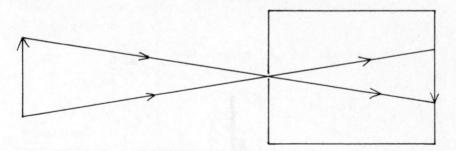

Figure 15.5 Standard diagram for a pinhole camera

An Arabic scientist, Al-Kindi, worked with a ray model to explain the formation of shadows and the production of images in the camera obscura. Centuries later, in another continent, Kepler worked on the problem of image formation through apertures. To understand the phenomenon, Kepler modelled rays of light by using threads. (This use of threads was well known to artists; see Pedoe, 1976).

One of the diagrams that Al-Kindi drew, using the ray model, was to explain the formation of a shadow by a point source (see figure 15.6). The point D represents a point source. DE is the height of the source above the bench. AB represents an opaque object, and DAG is the ray which grazes the top of AB. The distance BG then indicates the length of the shadow cast on the bench.

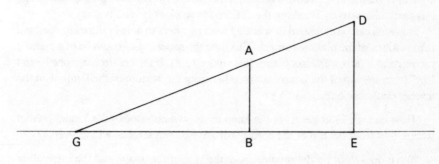

Figure 15.6 Al-Kindi's explanation of shadows

Children can set up a raybox and screen on a bench to see if Al-Kindi's model works, but it may be more effective to have them work with the model first. Children can be given paper cut-outs of a raybox and screen; they could 'borrow' Kepler's use of a thread to model a ray (see figure 15.7). The teacher could ask questions like:

'What does the model predict will happen to the length of the shadow if you . .

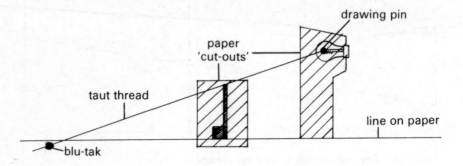

Figure 15.7 Using a thread to model a light-ray

. . . move the screen towards or away from the lamp?'
. . . move the lamp towards or away from the screen?'
. . . use a smaller or larger size screen?'

The children can use the thread 'ray' to make predictions and then go to the apparatus and see if, according to the model, their predictions were correct. If the teacher judiciously chooses the size of the paper cut-outs to match the size of the apparatus, then the children can make qualitative and quantitative predictions. Also, this particular activity is asking the children to work only with one ray.

This idea can be extended to working with two rays to help children understand explanations of the pinhole camera. This time the paper cut-outs can be of a pinhole camera and a carbon filament lamp (see figure 15.8). If the children use one thread 'ray' from the top of the lamp and the other from the bottom of the lamp, then the teacher could ask questions like:

'How can the light get from the lamp to the screen? Does your model predict where light from the top of the object will arive on the screen and vice-versa?'

'What does your model predict about the size of the image and the orientation of the image? Work with the model first and then go to the apparatus and test your prediction.'

'What will happen to the size of the image as the distance between the camera and lamp is made smaller or larger? Work with the model first to make a prediction and then go and test it with the apparatus.'

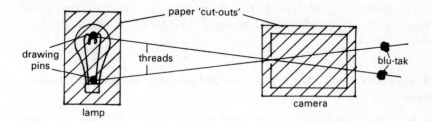

Figure 15.8 Using threads to model a pinhole camera

There are more possibilities that come to mind. Different colours for the two threads may help some children understand the image inversion, or with some children the teacher may ask them to try and use or adapt the model to see if it can help to explain how the brightness of the image alters with the distance of the object. The teacher may wish some children at some time to explore phenomena that are hard to explain with the model, so that the notion that scientific models have limits is raised. The important part is that with careful organisation the teacher should be able to encourage the children to move to and fro between practical experience and scientific model via evidence and prediction (see figure 15.2).

If children experience these activities, they are not only experiencing Attainment levels 6 and 7 of 'Scientific Investigations' but they are also working with AT 4, 'Physical Processes', where some knowledge of the ray model will be essential. They are learning to use and apply standard scientific models. This example draws on the history of science, but it isn't teaching children the history of science.

Al-Kindi's and Kepler's work are anachronistically juxtaposed to provide practical work to help the learning of a currently acceptable model. This doesn't stop a teacher telling the story about Al-Kindi or about Kepler and this may help children understand that scientific ideas have been created and developed in different cultures and in different times (see figure 15.3). These stories about science and scientists are important. Generally children enjoy them, teachers enjoy telling them and would like to know more of them, and they counteract negative images (or no images) of other cultures and people in the past. They also provide an experience appropriate to the general introduction for the PoS for the later years.

However, the prime motivation for creating the activity is for children to learn, use and understand the ray model of light. The other point of interest here is that the model is provided by the teacher. This is not to say that time shouldn't be spent eliciting children's ideas on how shadows and images are formed, but once they are elicited then they could test their ideas against the scientists'(teachers') model. It is my belief that children in school laboratories and with school apparatus will not rediscover or uncover many scientific theories. The teachers' role is to offer reasonable explanations which, in most circumstances, can be reasonably tested.

The teachers and children with whom this work was used on a trial basis found it worthwhile; the materials are now published in *Exploring the Nature of Science* (Solomon, 1991).

CASE STUDY TWO – Discussion work and role play: the story of Edward Jenner

The next case study concerns some curriculum materials called 'Jabs for James Phipps', which can be found in Solomon (1991). The specific topic is the story of Edward Jenner's work on vaccination. These materials help implement the programme of study for AT 2, which states children should study ' . . . how the body's natural defences may be enhanced by immunisation . . .', and also AT 1, which states ' . . . through activities which . . . involve the use of secondary sources . . . [pupils are encouraged] to appraise critically their investigation and suggest improvements to the methods'. Teachers have slotted the materials in with units on topics like microbiology or health.

There is a series of programmes produced for schools called *Scientific Eye* (Yorkshire Television, 1984). In one particular programme, called 'Minibeasts and Disease', is a short (approximately five minutes) cartoon of the story of Edward Jenner and the famous vaccination of the small boy called James Phipps. The style is 'jokey', but this does not detract from the fact that the main points of this scientific episode are raised. The experimental procedure is described in a clear chronological order. A rationale is also provided for Jenner's actions. The cartoon suggests with its imagery that James was not necessarily a willing volunteer to an 'untested' procedure. This (unintentionally?) raises ethical issues about this work. So here is a resource, common to many schools, which contains information about the introduction of a new idea, clearly describes the experiment and raises ethical and moral issues surrounding the procedure. It forms an ideal stimulus for some classroom activities about the nature of science.

The structure of the materials

The published materials consist of the following:

1 Telling a story

The first part is an activity to process the information in the cartoon story in the video. The children are split into groups of approximately four. Each group is given an envelope with jumbled chunks of text which describe the story. The group task is to put the chunks of text in the right chronological sequence. (See figure 15.9 for the ten chunks of text.)

Jenner's experiment

✂ --

Jenner puts cowpox pus into James's arm.

✂ --

Jenner sees that James doesn't get smallpox.

✂ --

JENNER HEARS THAT THE MILKMAIDS DON'T GET SMALLPOX.

✂ --

Jenner decides that having cowpox stops you getting smallpox.

✂ --

Jenner sees that James suffers from cowpox for a few days, and then gets well.

✂ --

JENNER TAKES SOME PUS FROM A SMALLPOX VICTIM AND PUTS IT INTO JAMES'S ARM.

✂ --

Jenner thinks that if he gives someone cowpox first they won't get smallpox.

✂ --

JENNER HEARS THAT MILKMAIDS OFTEN GET COWPOX.

✂ --

JENNER TAKES COWPOX PUS FROM A MILKMAID.

✂ --

Jenner thinks that having cowpox might stop you getting smallpox.

✂ --

Figure 15.9 Jenner's experiment
Source: Solomon, 1991

If some blanks are included in the envelopes then the children can add any bits of information that they think are important. The children can take part in the 'ordering' and the telling of the story. When the pieces of paper are in the right order they can then be stuck onto a large piece of paper to make an 'instant' poster detailing the events of the story in the correct temporal sequence.

The purpose of this activity is to provide an alternative way of processing the information in the cartoon – in other words, to retell the story in a different manner. If done in mixed-ability groups it provides an opportunity for all children to contribute to the telling of the story.

2 Evaluating an experiment

The second part of the activity is to then open a second envelope containing pieces of paper with the phrases 'making a hypothesis', 'observing', 'prediction', 'reaching a conclusion' and 'doing an experiment' (see figure 15.10). The children's task is then to match these words to the places where they think they occur in the story of Jenner's experiment that they have just put on the poster.

The purpose of this second activity is to help children to analyse the structure of the experiment. The words used are all found in AT 1, 'Scientific Investigations'. Teachers who have used these materials agree that the evaluation of Jenner's experiment happens, but it has also been reported that the analysis of the structure of the experiment has a transferability across to other scientific investigations. The following is an extract from an interview with a teacher:

> The amazing thing for me came in the next module along when the kids . . . were planning an investigation. . . . One girl came back, she had a series of flow diagrams . . . she had written on little boxes 'hypothesising here', 'testing here' and 'observing here' and I said, 'Where did you get all this from then?' She said she remembered it from the last unit that we did on the Jenner story. I went and had a chat with some of the other kids, and they had actually transferred the skills and ideas from ['Jabs for James Phipps'] to another [module], which to me is fairly successful. . . .'

> (Nott, 1992a: 222)

It appears that the children, having analysed (and criticised) the structure of experimental work as exemplified in the Jenner story, learned something about the structure of experiments. That learning had then been transferred to the planning of their own benchwork experiments. It may be that learning 'processes' through stories is as important as learning them by doing experiments. The processes of experimental planning could be seen as the identical processes in the Jenner story.

3 Values and experiments

Lastly, the children can be invited to discuss whether they think Jenner's experiment was a 'fair test'. They can suggest improvements to Jenner's experimental design. They can be asked to discuss whether all improvements would be right and proper in terms of whether they would be allowed to do them, or whether they felt it would be right to do them.

The purpose of this activity is to encourage the children to evaluate the experi-

Process words

OBSERVING

Meaning: **To watch carefully what is happening.**

(As well as using your eyes you can observe by listening, smelling, touching and occasionally tasting.)

MAKING A HYPOTHESIS

Meaning: **To have an idea about why something happens.**

(You can use this idea to design experiments.)

DOING AN EXPERIMENT

Meaning: **When you design and carry out a test for your hypothesis.**

PREDICTION

Saying what you think is going to happen.

REACHING A CONCLUSION

Deciding what your experiment shows.

(You might be deciding if your hypothesis is right or wrong.)

Figure 15.10 Process words
Source: Solomon, 1991

ment and hence to consider whether there are any ethical and moral limits on the nature of the experiment and hence medical experiments in general.

4 Role play

When children watch the cartoon they do so with interest and feeling. The cartoon implies that the procedure involved some risk and possible hurt to James. This is done in a way that is amusing, albeit darkly amusing. The materials contain a role play activity so that children can sympathise and empathise with the characters in the Jenner story.

Role play is one of the activities that science teachers are told is appropriate for teaching about the nature of science in the non-statutory guidance (NCC, 1989). (For a further introductory discussion on role play and drama in school science, see Bentley and Watts, 1988.)

The characters are the obvious characters in the cartoon – Jenner, James Phipps and Sarah Nelmes, the milkmaid. However, 'new' characters are also added. These are Mr and Mrs Phipps and James's aunt and uncle. These last two characters are fictitious; they are presented as two people who had James's interests at heart, and their views are constructed to represent contemporary arguments for and against Jenner's work.

A role card is available for each character, and questions at the end stimulate discussion amongst the children and make them start to build a character on the information they have (see figure 15.11 for examples).

A class can be split into small groups so that the roles can be built in groups and then one child from each group can act out the role – and even be prompted by her or his colleagues. (A concise background to the organisation of role play in science is contained in Williams, Hudson and Green, 1992.)

The pupils should spend time (approximately fifteen minutes) 'getting into role' in groups. Then one child from each group can play the part of the character. The scenario suggested in the published materials is a press conference where those not playing a role can act as journalists. This format has been seen to work extremely well – children are familiar with press conferences from the news. It should also be noted that a press conference is an anachronism but the point is to play a role where feelings and values can be explored, not to play a drama that looks for historical authenticity.

Press conferences observed have covered a range of issues that the role cards raise, such as:

- fatalism, i.e. if God chose you to get smallpox then that was your fate versus the motivation of Jenner that God would be benign and want people to be saved
- authority of experts on the risks of the experiment versus the risk of catching smallpox
- the ethics of the experiment, including issues of experiments on animals
- the influence of the employer/employee relationship between Jenner and the Phipps household

James

You are eight and three-quarters years old and love fishing. You have gone to Sunday school a few times but you usually manage to escape and go down to the river. You don't want to learn to read. You don't want to start work either, but you know you will have to as soon as you are nine.

When you were little you fell out of a tree and broke your leg. Your father got Dr Jenner to set the broken bone and it hurt very badly. You have always been scared of Dr Jenner from that time. Once he gave you a medicine to cure your fever which was made from bitter aloes. You couldn't get the taste out of your mouth for a week afterwards.

You don't know much about smallpox except that your aunt had it. Now her face looks horrible with large deep pits all over it. You cannot even bear to kiss her.

Now decide:

Did you understand what Dr Jenner was going to do?
How would you feel about asking the doctor questions?
Now that you are safe from having smallpox would you advise your friends to have the vaccination too?

James' Mum

You did not go to school but have worked with your husband in the fields for many years. Now that he is gardener to Dr Jenner things are much easier.

You have had nine children but two of them died when they were only babies. You have never forgotten that. Dr Jenner did come and give the babies some medicine but it did not help them. He was not able to help your sister either when she died in childbirth.

James is your youngest and you know you spoil him a little, but you can't help it. He is always out fishing when your husband wants him to help in the garden. A month ago your husband suggested that James should be given smallpox now to prevent him from getting it later. That seemed terribly dangerous. You didn't sleep for a whole week worrying about it.

Now decide:

How do you feel about doctors?
What did you think when Dr Jenner explained what he was going to do to James?
Did you talk it over with your husband? If so what did you say to him?

Figure 15.11 Examples of role cards
Source: Solomon, 1991

- the uncertainty whether the cowpox 'agent' would mutate into something more virulent inside James

And all of this in approximately ten minutes!

No work has been done with children on following up this classroom experience, but it does indicate that the materials stimulate a broad coverage and, in some cases, expression of some subtle ideas.

Teachers have been inventive and creative with it as well. One teacher reported creating the scenario for the role play as 'the Phipps' family tea' – familiar occurrence for children to use; and there have been children working the story up into 'the Jenner rap' (Nott, 1992a), and even a ballet!

The evidence appears to be that teachers have found this work to be very valuable both in exploring moral and ethical issues and in reprocessing the story and procedures of the experiment itself.

These materials deal only with a very narrow case, i.e. the experiment on James Phipps by Edward Jenner. It is important to add that the textbook impressions that it was solely Jenner who invented a safe technique of immunisation are wrong (see Smith, 1987). The story of immunisation in England is one that involves other cultures and a determined woman, Lady Mary Wortley Montague (Alic, 1986). There is also available some excellent classroom material, 'The long war against smallpox' (Science Education Group, York 1990), which adds to the historical dimension of the materials above and introduces the multicultural dimension. Both teachers and children learn about the nature of science from this.

CASE STUDY THREE – Demonstration work: working with different interpretations

The last section of this chapter is an opportunity to share some previously unpublished work written for school children on the topic of Brownian motion. The National Curriculum asks that children consider 'different interpretations of their experimental evidence'. Many teachers I have spoken with find this problematic – their experience is that children have difficulty in considering one interpretation, let alone two!

The National Curriculum also states that school children are expected to ' . . . make predictions, based on some relevant prior knowledge, in a form that can be investigated'.

It may be important that children learn that scientists have interpreted the same phenomena differently in order to understand that different interpretations are possible and even desirable. The materials, therefore, present children with one possible interpretation (Brown's original hypothesis) followed by our current interpretation; then the children have to suggest experiments and predicted results which will decide which of the two interpretations is correct.

The children work with Brown's ideas and then with our contemporary interpretation. The purpose is to work with both but to argue the case against Brown using our interpretation so that the contemporary scientists' model becomes more familiar and reasonable to the children.

The work described is targeted at AT 1, particularly with reference to consideration of different interpretations and at the programme of study for AT 3, where it is implied that children should be developing a particulate model of matter.

The materials thus stress figure 15.2 above, first-hand experience, but do it by providing participation in a story and a practical demonstration. This also provides the opportunity to share with children Brown's motivation for looking at pollen through a microscope – hardly a chance occurrence!

The school materials

It used to be the case that demonstrations and models of Brownian motion were commonplace in English schools, but recent personal experience with teachers suggests that it is a topic that is being squeezed out by the necessity to include so much in the National Curriculum.

I find this lamentable as the understanding and analysis of this phenomenon were critical pieces of evidence for the reality of atoms. The story, from Brown in 1827 to Perrin's Nobel Prize in 1926, is a long and discontinuous one. Some details of it can be found in a piece on the nature of science for schoolteachers (Nott, 1992b). Whilst I was researching and writing this piece, some ideas for activities that could be done with students both at schools and university were developed.

School textbooks never tell you why Brown was looking at pollen particles through a microscope. In fact, Brown had a clear research programme in mind, but it was nothing to do with atomistic theories. As a schoolteacher I had never known why Brown was looking at pollen, and in fact it had never occurred to me to reflect on his reasons.

In English secondary schools we have a piece of apparatus called a smoke cell (Nuffield Foundation, 1967). This is used in various years; children are expected to look at the smoke particles and explain their movement in terms of uneven bombardment from the air molecules in the cell.

In my schoolteaching experience and that of others (Rowland, 1991), this demonstration can be difficult for children to set up. When it is set up it is at first difficult for them to perceive what the teacher can perceive – a common experience for all with microscope work. When the small particles are discerned, the children need help to describe the motion and they then usually need some kind of model to help them grasp our understanding and explanation of what is going on.

The materials lead the children through Brown's research programme in stages and get the children to discuss it and evaluate Brown's work from as close to his perspective as they can. This enables them to work with his interpretations.

The next stage is the demonstration of the smoke cell and a three-dimensional kinetic model of a gas. At this stage the teacher can present the contemporary interpretation of Brownian motion.

The last piece of work is to ask the children to imagine that they could write to or telephone Brown, and their task is to explain to Brown the modern interpretation and to suggest experiments he could do to persuade him of the modern point of view.

The materials used are in appendix 15. A.

A report on the use of these materials

The materials described above have been used on a trial basis with two key stage 3 science classes. This chapter is about practical approaches to the nature of science, and in that spirit what follows is a report on the way that the materials were taught and the way that the children responded to them.

Two classes were taught: one high ability, the other average ability. They were 12-year-olds and mixed gender. Each class had two one-hour lessons taught consecutively on a Wednesday morning, as this was the way it was timetabled in the school. The classes were taught in consecutive weeks in their comprehensive school.

The children had done work on atoms and particle models before but had never experienced or heard of Brown or Brownian motion. I told them that this work was the kind of experiment that I did and that part of my job was to experiment with science lessons. I did not state or define any clear learning objectives at the beginning as, first, I wanted to see what the children took away from it. I introduced the topic as a topic about Brown and his experiments and how we now look at them.

The bits of the story were already in separate envelopes. The classes were split into six discussion groups with four children in each group. The first bit of the story was handed out. The story was read out by the teacher and then the children were asked to discuss the questions and statements at the end in their small groups.

The children proved to be very inventive in providing possible alternative explanations to Brown's for why the pollen moved. The range of alternatives were:

- pollen reacted with the water (both classes)
- pollen might be dissolving (class 1)
- pollen moved by wind (both classes)
- pollen moved by water (both classes)
- something to do with heat (class 2)/convection currents (class 1)
- pollen drowning (class 1)

When these were offered the teacher adopted the role of scribe and wrote the suggestions on the board. The children were praised for having so many ideas. When it came to the question of whether Brown would want to think of other ideas for why the pollen moved, only one of the small groups out of the twelve (each class had been split into six smaller groups for the discussion work) thought that he (or they!) might. Eleven of the twelve groups thought that if you were Brown then a positive result would make you think your theory is reasonable – no Popperians here!

It was surprising how short the discussion time needed to be – in the region of three minutes each time. During the discussion times the teacher didn't interfere but just circulated to note when discussion seemed to be exhausted within the small groups.

Task-orientated small group discussion of this kind was new for these children, and they were praised when they kept on task. They were also praised for their concentration and the range of ideas they had. At the end of each discussion 'bit' each small group was asked to report back, and those who spoke clearly were praised. The next bit of the story was handed out whilst the children made their responses.

Each time another bit of the story was revealed the teacher read out the text at the top of each sheet, and especially the one for sheet 5, as the length of this is daunting for some children.

After the discussion work came the demonstration of Brownian motion using the smoke cell. The classes were told that we use air and smoke particles in school as the motion is easier to see but basically it is the same kind of soot that Brown had used. A 'sponge' activity was used whilst the teacher set up the smoke cell; the children were asked to copy a diagram of the Brown experiment and the smoke cell demonstration from the board. There were only two smoke cells and the following technique was used to demonstrate Brownian motion to the whole class.

In each class two girls were asked to come and look down the microscopes. They were then asked to answer the teacher's questions so that the rest of the class could hear their replies. They were asked what they could see; if they said 'nothing', they were asked to look for tiny dots of light – like very distant stars. This simile worked, and then they were asked to describe what the dots of light were doing and describe their motion. Words like 'jiggling' and 'jerking about' were used; then they were asked if they could see what was making the particles jerk about and to describe to the rest of the class if the smoke particles were hitting each other or not. They said not – by this time the rest of each class was intrigued and paying attention and very curious to have a look. They now knew what to look for, and it took no more than half a minute for each child to look down the microscope and see the motion.

The science teacher present said that this technique worked much better than asking children to look down the microscope with no prompting about what to see and that he would use the technique when appropriate.

Then the three-dimensional kinetic theory model was used by the teacher to explain our ideas (Nuffield Foundation, 1967). As has been noted, the children had done work on atoms and particles before and the teacher thought that this work provided a good reinforcement of previous work. It allowed the children to revisit the concepts and also exercise their abilities in terms of knowledge of scientific investigations.

The last exercise was the letter to Robert Brown. The small groups worked together on the letter, and then one person from each group read out a draft letter. By the time the second class were being taught it was realised that this was a superb opportunity to spot serious misconceptions that the children may have. As the letters were read out, the skills and knowledge demonstrated were publicly praised, but the teacher mentally noted serious errors in understanding. Then, when the groups had been set the task of writing letters as individuals, the teacher could go to the groups that needed attention and provide some kind of remediation in a private rather than public manner.

The children's reactions to the work and their thoughts on what they had learned were obtained by questionnaires which took between five and ten minutes at the end of each lesson. Some responses are given below.

What they enjoyed

- 'I enjoyed working in groups, using the theories + discussion' (girl, class 1)
- 'I enjoyed group work and discussion for it enables you to have your own say' (boy, class 2)
- 'I enjoyed looking down the microscope' (girl, class 2)

What they didn't enjoy

- 'too much sitting and discussing' (boy, class 1)
- 'trying to think about what Robert Brown had done' (girl, class 2)

What they thought they learned

- 'I learned that there are different answers to explain things about something' (boy, class 2)
- 'about Robert Brown and what he thought' (girl, class 1)
- 'I learned about Robert Brown's experiments and theories. I learned more about atoms and the kinetic theory' (girl, class 1)

When they thought they were being scientific

- 'discussing the theory' (girl, class 1)
- 'we learned scientifically that pollen does not really move' (boy, class 1)
- 'I thought about the particles under the microscope scientifically' (girl, class 2)
- 'I thought about this as if I was there and I was a scientist' (boy, class 2)

How they would improve the work

- 'Do more practical work e.g. setting up the pollen and water experiment' (boy, class 1)
- 'Not a lot, I enjoyed it, a bit less discussing' (girl, class 1)
- 'I think less talking by the teacher could improve this lesson' (girl, class 2)

These comments illustrate a range of opinions and were selected as typical of the range of responses from the children. It is interesting that 'being scientific' can be seen as discussing theory as well as doing practicals. The point of this work was to teach children a story from science, to discuss different theoretical interpretations of evidence and to learn the 'standard' interpretation of Brownian motion. The evidence above supports a verdict of success.

SUMMARY

This chapter has provided three cases of classroom materials which allow teachers and children to explore and investigate the nature of science in their classrooms. The intention has been to provide enough detail and information so that the reader can experiment with a range of teaching strategies that teach children science and the nature of science.

The above cases are based on stories of four scientists. How many does one need to know? The answer is not many. A teacher only needs a small range of stories to convey the key ideas of the nature of science to children. Not every lesson is going to be, nor needs to be, based on historical information. An expectation that science teachers will be fully conversant with an accurate sociology, history and philosophy of science is unrealistic. The classroom resources cited and given in further reading below will provide any teacher with a good half-dozen ideas and stories to get going.

It is important to have some stories and to recognise that stories are an important part of the culture of science. As Peter Medawar said: 'Scientific theories are the stories that scientists tell each other.'

EPILOGUE: ARE WE STILL TEACHING SCIENCE?

Many teachers, on first reading, think of the nature of science as the formal study of the history and philosophy of science. They see little opportunity for experimental work unless it is repeating the experiments of scientists in the past, for example doing similar experiments to Pasteur. This is laudable and can be worthwhile. However, it is not always possible to repeat experiments either because they are difficult to replicate or they are patently unsafe to do!

The non-statutory guidance argues that it should not be inferred that children are doing either the history or the philosophy of science. Teachers should use examples from the history of science to illustrate the nature of science.

This is also a point where there is a real tension between the teachers of science and the historians of science. Teachers work with pedagogic objectives in mind. Their purpose is to ensure that children learn the currently acceptable content and processes. Historians work with a different set of objectives. They seek to understand why people did what they did and why they believed what they did. So if a child repeated Black's experiments on heat capacities, the teacher may want the child to use the concept of energy in learning about heat capacities, whereas a historian may want a child to see the problem through Black's eyes and use the concept of caloric and hence understand why the word 'capacity' may have been used in the first place (see Roller, 1950).

Similarly, although reflection is a philosophical activity, it would be a mistake to see the nature of science as a course in the philosophy of science. Children's experiences are more direct. There is little value in 14-year-olds perceiving themselves as naive falsificationists or discussing whether they are in a degenerative research programme or not!

Teaching science and teaching the history and philosophy of science may share the same activities but not necessarily the same objectives. This chapter has taken the science teachers' objectives as paramount whilst trying not to do too much of a disservice to the history or philosophy of science (for further discussion of these points see Shortland and Warwick, 1989, and Brush, 1974).

APPENDIX 15. A: MATERIALS ON BROWNIAN MOTION

Brownian motion teachers' notes

It is intended that this work will fit in with a scheme of work on the particulate nature of matter or kinetic theory. It is intended to supplement the 'traditional' work on the smoke cell, not to replace it.

The objectives of the work are that children:

- should be able to discuss and understand different interpretations of experiments
- be introduced to some of the stories of science and the scientists involved
- be able to offer the 'standard' scientific explanation of Brownian motion

The class should be split into groups of four for this exercise.

The resources should be photocopied and put into separate envelopes marked 1, 2, 3, 4, 5 and 6. Each group of children will need a set of 1 to 6. The resources do not need to be marked or written on in any way, so they may be re-used.

Management

Arrange the groups. Explain that today they are going to look at how a scientist's interpretation of an experiment can suggest new experiments and how those in turn may change the interpretation. They are going to have to imagine themselves in the position of the scientist.

Later they are going to do an experiment and look at a model to see if they can understand an explanation of the experiment.

Whilst you are saying all this, put a set of envelopes into the middle of each group and explain that they are going to discuss the story bit by bit and that you would like to control the pace at which things are opened!

Tell them to open envelope 1. Ask them to read the information and discuss the questions as a group. Spend a short while collecting responses. These could be put on the board or a transparency. (Total time ten minutes.)

Tell them to open envelope 2. Repeat as for envelope 1. (Same amount of time.)

Repeat this process for envelopes 3 and 4. (Same amount of time for each one.)

Now move to envelope 5. This contains the denouement of the story. It is strongly recommended that the teacher reads this out loud while the children read through the material at the same time. It is felt that not only will this reduce time spent on the activity, it will also reduce demands on the children's reading and ensure that they all hear the same story. If they are listening(!), it may ensure some kind of commonality of experience. Again a short discussion of the questions and a plenary feedback should mean this activity takes about ten minutes.

The last part is part 6, which is intended to be the standard lesson on Brownian motion using the smoke cell. In addition to this, it is essential that the children see the model that explains this motion, i.e. the three-dimensional kinetic theory model plus a polystyrene ball! (If you are not familiar with this then see Nuffield Physics Year 2 or Year 4 texts – either the original texts or the revised pupils' guides.)

The smoke cell part itself takes about twenty minutes if the microscopes are set up. Most of the time is spent ensuring that the children have seen it. As with most microscope work, they need to be guided into what to look for!

It is suggested that the part where they do the discussion of writing or talking to Brown could be done either as a homework or as an aproximately 25-minute group discussion and group presentations at the next lesson, i.e. :

- Teacher reminds the groups of the last lesson's work. (Five minutes.)
- Groups discuss questions and what they would need to say to Brown. (Five to ten minutes.)
- Each group or spokesperson from the group gives a quick oral report on what they would say. (If, say, six groups at approximately a couple of minutes each: approximately 15 minutes.

Brownian motion – Part 1

Story

Imagine you are a scientist like Robert Brown. You are an expert with a microscope, and in the summer of 1827 you are curious to do some experiments on plants.

You have a theory which is this:

Plants have male parts and female parts. They reproduce by the male part and female part meeting and somehow mixing. You know that the pollen – the male part – gets to the ovulum – a female part. You guess that the pollen is 'vital' – that it moves itself to the ovulum. It is natural that the male parts of the plants will be active.

You guess or hypothesise that:

if the pollen is active or vital it will move.

As the pollen is so small, this motion can only be seen under a microscope. So you set up your microscope, slides and bits of pollen in water to test your hypothesis.

When you look through the microscope at the pollen bits you see them moving and twisting and turning in the water.

Discussion

Imagine you are Brown.

- After these results, would you think your theory is a reasonable one? Can you give reasons why?
- Could you think of other explanations for why the pollen moved?
- Would you want to think of other reasons why the pollen moved?

Brownian motion – Part 2

Story

Another scientist has suggested that the motion of the pollen may be a permanent part of its masculinity. In other words, it doesn't matter whether the pollen is from a live or dead plant.

Discussion

Imagine you are Brown.

- What kind of experiments would you like to try next to test this further idea?
- How would you go about setting them up?

Brownian motion – Part 3

Story

Brown tried pollen from plants ranging from those that were 'just dead' to those that had been dead for over 100 years! All the time he saw the bits of pollen moving.

Discussion

Imagine you are Brown.

- How do you think you feel now about your original hypothesis?
- Will you think it's a reasonable one to believe and why?
- Does this new idea you have tested change or modify your original hypothesis?

Brownian motion – Part 4

Story

One of the things you have done a lot of research on is the sexual parts of plants. In fact, you are one of the leading experts in this topic. Some plants have not had their male and female parts properly identified. Your experiments and your hypothesis suggest to you a method for identifying whether the part of the plant is female or male.

Discussion

Imagine you are Brown.

- You thought that the natural thing for the male part is to be active. Can you suggest what experiment you might do next to see if you can distinguish between male and female parts?
- Can you make predictions about what you would expect to see when you look down your microscope?

Brownian motion – Part 5

Story

Brown went on to test different parts of plants, and to his surprise he found that any part of a plant showed this motion *provided it was small enough*.

His next hypothesis, therefore, was another that was around at the time:

All animals and plants contain minute particles which carry the vital life forces.

Brown looked at small particles from animals and vegetables and again found the motion. He decided to look and see if this 'vitality' lasted even when the animal or plant was dead.

Again he found the particles to be moving. He tested fossilised plants – coal – and found London soot to be particularly active!

His curiosity drove him to ask if vegetable matter which he no longer considered organic would also show the motion – so he tried looking at small particles of fossilised wood. (In this material all the carbon-based matter has been changed to other elements.) Again he observed the particles to be moving.

He decided to investigate a range of *inorganic* materials he had on his shelves, including particles from a bit of the nose of the Sphinx! Same result: the small particles moved.

Brown's conclusion was that all bodies, wherever they come from, contain tiny active particles. The reason why they are active is unknown, but it cannot be used to tell 'living' from 'non-living' or 'the never lived'.

Discussion

Brown's experimental set-up was a powerful microscope and small particles of matter suspended in water.

Brown thinks that one bit of the apparatus has no effect on the motion. Which bit is it?

Brownian motion – Part 6

Experiment

In school we do an experiment similar to Brown's called the smoke cell experiment.

Listen to your teacher explain what to do and his or her explanation of what you see.

Your teacher may use a model to explain her or his ideas.

Imagine you could write or talk to Robert Brown about his experiments and conclusions.

- How would you explain your ideas and suggest to thim that they were reasonable?
- How would you persuade him to accept your explanation?

REFERENCES AND FURTHER READING

Alic, M. (1986) *Hypatia's Heritage* London: Women's Press.
Bentley, D. and Watts, M. (1988) *Teaching Science: Practical Alternatives*, Milton Keynes: Open University Press.
Brush, S. (1974) 'Should the History of Science Be Rated X?', *Science*, 183: 1166–72.
Children's Learning in Science Project (CLISP) (1987) *CLIS in the Classroom: Approaches to Teaching*, Leeds: CSSME, University of Leeds.
Department of Education and Science/Welsh Office (DES/WO) (1989) *The National Curriculum: Science*, London: HMSO.
—— (1991) *The National Curriculum: Science*, DES Circular 17/91.
Driver, R., Guesne, E. and Tiberghien, A. (1985) *Children's Ideas in Science,* Milton Keynes: Open University Press.
Futtock, K. (1991) *Louis Pasteur*, in the Nature of Science series, Hatfield: ASE.
Hesse, M. (1973) 'Models of Theory Change', in Hesse, M. (1980) *Revolutions and Reconstructions in the Philosophy of Science*, Brighton: Harvester Press.
Hodson, D. (1990) 'A Critical Look at Practical Work in School Science', *School Science Review March 1990*, (71): 256.
National Curriculum Council (NCC) (1989) *Non-statutory Guidance for the National Curriculum* York: NCC.
Nott, M. (1992a) 'History in the School Science Curriculum: Infection or Immunity', Proceedings of the Second International Conference on the History and Philosophy of Science and Science Teaching, Kingston, Ontario: Queen's University.
—— (1992b) *'The Nature of Science or Why Teach Brownian Motion?'* in Atlay, M. *et al.* (eds) (1992) *Open Chemistry*, London: Hodder & Stoughton.
Nuffield Foundation (1967) *Nuffield Physics: Guide to Experiments III*, London/Harmondsworth: Longmans/Penguin.
—— (1971) *Nuffield Combined Science*, London/Harmondsworth: Longmans/Penguin.
Pedoe, D. (1976) *Geometry and the Liberal Arts* London: Penguin.
Roller, D. (1950) *The Early Development of the Concepts of Temperature and Heat; the rise and decline of the caloric theory*, Case 3, Harvard Case Histories in Experimental Science, J. B. Conant, (ed.) Cambridge, Mass. : Harvard University Press.
Rowland, M. (1991) 'The Great Brownian Motion Swindle' *New Scientist*, 3 April 1991: 49.
Science Education Group, University of York (1990) *Science: The Salters' Approach. Key Stage 4. Unit Guide: Keeping Healthy*, London: Heinemann.
Smith, J. R. (1987) *The Speckled Monster*, Chelmsford: Essex Record Office.
Shortland, M. and Warwick, A. (1989) *Teaching the History of Science* London: BSHS/Blackwell.
Solomon, J., Hunt, A., Johnson, K. and Nott, M. (1989) *Teaching about the Nature of Science Science*, Hatfield: ASE.
Solomon, J. (1991) *Exploring the Nature of Science: Key Stage 3*, Glasgow: Blackie.

Soloman, J., Duveen, J. and Scott, L. (1993) *Exploring the Nature of Science: Key Stage 4,* Hatfield: ASE.
Williams, S., Hudson, T. and Green, D. (eds) (1992) *Active Teaching and Learning Approaches in Science*, London: Collins Educational.
Yorkshire Television (1984) *Scientific Eye* Leeds: YTV.

16 Using informal learning to enrich science education

Many people associate learning in science with the formal science curriculum. Yet much, if not most, of children's learning about science takes place outside the confines of a timetable and a school. There is a mound of evidence to show that this 'informal' learning is both powerful and tightly held onto. This chapter considers children's out-of-school learning sources and studies in detail two ways in which teachers can make use of such sources.

FORMAL AND INFORMAL LEARNING

All people learn science from a variety of sources, in a range of different ways, and for a number of different purposes. In other words, the reasons, sources and favoured modes for learning science vary from one individual to the next.

There are two different sources of or areas of learning that must be considered in science education – these can be called *formal* and *informal* learning. The main features of the two areas are summed up in table 16.1.

Formal learning takes place largely through the medium of the National Curriculum. It is compulsory, highly structured and regularly assessed. In contrast, informal learning is voluntary, sometimes accidental, haphazard and un-assessed. Therein lie its advantages as well as its drawbacks. It also has the advantage of being spontaneous, sociable, learner-led and open-ended but with the consequent drawbacks of being unpredictable, unsequenced and undirected. The distinction between them is not always clear-cut, however, nor should we assume that formal learning is always confined to school with informal learning always occurring outside. Much valuable informal learning takes place in school, while some formal learning occurs out of school.

One thing is clear. In the 1990s and beyond, informal and undirected learning in science will be of increasing importance – the so-called IT revolution will ensure this. Learning will take place in a variety of contexts and through an increasing number of media. Learning outside of school is certain to be of growing importance

Table 16.1 Features of formal and informal learning in science

Informal learning	Formal learning
Voluntary	Compulsory
Often haphazard, unstructured, unsequenced	Structured and sequenced
Non-assessed, non-certificated	Assessed, certificated
Open-ended	More closed
Learner-led, learner-centred	Teacher-led, teacher-centred
Outside of formal settings	Classroom and institution-based
Unplanned	Planned
Many unintended outcomes (outcomes more difficult to measure)	Fewer unintended outcomes
Social aspect central, e.g. social interactions between visitors	Social aspect less central
Low 'currency'	High 'currency'
Undirected, not legislated for	Legislated and directed (controlled)

in relation to the formal school curriculum. This will perhaps be as true in science, in our so-called 'scientific and technological society', as in any of the other National Curriculum subjects

Using and understanding informal learning

My view is that the realm of 'informal learning' in science is an under-used and under-studied area. If we knew more about it, or simply took more notice of it, children's science education could be greatly enhanced.

There is already evidence to suggest that 'factors outside of schools have a strong influence on students' educational outcomes, perhaps strong enough to swamp the effects of variations in education practices' (Schibeci, 1989: 13). More knowledge of, and attention to, 'informally acquired ideas' (Lucas, *et al.*, 1986) could thus be used to enrich science education and the work of classroom teachers: 'If the process of acquiring these ideas were examined carefully, information could become available that would be of use to teachers in their day-to-day work' (Lucas, *et al.*, 1986: 341).

Lucas (1983) provided an excellent review of sources of informal learning and their influence on so-called 'scientific literacy'. His analysis offers valuable guidelines in considering out-of-school learning in science. He distinguishes, for example, between intentional and unintentional sources of learning, and between accidental and deliberate encounters with learning sources. These distinctions

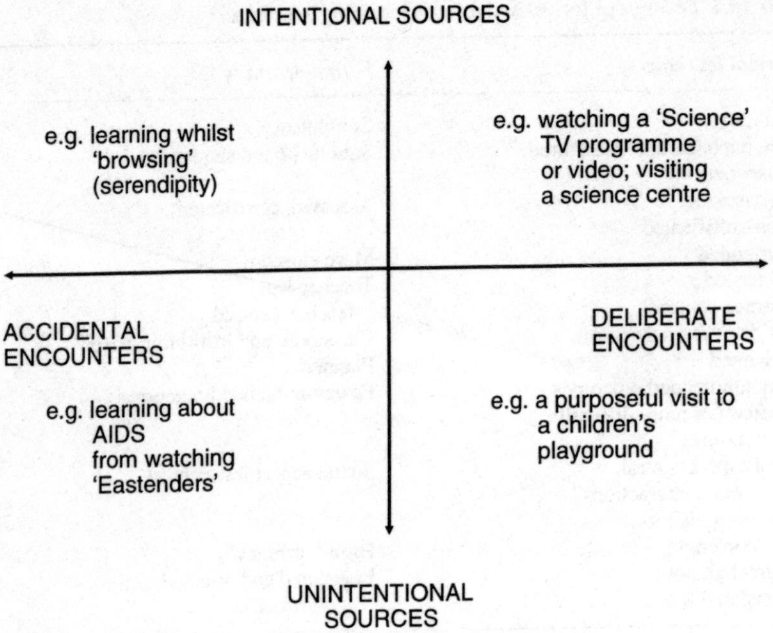

INTENTIONAL SOURCES

e.g. learning whilst
'browsing'
(serendipity)

e.g. watching a 'Science'
TV programme
or video; visiting
a science centre

ACCIDENTAL
ENCOUNTERS

DELIBERATE
ENCOUNTERS

e.g. learning about
AIDS
from watching
'Eastenders'

e.g. a purposeful visit to
a children's
playground

UNINTENTIONAL
SOURCES

Figure 16.1 Classifying informal sources of learning in science

present various interesting permutations (figure 16.1). Thus a casual visit to a children's playground may be called an accidental encounter with an unintentional source of learning, for example a roundabout. Interestingly, this encounter may lead children to believe in the centrifugal force on an object which physics teachers later inform them is fictitious. Encounters with science take place in an interactive, 'hands-on' science centre – these are likely to be deliberate encounters with an intentional source.

There is clearly a huge variety of informal sources of learning that impinge on science education:

- everyday experiences, such as slipping on ice; fastening a seat belt; visiting Alton Towers; riding on a bus; eating, drinking, cooking; gardening; riding in a lift; sweating; boiling a kettle. . . . The list is endless.
- the media: television programmes, some deliberately educational, some providing 'accidental learning'; radio; newspapers
- visits to museums, science centres, workplaces, etc.

These and many others make up the so-called informal learning which can sometimes support, but occasionally conflict with, the process of the formal science curriculum. In this chapter there is only room to consider briefly two sources of 'informal' learning in science: text and print encountered out of school, be it supermarket, publicity leaflet, advert. or news cutting; and interactive science centres of various kinds.

EXAMPLE ONE: USING 'INFORMAL' SOURCES OF TEXT IN SCIENCE TEACHING

This section discusses the way in which print and reading from any outside source can be used in science education, although the main focus is on text from newspapers.

The science presented in newspapers can be of value in the school science curriculum but only if used carefully and critically. In addition, one of the aims of science education should be to develop in students both the will and the ability to read 'newspaper science' with a critical eye and with healthy scepticism. For a number of pupils the only science they will encounter in written form after leaving school will be in the tabloid newspapers – hence the necessity of learning to read with care and purpose. Finally, both newspaper science and the formal science curriculum act as 'media' between the scientific community at one level and the general public at the other (this idea is shown in figure 16.2). Both contribute in some way to the public understanding of science, although their interaction may not always be productive.

Based on these premises, this section offers notes and suggestions related to the use of news cuttings and printed material from other sources in science lessons.

Why use material from newspapers in science education?

In addition to the general aim outlined above, using newspapers and other printed matter can help to meet the following objectives:

1   to meet general National Science curriculum requirements in the PoS, for example to relate science to everyday life, to develop communication skills in 'responding to information'; to encounter a variety of 'sources from which they can gain information'; 'to read purposefully an extended range of secondary sources'; to engage in 'the critical evaluation of data'; to use 'secondary sources as well as first-hand observation'.

2   to provide material directly related to the attainment targets of the National Curriculum. Content analysis of the newspapers has shown that newspaper space is devoted to medical issues, the environment, space, food and diet, energy sources, pollution and waste management, and many other topics that relate to specific statements of attainment (Wellington, 1991).

3   to act as a starter in exploring some ideas about the nature of science in the National Curriculum, i.e. to 'distinguish between claims and arguments based on scientific considerations and those which are not'; 'to study examples of scientific controversies and the ways in which scientific ideas change'; to appreciate the tentative nature of conclusions and the uncertainty of scientific

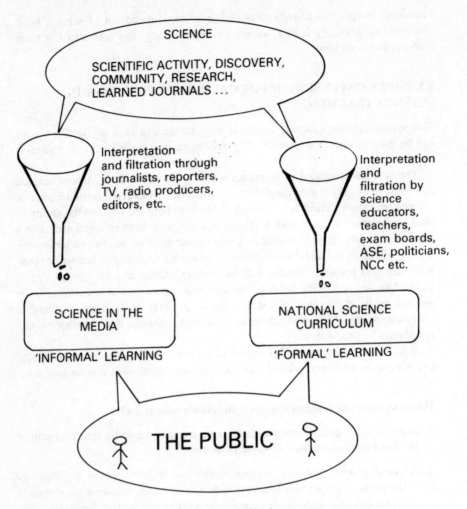

Figure 16.2 Media science and school science as filtering systems

evidence. Current issues, and those from the recent past such as BSE and cold fusion, can be used here as a complement to material from the history of science.

4   Newspaper material can also be related to the cross-curricular themes of health education, environmental education, citizenship and industrial and economic awareness.

5   to teach pupils to read critically and actively, and to develop an interest in reading about science; to allow group reading, analysis and discussion

6   to raise awareness and interest in current issues related to science, many of which are controversial. By the same token pupils can become aware of some

Table 16.2 Using newspapers in science education

A: Possible ideas for class work

1   *Issue raising/introducing an issue*
    for example, controversial issues
2   *Starter activity*
    for example, for a new topic
3   *Prompt/stimulus*
    for example, for discussion/role play; a stimulus to writing
4   *Directed reading*
    for example, comprehension, examining key words
5   *Information/data extraction (and presentation and analysis)*
    for example, making a graph from data in the text; interpreting a graph
6   *Vocabulary/terminology study*
    for example, examining the language in an article; picking out difficult words
7   *Poster making/collage/display creation*
    for example, on the environment; collections of headlines; articles from two papers
    on the same topic

B: Homework ideas

1   *Content analysis*
    for example, pupils analyse one week of the paper taken at home (if there is one)
    for its 'science content' – this illuminates their interpretation of what 'science' is.
    Pupils then bring their analysis to the following week's lesson
2   *Making an activity for others*
    for example, selecting a cutting on science/a scientific issue and devising questions /
    activities on it for other pupils
3   *Searching for cuttings on a particular topic*
    for example, space, diet, environment, disease, flight, drugs, etc.

(NB: The pupils are probably the best source of newspaper material for the classroom!)

of the values and interests inherent in the development of science, and be enabled to see the limitations of science.

How can they be used?

Newspaper cuttings, and indeed other written material from magazines, supermarket leaflets and even pressure groups (such as UKAEA, Friends of the Earth) can be adapted for classroom use. Table 16.2 provides a list of possible ideas for class and homework which I am sure could be added to.

Finally for this section, I would stress the importance of the role of the teacher in encouraging systematic analysis and careful criticism – teachers should not fall into the trap of seeing any of the above as totally independent learning activities.

Which cuttings are best?

I have bought and sometimes reviewed classroom material using news cuttings drawn entirely from the so-called quality press and from *New Scientist*. While such cuttings can give the basis for good classroom activities, they invariably have a reading age higher than the pupils' chronological age and unless heavily edited or used in a very step-by-step, structured way will be unsuitable, even at key stage 4. The quality papers, therefore, need to be handled with care.

This is also true of the tabloids, though for different reasons. I would argue that cuttings from the tabloids (and that includes the *Sun* and *The Mirror*) should be used: first, these are the papers that the majority of school students and adults actually read; secondly, they present science and scientists in a way which needs to be challenged. Science in the media is so often presented as whiz-bang and dramatic, as certain, as an individual rather than a collective activity, as 'sudden' and unrelated to previous work, as carried out by crackpot and unorthodox discoverers (see Wellington, 1991, for a fuller discussion of these points); thirdly, from a purely practical point of view, they are more readable and often shorter and more snappy than the quality coverage, which can sometimes go into inappropriate depth.

How should they be adapted for classroom use?

Certain rules can be followed in choosing and using text:

1   In line with the above comments, the cutting itself needs to be carefully chosen. The total text needs to be fairly brief (perhaps less than half of one A4 side) and, of course, readable. Diagrams, tables, pie-charts and other illustrations will help, especially if one of the aims is to interpret data and look at it critically.
2   If questions are directed at the text a closed, simple question which merely asks for an item of information or a word from the passage should be placed first. It should be a question which every member of the class can answer. More difficult and perhaps open-ended questions can be left until later. This may seem an obvious point, but how many sets of questions in teachers' worksheets and even in textbooks start off with open-ended, difficult questions which half of a group struggle with and act as a deterrent to continuing?
3   Questions which ask them to pick out and identify certain words in the passage can be used early on. Once pupils have found and highlighted important words, they can then be set the task of finding out (either from each other, a teacher, a textbook or dictionary) what those key words mean.
4   Open-ended questions which ask for an element of discussion and evaluation should be left until the end, once pupils have got to grips with the passage.

To sum up points 2, 3 and 4, questions should be graded from simple to difficult and from closed to open – an obvious rule, but one which is surprisingly often ignored.

5   With more difficult passages, such as from *New Scientist*, teachers may choose to read through an article with a class, and then discuss its main points before

embarking on the activities. With other material, teachers may simply let the class work in small groups, or individually, and then bring them together later to compare answers or points from discussion.

In all cases I feel that some teacher intervention is needed to bring out the point behind the activity. This is particularly true in activities aimed at raising questions about the nature of science, such as why do scientists disagree? Are some scientists biased? What counts as a fair test? How are scientists portrayed in the media . . .? and so on.

6 Finally, activities of this kind can very often be used as examples of the presentation of science, for example the way that data and statistics are presented in papers to make certain points or support certain arguments; the way in which science generally is presented to the public. Pupils can thus be encouraged to look critically at the presentation of science by the media – this is surely an essential prerequisite for participation as a citizen in a science-based democracy.

EXAMPLE TWO: THE INTERACTIVE SCIENCE CENTRES

In a relatively short time, and with limited funding and support, an impressive number of science centres have grown up in the UK and abroad. They include the Exploratory in Bristol, Techniquest in Cardiff, and Launch-pad, which forms part of the Science Museum in London (see Appendix A for full details). Further afield, there are centres in all the major cities in Europe and a wide range in the USA (including the early pioneer in San Francisco, the Exploratorium, and the Children's Museum in Boston). The centres each have their own distinctive flavour and emphasis, but they all have certain features in common:

- All provide interactive, hands-on learning of science using a range of activities/events/'plores' (the Bristol term) rather than untouched exhibits in glass cases.
- They all emphasise play and enjoyment as an essential element of learning.
- The stress is on doing, seeing and experiencing rather than formal understanding and explanation. Although each 'event' carries a short explanation or caption, the evidence is that these are hardly ever read – in addition, the use of formal, structured worksheets in the centres is uncommon, if not discouraged.

What can such centres contribute to science education, especially if (as the critics are quick to point out) they emphasise playing and enjoyment rather than reading and understanding? First, they can provide direct experience of different phenomena which may not be experienced elsewhere. They may not be explained or understood but they can provide little islands of experience which can be built on later. This is a kind of 'rubbing-off' effect of hands-on science. Children visit a centre and do and see an enormous number of things in a short space of time. They often see, hear or do something which rubs off and sticks – this informal learning may resurface weeks, months or even years later and may just provide that trigger of interest and experience that can make a 'formal' science lesson more meaningful (like Ausubel's advance organiser).

The second main contribution is in the so-called 'affective domain'. A visit to an interactive science centre can develop interest, enthusiasm, motivation, eagerness to learn, and general openness and alertness. The affective area is often neglected in formal science education. By developing motivation and interest for science, centres can ultimately contribute to the understanding of science.

BRINGING INFORMAL, OUTSIDE LEARNING INTO THE CLASSROOM

We have considered just two examples of how 'informal' sources can be linked with formal science education. There are clearly many others that can contribute. One of the dangers, of course, is to try to over-exploit outside experiences or sources, resulting in what teachers call 'overkill', i.e. trying to make too much of a good thing. Given this qualification, however, there are several ways in which teachers can link the domains of informal, out-of-school learning and formal, structured learning:

- in introducing a lesson or a new topic, such as by starting with the pupils' experiences of that topic
- in basing a lesson around an out-of-school activity, such as a visit, a TV programme, an advertisement
- in providing ideas for project work and independent learning
- by using 'everyday' materials (such as bleach, washing powder, food colourings) to replace or use alongside laboratory materials
- in overtly valuing children's contributions to classroom discussions of everyday anecdotes about science experience
- in displaying posters and adverts about the use of science in everyday life, for example plastics, chlorine, drugs
- in placing practical problem-solving tasks in everyday, relevant contexts

LOOKING TO THE FUTURE

One of the founders of the San Francisco Exploratorium, Frank Oppenheimer (brother of Robert), argued more than fifteen years ago for the value of informal learning in promoting science education and science, and against the dominance of formal, certificated (see table 16.1) education:

> . . . no-one ever flunks a museum or a television program or a library or a park, while they do flunk a course – they do 'flunk out of school'. Only schools can certify students; only certified students can progress. As a result only schools are conceived as public education. I would like to suggest that the current mechanisms for certification are not only stifling to educational progress but

that they are also extraordinarily costly and wasteful. Certification is an impediment.

(Oppenheimer, 1975)

Perhaps Oppenheimer was overstating the case for informal, out-of-school education as against the certificated, formal curriculum. But the importance of such learning is certain to grow in the future – teachers need to be aware of it, to nurture it and to use it whilst avoiding overexploiting it.

APPENDIX 16. A: Interactive Science Centres

Some of the interactive centres around the UK are:

The Archaeological Resource Centre (ARC), St Saviourgate, York YO1 2NN, Tel: 0904-654324.

Catalyst, Mersey Road, Widnes, WA8 ODF. Tel 051-420 1121.

Curioxity, The Old Fire Station, George Street, Oxford OX1 2AQ, Tel: 0865–794494.

Eureka!, Discovery Road, Halifax, HX 1 2NE. Tel 0422-330275.

The Exploratory, The Old Station, Temple Meads, Bristol BS1 6QU, Tel: 0272–252008.

Great Explorations, International Festival Park, Otterspool, Liverpool, L17 7HJ Tel: 051-728 8686.

Green's Mill and Centre, Belvoir Hill, Sneinton, Nottingham NG2 4LF, Tel: 0602–503635.

Hampshire Technology Centre, Romsey Road, Winchester SO22 5PJ, Tel: 0962–63791.

Jodrell Bank Science Centre, Macclesfield, Cheshire SK11 9DL, Tel: 0477–71339.

Kaleidoscope, Milford Marina, Milford Haven, Dyfed, SA73 3AF. Tel: 0646-695374

Launch Pad, Science Museum, Exhibition Road, London SW7 2DD, Tel: 071–938 8222.

Light on Science, Museum of Science and Industry, Newhall Street, Birmingham B3 1RX, Tel: 021–236 1022.

The Micrarium, The Crescent, Buxton SK17 6BQ, Tel: 0298–78662.

Satrosphere, 19 Justice Mill Lane, Aberdeen AB1 2EQ, Tel: 0224–213232.

Science Factory, Museum of Science and Engineering, Blandford Square, Newcastle Upon Tyne NE1 4JA, Tel: 091–232 6789.

Scope, Sheffield Hallam University, 36 Collegiate Crescent, Sheffield S10 2BP, Tel: 0742–720911 extn. 2201.

Snibstone Discovery Park, Ashby Road, Coalville, LE67 3LN. Tel: 0530-510851.

Techniquest, 72 Bute Street, Pier Head, Cardiff CF1 6AA, Tel: 0222–460211.

Xperiment!, Museum of Science and Industry, Castlefield, Manchester M3 4JP, Tel: 061–832 2244.

REFERENCES AND FURTHER READING

Formal and Informal Learning

Lucas, A. M. (1983) 'Scientific Literacy and Informal Learning', *Studies of Science Education*, 10: 1–36.

Lucas, A. M., McManus, P. M. and Thomas, G. (1986) 'Investigating Learning from Informal Sources: Listening to conversations and observing play in science museums', *European Journal of Science Education*, 8: 341–52.

Schibeci R. A. (1989) 'Home, School and Peer Group Influences on Student Attitudes and Achievement in Science', *Science Education*, 73: 13.

Using 'outside' text or photographs in the classroom

Association for Science Education (ASE) (1991) *Race, Equality and Science Teaching*, Hatfield: ASE (contains an excellent section on choosing and using photographs in the classroom with examples that can be taken from newspapers, books, magazines, etc. The aims behind the activities include making science learners into 'critical observers' of the images of people and places presented by photographs).

Wellington, J. J. (1986a) (ed.) *Controversial Issues in the Curriculum*, Oxford: Basil Blackwell.

—— (1986b) *The Nuclear Issue*, Oxford: Basil Blackwell.

(Both discuss the value of using controversial issues in developing certain skills, and suggest strategies for the classroom. *The Nuclear Issue* also contains examples that can be photocopied for classroom use.)

—— (1991) 'Newspaper Science, School Science: Friends or Enemies?', *International Journal of Science Education*, 13 (4): 363–72 (contains a recent example of content analysis and a review of past news coverage).

Science Centres

Oppenheimer, F. (1975) 'The Exploratorium and Other Ways of Teaching Physics', *Physics Today*, 28 (9): 9–13.

Quin, M. (ed.) (1989) *Sharing Science: Issues in the Development of Interactive Science Centres*, London: Nuffield Foundation/COPUS.

Shortland, M. (1987) 'No Business Like Show Business', *Nature*, 328: 213–14 (a critical look at 'hands-on' science).

Wellington, J. J. (1989a) 'Attitudes Before Understanding: The role of hands-on centres', *Sharing Science*, London: Nuffield Foundation/COPUS.

—— (1989b) *Hands-on Science: 'It's fun, but do they learn?'*, video with notes, Sheffield: University of Sheffield Television Service.

—— (1990) 'Formal and Informal Learning in Science: The role of the interactive science centres', *Physics Education*, 25: 247–50.

Index